LEN SENATER

PHOTOGRAPHY BY KSENIJA HOTIC

PUBLISHED BY SIMON & SCHUSTER

NEW YORK   LONDON   TORONTO   SYDNEY   NEW DELHI

A BOOK WHERE
INTERESTING
FOOD THINGS HAPPEN

DEPANNEUR
COOK BOOK

100 RECIPES
100 COOKS

STORIES FROM CANADA'S
UNLIKELIEST RESTAURANT

A Division of Simon & Schuster, LLC
166 King Street East, Suite 300
Toronto, Ontario M5A 1J3

This Simon & Schuster Canada edition March 2024

SIMON & SCHUSTER CANADA and colophon are trademarks of Simon & Schuster, LLC

Simon & Schuster: Celebrating 100 Years of Publishing in 2024

For information about special discounts for bulk purchases,
please contact Simon & Schuster Special Sales at
1-800-268-3216 or CustomerService@simonandschuster.ca.

Manufactured in the United States of America

1   3   5   7   9   10   8   6   4   2

Library and Archives Canada Cataloguing in Publication

Title: The Depanneur cookbook : stories from Canada's unlikeliest restaurant / Len Senater.
Names: Senater, Len, author.
Description: Simon & Schuster Canada edition. | Includes index.
Identifiers: Canadiana (print) 20230217931 | Canadiana (ebook) 2023021794X |
ISBN 9781668002650 (softcover) | ISBN 9781668002735 (EPUB)
Subjects: LCSH: Depanneur (Restaurant) | LCSH: International cooking. | LCSH: Cooking–Social
aspects–Ontario–Toronto. | LCGFT: Cookbooks.
Classification: LCC TX725.A1 S46 2024 | DDC 641.59–dc23

ISBN 978-1-6680-0265-0
ISBN 978-1-6680-0272-8 (hc)
ISBN 978-1-6680-0273-5 (ebook)

The Dish With One Spoon is a treaty
between the Anishinaabe, Mississaugas,
and Haudenosaunee that bound them to
share the territory and protect the land.

Subsequent Indigenous Nations
and Peoples, Europeans, and all
newcomers have been invited into
this treaty in the spirit of peace,
friendship, and respect.

The Dish With One Spoon reminds us
that we are all responsible for keeping
the dish full. That those who would
eat from the dish must share the
spoon if it is to feed us all. That if we
eat together, we are connected.

Miigwech—thank you—to all those who
have shared this land with me.
I seek to honour and live the
wisdom, generosity, and hospitality
embodied in this knowledge.

I shall strive to better understand its dark
past, to engage with its flawed present,
and to work towards its better future.

DEPANNEUR

where interesting food things happen!

est. 2011

Lunch & Learn
MONDAY + FRIDAY
10AM-1PM

Cooking Classes
SUNDAY + MONDAY
6:30PM

Drop-In Dinner
WEDNESDAYS
6-9PM

follow
[Instagram] [Facebook] [Twitter]
@thedepanneur
thedepanneur.ca

Supper Clubs
SATURDAYS
7:30PM

available for
DINNER PARTIES,
PRIVATE EVENTS,
TEAM BUILDING
WORKSHOPS!
thurs + fri

TORONTO
FOOD
FILM FEST

Watch. Learn,

The *DEPANNEUR* Cookbook

Table of Contents

FOREWORD

David Sax

When you are from Toronto and work in food (cooking it, selling it, writing about it), the question you constantly have to grapple with is what makes this food, or this restaurant, or store, or cuisine, distinctly "Torontonian." While other cities have clearly defined local dishes, regional palates, spice mixes, and aromas, all Toronto can boast is its stunning cultural diversity, which of course makes its essential deliciousness impossible to pin down. Whenever I write about the city's food scene for American publications or appear as some talking head on a TV show, I am asked what makes Toronto's food quintessentially from Toronto. No matter how eloquently I frame my answer, it is always so full of qualifiers and hedged statements about the city's impossible-to-pin-down taste, that no editor is ever satisfied.

"Yes, yes, sure, but what's one restaurant, or food, that's truly uniquely Toronto?"

What am I supposed to say? Moderately overpriced street hot dogs? The peameal bacon sandwiches, which no one I know ever eats? Some place that was hot a year ago, but now closed? Better just to dodge the question.

For much of the past half century, Toronto has been defined not by a single culture or a shared history, but by the sheer pace of its growth, as people from across Canada, and increasingly every corner of the globe, come here to work, invest, raise families, live, love, create, and do all the things people do in great cities.

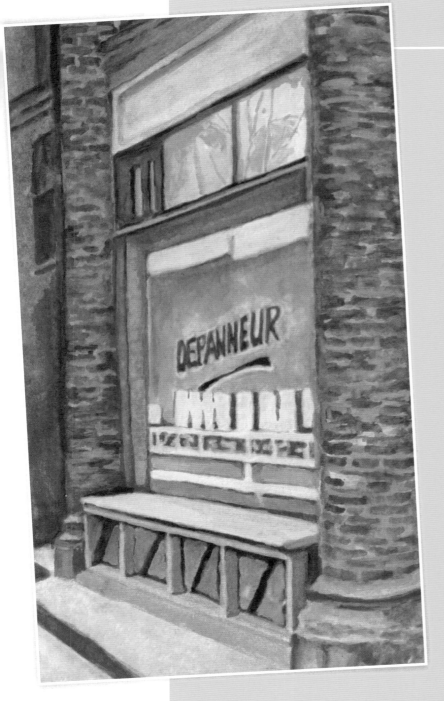

Watercolour by Jeanne-Marie Robillard

viii

We don't have the defining geography of Vancouver or San Francisco, the history of Montreal or Rome, or the sexiness of New York or Rio. What we have is a relentless restlessness driven by economic growth and immigration, defined by rapidly changing neighbourhoods and faces, sprawling suburbs, and hideous condominiums, and all the joys and pains of being the place where people come to with ambition to spare.

When I think back on it now, for a brief moment in time, Len Senater's Depanneur captured all of that: the soul of Toronto, in one small, beautiful place.

I met Len by chance one day, walking on College Street with my wife, shortly after I'd moved back home from New York. He was selling things out of this little shop, and we got to talking (which is a hazard . . . Len's gift of the gab is legendary). He told me about this crazy dream to build a kind of community kitchen, where cooks and chefs (but also anyone really) could come and cook and others could eat, and really it would just bring people together around food. He would call it The Depanneur, after the scrappy little corner stores in Montreal that sell beer and cigarettes and chips, but sometimes also really good hot dogs and tandoori chicken.

This was the golden age of pop-ups, when hot chefs and brands were doing cool things in weird spaces, but Len wanted something more wholesome and lasting. A place for everyone, within reach and totally accessible, where Toronto could cook and eat together. Like most great things that happen in this city, especially around food, The Depanneur was small and unpretentious, a flower growing from a crack, rather than a big bouquet. Sure, there were lauded restaurants with

million-dollar design budgets downtown, where bankers and other executives enjoy five-star service and precise cuisine. The Depanneur, on the other hand, was built from donated and salvaged parts . . . random chairs and mismatched plates, old stoves, and beaten tables . . . like some grad student's university apartment that oozed thrifty charm.

True to his promise, Len built The Depanneur around the city's greatest resources, the people who live here, with roots in every single culture on earth, combined and shaped by travel, history, ideas, and experiences. Each night, one of these people would take the reins at the stove and cook what they wanted to cook. The city's hungriest eaters had already been hunting out this tasty randomness, in far-flung suburban strip malls, where, say, an India-born chef ran a stellar Bavarian restaurant, or a Jamaica-born kid from a Chinese family was starting to mix those halves of his identity. Now, thanks to Len and The Depanneur, anyone could pop in, with little commitment and cost, and add to the city's culture: vegan Jewish deli, Georgian dumplings, Oaxacan tamales, and innumerable creative combinations. Every night was different. Some were great. Others, well, experiments. But the randomness was the key.

Quickly, The Depanneur became a sort of home: for the cooks and chefs, for the regular diners, for the neighbours (who stopped by for coffee and muffins at the start), and anyone who came into the space. After a while, however, The Depanneur achieved an act of magic that Len had set out for . . . it built a community, open to all, in a city where that is increasingly hard to find.

I experienced it during several meals

1970s

1986

2004

2010

2012

1986–2010 archival photos: Patrick Cummins

Photo: Sandy Nicholson

at The Depanneur over the years, as I shared plates and tables with friends and strangers, breaking bread and opening up in a way that was distinct from restaurants, right at the same time the city was opening too. Toronto had been infamous for being a cold place . . . unwelcoming and tight-lipped. Whether this was warranted or even true is debatable, but by the time Len got the place going, that was clearly changing. The old image of Toronto as a hotbed of prim, sensible Scottish Protestant living was as relevant as that peameal bacon sandwich as its defining food. This was the age when Drake became the poster child for the city's global reputation, a boastful, culturally diverse global superstar who made no apologies for what his Toronto looked and sounded like. It was the wild years of Rob Ford's trainwreck mayoralty, a nail in the coffin of quiet, competent Toronto, which revealed us as just as flawed and imperfect as other great cities led by schmucks. We shed something in that time, and The Depanneur was there, quietly leading the way.

My abiding memory of The Depanneur captures all of this. It's the middle of a Tuesday and half a dozen Syrian refugees from the Newcomer Kitchen are gathered inside on this winter day, making fattoush salad, *ma'amoul* cookies, and cumin-scented chickpeas and lamb meatballs in tomato sauce. In the midst of this, the de facto leader of the women, Rahaf Alakbani, a young musician, begins to sing, and everyone quickly joins in. Far from stopping, the cooking picks up in pace in time to the music, as the chopping of the parsley, the rolling of meatballs, and the *thwack* of the date-filled cookie dough emerges from an old wooden *ma'amoul* press someone dragged through hell to bring to their new home. I was there to write about this place for the *New York Times*, but all I could do in that moment was sit, watch, and listen . . . smell and smile as a current of warm energy filled the room.

Like so many great things about this city, The Depanneur is gone. Toronto's dynamism, its defining feature, means that we have to accept constant change, whether that means evolving flavours and influences, or just the steady upward pressure of real estate values and the associated rents. That's okay. Because the things The Depanneur stood for are stronger than ever. Diversity. Surprise. Openness. Randomness. Deliciousness. And fun.

Nothing could be more Toronto.

PREFACE

Even though thousands of people ate there over the years, The Depanneur (The Dep) was never really a restaurant. Located in an old corner store in a largely residential Toronto neighbourhood, it was an unlikely social and culinary experiment that ran from 2011 until 2022. I would invite guest cooks, mainly enthusiastic amateurs, to host different kinds of pop-up food events, everything from dinner parties and cooking classes to brunches, lectures, and even the odd wedding. It was an overstuffed little space that disgorged a ridiculous clown-car's worth of delicious food, interesting events, and lasting friendships. In 2016 it became the incubator for Newcomer Kitchen, a remarkable non-profit project with newly arrived Syrian refugee women, which thrust us onto the national and international stage. This book hopes to tell a bit of the story of how this peculiar project came to be, celebrate the multiplicity of amazing talents and stories it was home to, and share a few of the lessons it taught me about how food connects us all.

A Note on the Recipes

Hundreds of cooks from more than eighty countries have cooked at The Dep over the years and offered a unique window into the remarkable diversity of food in Toronto. Many of the people who cooked here had no prior professional kitchen experience. For some it was the first time they had ever cooked for strangers. Most didn't follow a recipe, and I'm certain the vast majority had never attempted to write one. In our kitchen they each shared a bit of themselves, their personality and memories, history, and culture. I've done my best to let their individual voices shine, while a valiant team of testers strove to ensure that the recipes actually worked. I hope they bring as much joy to your table as they brought to mine.

DEDICATION

To everyone who ever cooked and ate at The Dep.

To the women of Newcomer Kitchen who filled my heart.

To all the Kickstarter supporters who made this book possible.

My nieces, Lucy and Grace, 2011

APERITIF

A drink taken before a meal to stimulate the appetite, from the Latin aperire *"to open."*

WHEREIN I TELL THE STORY OF HOW THE DEPANNEUR CAME TO BE

A PLACE WHERE INTERESTING FOOD THINGS HAPPEN

My enthusiasm for food goes back a long way.

I have always gone through life stomach-first. It has led me on a long, circuitous journey from Montreal and Toronto, around the world, and back again, away from a desk job and into the old corner store that would become The Depanneur.

As a teenager I had a precocious entrepreneurial streak and used it to help fund backpacking trips to Europe, culminating in a semester as an exchange student in France. A few years later, after graduating with a degree in photography in Montreal, I spent about a year wandering from Bali to Delhi. These voyages changed me, igniting a cultural and culinary curiosity that never abated. I returned from them with a conviction that this was the end for which the rest of my life was the means. Although I had the good fortune and privilege to travel a bit more here and there, over the years what had once been a bright fire burned down to dull embers.

As I reached the end of my thirties, working as a partner in a small design firm in Toronto, I found myself wrestling with a kind of formless discontent. I had lost my enthusiasm for my work, and had begun to chafe in my role as a marketer, a cog in the machine of buying and selling ever more stuff. The friction ultimately burned through my partnership and I found myself without a job, living in an unfinished shell of a house. I struggled to find direction as I grappled with my first dark and bitter encounter with depression. It led me to new questions about what things I cared about, what actually made me happy.

When I was sixteen, I spent a summer train-and-biking around Europe, getting addicted to the thrill of travel.

Two years later, I moved back to Montreal to study photography. Here I'm at the now-posh Atwater Market, back when it was mainly a scrappy bunch of farmers' stalls.

After graduating, I spent a year travelling from Bali to New Delhi. In Varanasi I rented this water taxi from its owner so I could cross the Ganges to go swimming. By my reckoning, now I'm immune to everything.

I was unsure how to proceed, but one could say I followed my gut. Food, and the communion it offered with other people and cultures, felt to be part of the answer. But how to weave these things back into the fabric of my life? The idea of becoming a chef, of frantically cooking the same thing every day for people I would never meet, held no appeal. Nor did the values, economics, and aesthetics of fine dining. When I thought about the kind of food experiences that I cherished the most, they were not the ones I had spent the most money on. Rather, they were the ones centred around home cooking, cultural discovery, the conviviality of shared meals, and the human experiences that came with them.

How could I foster these kinds of experiences? Was there a way I could keep the things I loved about food while avoiding the things I disliked about restaurants? Over time, an idea slowly began to take shape: something involving food and community and entrepreneurship, something built around human connections rooted in the place where I lived. **Whatever it was, it didn't look like a traditional restaurant; it would be a place where interesting food things could happen.**

This was around 2010, and "pop-up" dining was becoming a thing: spontaneous micro-restaurants, quasi-public dinner parties, underground food markets— clearly there was much more fun to be had with food than simply eating at a restaurant. But there seemed to be so very little of this in my own city of Toronto, and I set about trying to figure out why.

I discovered that one of the key factors was the cost; it was just way too expensive to set up all the infrastructure needed to host a one-off pop-up food event. This was also around the time that co-working spaces were starting to take off, and there was much talk of the emergent "sharing economy." I thought, "What if there was a dedicated space, equipped with everything you needed to host pop-up food events, so that people did not have to reinvent the wheel every time?" This could dramatically lower the barrier to participation, allowing for a much broader range of cooks to participate. This, in turn, could make the resulting events much more affordable, meaning there could also be a more interesting and diverse range of diners as well.

If it had an inspected kitchen, in a licensed and insured commercial space, part of a legitimate, tax-paying business, it could mitigate a lot of the risks involved. It'd be better for both cooks (no running afoul with the City bureaucracy) and guests (no health and safety concerns). It could lower the barriers to entry and encourage fledgling entrepreneurial ambitions by helping lift pop-up and underground food events out of the grey-market shadows.

But where to begin? If only there were a sign . . .

What a sign it was!

2011

DEPANNEUR
1033A COLLEGE ST

With bars on the windows, chains on the doors, and random hours, it was more of an inconvenience store.

SINGLE CIGARETTES, EXPIRED CLAMATO, AND VERMIN

J&S was a moribund, dismal-looking convenience store a few blocks from my house. With bars on the windows and chains on the doors, it was rarely open. But beneath the grime, graffiti, and charmless signage were the outlines of a once elegant, dignified building. After seeing a cryptic "store for sale" message scrawled in the window, I began calling the number and coming by at various times in hopes of learning more.

Who knows how many attempts I made, but when I finally managed to get inside one afternoon in December, the scene was not promising: off-brand crackers and Spam sat next to a bottle of Clamato that had expired six months previously. Someone came in and negotiated the purchase of two single cigarettes at a quarter each; both the customer and the cashier seemed a bit confused by the whole transaction. It was all more than a little sketchy, but I introduced myself, and mentioned that I had noticed the business for sale sign outside.

The African woman at the cash register informed me that she was the owner and if I was interested, this filthy, dingy disaster of cobwebs, grime, and mouse turds could be all mine for only $10,000. However, she had four years remaining on a five-year lease at a price that seemed impossibly low for Toronto, and that was enough to light the fire of my imagination. The next step involved seeing if I could get the lease sorted out, and that meant meeting the landlord, Tony.

Tony was what one might charitably call a "character." For nearly fifty years he had let the building slowly decay; paint peeled, bricks cracked, and ceilings leaked. Tony was embroiled in acrimonious battles with various City departments due to countless violations of building, fire, and municipal codes. Any mention of the City or building inspectors would set off a loud, largely unintelligible tirade punctuated by shouts of "Mafia!," "Nazis!," "Faschistas!," and "Bang! Bang! Bang!" with accompanying finger guns.

For all of his pronounced eccentricities, and the twin challenges of trying to understand whatever point he was vigorously making, and ensuring he actually understood whatever I was trying to convey to him, he wasn't a bad guy. Whatever his flaws, Tony was not greedy. His compulsive cheapness made him a slumlord, unwilling to do anything but the most absolutely necessary, mandated-under-threat-of-legal-action maintenance. The upside of the dismal condition of the building was that it was really, *really* cheap.

Tony and I worked over a crumpled, tenth-generation photocopy of a boilerplate commercial lease form, hashing out a five-year agreement, and from there things moved quickly. By mid-December I had agreed to purchase the "business" from the owner. Starting January 1, 2011, I would own a corner store.

I did not have much more than a loose, amorphous idea that I hoped could be turned into some kind of viable business plan. I came up with a short-term strategy: do the minimum to clean it up and make the space usable, then sublet it as a pop-up shop to a friend for a few months. This would cover some of the rent and buy some time to get my act together. I'd clear my decks by spring, come back to finish the renovation, and be open in time for summer. Hopefully by then I'd have figured out what I was doing.

Random inventory of dubious vintage

LE CUL ENTRE DEUX CHAISES

By this time, I had been living in Toronto for around fifteen years. I was born in Montreal, but grew up in Toronto in the '80s, then returned to Montreal to study after high school. It was a formative era for me, a time when my personality, aesthetics, and values came into focus. Montreal was an artsy, bohemian city where you could afford to be broke. Jobs were scarce, so people had more time and less money; it was creative, quirky, resourceful, relaxed, sexy, and cool.

After my time in Montreal (followed by a transformative year of travel), I relocated back to Toronto. I sensed the difference immediately; Toronto was a magnet for the ambitious, and it bustled with energy and money. It was diverse and cosmopolitan, every streetcar ride felt like walking into the United Nations cafeteria. But it was expensive, and people were very preoccupied, hustling hard just to make rent. This left much less for creative folk to reinvest in themselves and their community. The city felt much more status-conscious, with everyone jockeying for a position in the cultural and social landscape.

Over the years I would come to identify as an ex-Montrealer living in Toronto, a situation the French sometimes call *avoir le cul entre deux chaises*—to have one's ass between two chairs. But now I had put down roots, and with this new chapter I began to wonder if I could bring a bit of what I missed about Montreal to my new home. As a nostalgic Montrealer with a corner store, calling it a *dépanneur* seemed like an obvious choice.

In Montreal, a *dépanneur* ("dep" for short) is what you call a small neighbourhood convenience store. Its etymology is a bit oblique: if your car suddenly breaks down, one might say *"Je suis en panne,"* meaning "I'm stuck," or "in a jam." Hence to *dé-panner* is to help someone get un-stuck; a *dépanneur* is a problem-solver, fixer, or trouble-shooter. (More colloquially, in France *une dépanneuse* is a tow truck, and *un dépanneur* its driver.)

An old-school Montreal dépanneur

But somewhere in '60s Quebec, someone was like, "Damn, it's 10:30 p.m. and I really need smokes, beers, and a May West.*" Whatever local corner store was open late got them "un-stuck," and so a nugget of Quebec's distinctive French dialect was coined.

Perhaps I also felt that Toronto in general, and its pop-up food culture in particular, was a bit *en panne*, and maybe I could help *dépanner* it. And so, my corner store became The Depanneur, my messy Franglais love letter to the things I missed about Montreal, an experiment in how to connect people with each other inspired by the city where I first connected with myself.

*An iconic Québécois snack cake by Vachon, similar to a Jos Louis or a Hostess Ding Dong.

THE CRACK IN EVERYTHING

Ask, and ye shall receive.

I arrived the first week in January to begin to take stock of my new reality. With the filthy shelves, dank appliances, and garbage bags full of expired chocolate bars and sports drinks, I certainly had my work cut out for me. This was going to be more of an exorcism than a renovation.

I dove in and began clearing out and fixing up the space. What I could not sell, I gave away, and the rest I threw out. The accumulated filth was astonishing, from opaque grime on abandoned windows to fossilised mouse skeletons in the baseboard heaters. I made the space inhabitable enough to serve as a temporary home to a pop-up vintage shop run by my old friend Sue and her son, Axel. By mid-March it was warm enough outside to tackle the next big task, taking down several generations of exterior signage. The signs and rusted metal bars that covered all the windows gave way to reveal beautiful Victorian tinwork. When we were finally done, I sat back and watched the afternoon sun pour through the beautiful prismatic glass transoms for the first time in at least sixty years.

My concept was starting to come into focus: a combination cafe/corner store with a weekend brunch that would double as a venue for pop-up dinner parties in the evening. The room was cleaned up, the bathroom, electrical, plumbing, ceiling, and floor all replaced, but I still needed to outfit the kitchen and dining room. With funds running low, I had to be especially resourceful. In my Montreal days, every kitchen was a hodgepodge of mismatched plates and flatware, a mix of hand-me-downs and garage sale scores—and never once did it diminish the pleasure of sharing a meal with friends. Would anyone really care if their fork and knife did not match? I didn't think so, so I came up with the idea of a Kitchen Drive, kind of a reverse garage sale.

I put up a poster in the window announcing the arrival of a new community food spot, and listed the kinds of things we needed: plates, glasses, cutlery, pots, pans, bowls, etc. Everyone was invited to attend an open house weekend where they could donate any surplus kitchenware that they had lying around. Sure enough, there turned out to be enough stuff languishing in people's cupboards, basements, and garages to fill half a dozen kitchens. It offered a novel way to get the neighbourhood involved,

---

The Dep Kitchen Drive on Saturday, Aug. 6, 10am-4pm

What We Need

Plates, dishes or bowls; anything, as long as it's white

Glasses; water, 10oz+ (big-ish) & wineglasses, clear

Cutlery; steel

Mugs; anything goes

Large serving dishes & platters; non-plastic, please

Salad & mixing bowls

Pots & pans; preferably large and not non-stick

Baking stuff; cookie trays, baking sheets, pie plates, etc.

Colanders, salad spinners, sieves

Measuring cups & spoons

Miscellaneous kitchenware; spatulas, whisks, wooden spoons, ladles, tongs, serving utensils, peelers, graters, pepper mills, cutting boards, etc.

Small appliances; hand blender, blender, food processor, toaster/toaster oven, pasta mill, kettle, pressure cooker, food mill, juicer, etc.

1L 'yogurt'-style plastic containers; clear only, please

Large Tupperware/Rubbermaid-style storage containers

Jars; mason jars, jam jars, pickle jars, etc.

Wishful thinking; Hobart mixer, Robo-coupe, deli slicer, commercial dishwasher, fridge or freezer, bread slicer, samovar/coffee urn, chafing dishes, induction hot plate, commercial food storage bins (clear or stainless)

Hey, we can dream, can't we?

and for people to feel connected to this peculiar new business. It contributed to an intentionally "un-designed" sensibility, a lightly curated mix of thrift, serendipity, and opportunism.

I was getting closer, but behind the scenes I was still scrambling to understand what felt like a million new bureaucratic constraints. Part of the point of The Dep was to provide a clean, safe, inspected, legitimate venue for non-professional cooks. In my mind, I was doing the City a solid: I was creating a place where pop-ups could operate with confidence and transparency while also offering customers the peace of mind of a kitchen that passed public health scrutiny. Pretty quickly I realized that there was going to be friction between theory and practice.

For instance, even though I didn't drink myself, it was pretty clear to me that completely dry dinner parties were going to have limited appeal. But getting a liquor licence presented a daunting gauntlet of regulations, permits, and inspections, some of which threatened to be insurmountable. There was very little wiggle room; a fundamentalist reading of Ontario's outdated liquor laws expressly forbade anyone to drink anything alcoholic, anywhere, under any circumstances, except in a licensed bar, restaurant, or private residence. **Apparently, those in charge felt that if they were to let people have a glass of wine with their dinner, the very fabric of civilization might begin to unravel.**

In many Montreal restaurants, there was a long-standing BYOB tradition, something entirely non-existent in Toronto, a by-product of a puritanical history that once earned it the backhanded moniker of "Toronto the Good." I recalled

a few especially sketchy Montreal bars that purported to be "private gentlemen clubs," where a $5 membership card bought patrons the right to drink after hours. Thus inspired, I founded the Rusholme Park Supper Club (Rusholme Park Crescent being the cross street at which The Dep was located).

The Supper Club was to be a "private members association" for people interested in convivial social dining. In this "club," guests would purchase a "membership" to attend a private "meeting" where a "free" meal would be served. No alcohol would be bought or sold or served, nor would any corkage fee be charged. However, if members decided they wanted to bring their own beverages to their own meeting, who was I to tell them how to run their meetings? Alas, memberships only lasted one day, so those wishing to attend another meeting would have to "renew" their membership at that time.

It was a pretty transparent hack, and if push came to shove, I doubt it would have held up under scrutiny. Creativity sometimes requires a degree of foolhardiness. Not for the last time, I banked on it being easier to ask for forgiveness than for permission. Little did I know how many more challenges were still to come—there would be plenty more forgiveness to ask for.

Decades worth of signage came down to reveal the original Victorian tinwork.

These original leaded-glass transoms, hidden behind particleboard and caked in decades of paint, were one of the many unexpected treasures I discovered during the reno.

2013

HOW HARD COULD IT BE?

By this point The Depanneur had an optimistic sketch of a business plan, a Facebook page, a domain name, and a newly minted location, but it did not yet have a visual identity. In my years as a designer, I had come to understand that a brand was more than just a logo; it was the embodiment of an idea across all the forms that idea can take: conceptual, experiential, visual, and tangible. As a typography aficionado, I adored the hand-drawn retail signage of the early and mid-twentieth century, and as a resident of Toronto that inevitably pointed to one place: Honest Ed's.

For anyone who lived in Toronto in the second half of the twentieth century, there were probably few landmarks as iconic as Honest Ed's. Located at the high-traffic corner of Bloor and Bathurst Streets, in the heart of central Toronto's Annex neighbourhood, Honest Ed's extended a full block west to Markham Street. Its exterior was a blazing, blinking marquee of more than twenty thousand incandescent light bulbs interspersed with huge red-and-yellow billboards of corny puns and slogans: *Honest Ed's a nut, just look at the "CASHEW" save!*

The product of the ambition and hustle of Ed Mirvish, a poor Jewish immigrant, Honest Ed's loud, garish, vaudeville sensibility was a none-too-subtle middle finger to the city's stuffy, snobbish old guard. Using self-effacing humour, radical unpretentiousness, and genuine generosity as a kind of anti-gentrification, he created a place where Toronto's fast-growing immigrant community could feel truly welcome.

In the windows, and throughout the chaotic, multi-level warren of Honest Ed's store, were thousands of hand-painted paper signs with the names and prices of products. Ed's small army of sign painters created an iconic, primary-coloured typographic style that would become embedded in the imaginations of generations of Torontonians. **In a city so young, so mutable, with so few cultural landmarks to connect its citizens, this was one of them.**

I managed to track down Dougie Kerr, one of Honest Ed's original sign painters. Within a week he showed up with his small kit of paints and brushes, and by the end of the day he had painted both large plate glass windows at The Dep. I got something so much better than I could have designed myself: something that connected me to the place where I lived and came with a fabulous backstory. It embodied the hidden talents and personal stories that The Dep was all about.

The Dep opened, softly, in August 2011. I was still uncertain how many things would work, so it was pretty low-profile,

Photo: mikecphoto via Shutterstock

Dougie Kerr touching up his original hand-painted sign after several years of wear and tear.

which was fine—I wanted something that felt like a small discovery, a hidden treasure. I hired a skeleton staff and leapt into the fray. By October we were ready to roll out the first official "meetings" of the Rusholme Park Supper Club.

The Supper Club also reimagined the traditional relationship between restaurants and cooks. The pop-up events were built on a shared-risk/shared-reward model: cooks received a percentage of sales (50 to 60 percent depending on the kind of event), and half of any tips. The cooks bought their own ingredients and used The Dep's inspected kitchen to prepare their food. I marketed and promoted the events and handled ticket sales and

front-of-house service. If we had a good turnout, we both made money; maybe not a lot, but typically more than one might make working a comparable shift in a regular restaurant. If it was a slow night, we each absorbed our share of the loss. This arrangement incentivized cooks to co-promote events. As each cook told their friends and family, this spread the word of The Dep further than I could ever have done on my own.

Overall, it felt fundamentally more equitable, respectful, and collaborative than the kind of arrangement one typically finds in restaurants. I still feel this model hints at alternatives in an industry rife with exploitation and labour/management conflict. Although I had no way to know it at the time, it also laid the foundation that would later make things like the Newcomer Kitchen project possible.

In November I started experimenting with our first Cooking Classes, and by the end of the year The Depanneur felt like a real living, breathing thing: serving food, hosting dinners, renting kitchen space, selling products, making brunch, getting press. As we rolled into 2012, I experimented with cooking one night a week. I was no chef, but felt confident I could at least whip up a pot of something tasty once a week and, significantly, was willing to do it without getting "paid." These casual, spontaneous meals became the first Drop-In Dinners. At first, I wasn't that concerned with the daytime cafe business; there were a million little cafes in Toronto—how hard could it be? (Spoiler alert: It is really, really hard.)

When Honest Ed's closed in 2016, thousands of people lined up to buy the signs as a souvenir of one of Toronto's most iconic and beloved landmarks.

Photo: Amy Wilson

2014

*Out of the frying pan,
but not out of the fire*

CUT YOUR LOSSES

While the outward face of The Dep was about interesting food things, behind the scenes the first few years were defined by an ongoing battle with an antagonistic bureaucracy that seemed hell-bent on shutting me down. Granted, I was trying to squeeze some iffy stuff through the regulatory cracks—the BYOB Supper Clubs were built on shaky ground at best—but I had not anticipated the multi-year conflict that would ensue. Ironically, in all the years I wrestled with the system, liquor was the one thing that never actually caused any issues.

The first big hurdle was the initial Toronto Public Health inspection, which I thought I had managed to ace without any issues. Then, just before leaving, they informed me that if I wanted to maintain my seating, I would be required to install a *second* washroom. Oh, and since I was on the ground floor, it would have to be wheelchair accessible. I couldn't even begin to figure out where to start with this. There was nowhere to put another bathroom in my tiny, 450-square-foot space. **In the end it took a combination of luck, privilege, and testicular brass to come up with a solution.**

Just below The Dep, there was a dark and squalid one-room apartment. It had recently been abandoned by a particularly odious tenant, who had smoked the walls to a grim beige—but it had a bathroom. If I took over the unit, maybe I could get the city to consider its bathroom part of The Dep. I was already in over my head, but I decided to lease it. To offset the additional cost, I planned to convert it into a rental kitchen for food entrepreneurs, a kind of co-working space for cooks. (This was well before "ghost kitchens" became a thing.)

It was a big gamble, but I did not see any other possible solution.

In record time I ripped everything out, slathered it in high-hiding, odour-blocking paint, and kitted it out with a stove, an oven, a few sinks, fridges and freezers, some shelves, and a giant central prep island. After a fair bit of cajoling, the health inspectors eventually agreed to consider it The Dep's second washroom (even though it was pretty clear to everyone that no customer would actually ever need to use it). But they then told me that now that it was a customer washroom, customers were not permitted to enter the food preparation area, so I'd have to build a hallway from one corner of the room to the other! It was completely absurd. Despite much personal agonising, eventually the City seemed to forget all about it.

Over the next ten years The Dep's shared kitchen would become an incubator for scores of local food businesses—an affordable entry point where new food entrepreneurs could plant the seeds of their food dreams and nurture them until they could stand on their own. You'll encounter some of their stories—and recipes—throughout this book.

It seemed the moment I looked up from the bathroom crisis, I was served a new infraction notice from the City's Municipal Licensing & Standards division informing me I was not actually allowed to have seating at all. I was licensed as a "Retail Food Store with Refreshments" (aka corner store), which allowed me to make and sell food. I was now told that if I wanted to have seating, then I'd have to get a new "Eating Establishment" (aka restaurant) licence, a bureaucratic Pandora's box I had been trying very hard to keep shut.

When I applied for the new licence, I was told my application would need to first be approved by Zoning. This itself did not seem like a big deal; The Dep sat on College Street, a major commercial thoroughfare that is home to over a thousand businesses, and easily over a hundred restaurants and bars. The Dep's building had originally been a bank in the 1800s and had operated continuously as a business of one kind or another for more than a century.

So, when they rejected my application, it took me a while to figure out why. It turned out that due to some unexplained historical anomaly, the *one block* that The Dep sat on was zoned "R" (Residential) instead of "MCR" (Mixed Commercial Residential). The previous corner store business had been grandfathered in.

The official way to address this was to go through the Committee of Adjustment for a Zoning Variance. But for a business, this costs upwards of $10,000 just to apply, and comes with no guarantee it will work out in your favour. Besides, the official City plan was supposed to be addressing these kinds of zoning anomalies eventually (though no one could tell me when). It was insane: I was being forced to spend a huge amount of money I did not have, to do something they were going to do anyway, just so I could be allowed to do what I was already doing.

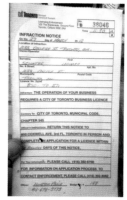

To give you some hint of how old these bylaws were, the infraction was for operating a "Victualling House . . . where fruit, fish, oysters, clams or victuals are sold to be eaten therein." On the other hand, my "Retail Food Store" licence explicitly allowed me to sell horse meat, but only in quantities less than a quarter carcass!

The Dep's basement rental kitchen was an incubator for scores of fledgling food entrepreneurs.

This was an authentic, old-school, jerry-rigged death trap of a Montreal delivery bike that I brought to Toronto. Bikes like these, custom-built to fit exactly four 24s, used to ply Montreal neighbourhoods in the '70s and '80s, delivering groceries and beer before most UberEats drivers were even born. I christened her Céline, and too dangerous to actually ride, she lived parked outside the front door, the unoffical mascot of The Depanneur for years.

Frantic, I lobbied my city councillor for months, and finally a meeting was brokered with representatives from Zoning, Municipal Licensing & Standards (MLS), and the councillor's office. The person from Zoning arrived with his foot-thick binder of city bylaws, opened it to the relevant page, and told me that any "change of use" (e.g., from corner store to restaurant) required zoning approval. Since it was currently zoned Residential (regardless of the city's plans to address this anomaly), no other use was allowed, so no approval would be given. The person from MLS said they were unwilling to waive the recently introduced "No Seating Allowance" condition of my existing licence, even though I provided examples of other businesses in the area with the identical licence that had been operating with seating for years without any issues.

I would not be allowed to operate with the licence I had, and they refused to issue me the licence I needed. I had just invested my life savings to build a new business from scratch, turning a decrepit eyesore into a flourishing community space. I asked the zoning official what he thought I should do; his response was: "Cut your losses."

Asking for permission hadn't worked. In the end, it would take five more years, dodging summonses and petitioning councillors, co-founding a Business Improvement Area (BIA), and eventually getting the entire neighbourhood rezoned before The Dep would finally win its right to, officially, simply exist.

2015

SOME DAYS YOU HAVE CHICKEN, SOME DAYS YOU HAVE FEATHERS

Undeterred, I celebrated the one-year anniversary in August 2012 with a BBQ party and a one-ton crate of watermelons that took several days to slice up and give away to passersby. It was a chance to thank the people who had worked so hard alongside me to get this far, and celebrate with the incredible community who were coalescing around The Dep. These people inspired a pride in me in a way my previous work never had; I was now doing this as much for them as for me. But July and August are very slow months for food businesses in Toronto, and by the end of the summer I was facing a new dilemma, one without a convenient enemy: I was completely broke.

The daytime cafe/corner store was simply not generating enough revenue to cover its costs. Brunch barely broke even,

slow days eating up whatever slim profits were earned on busier days. The Drop-In Dinners were unpredictable; an unexpected rain could turn a promising night into a mountain of leftovers and leave both me and my guest cooks out of pocket. Even the Supper Clubs proved reliably unreliable, with some events selling out immediately, others languishing until the last minute or even getting cancelled altogether for lack of sales.

This unpredictability was the single hardest thing to get used to. At the time, it was an intense roller coaster from elation and validation to panic and despair. For a tiny business built on the values I cherished, there was no way to not take it personally. Chef Greg Couillard (see page 125) once related an old saying from Mexico that translates roughly to: *"Some days you have chicken, some days you have feathers."* It would take me many more years to be able to face this kind of uncertainty with any sort of equanimity.

Even though I had not expected to make a profit out of the gate, I had imagined breaking even eventually. But the hard reality was I was now considerably deeper in debt than when I started. Despite the way-below-market rent, despite the modest-but-not-minimum-wage salaries, despite my uncountable unpaid hours, there was simply no more money to lose. Dogged by relentless bureaucratic nightmares, **frazzled, and broke, I did not have enough funds to make payroll, the entrepreneur's ultimate anxiety dream.** The project was a failure, and I could not help but feel that by extension, so was I.

The Depanneur was deeply *en panne*. I had to pivot, very hard and very fast.

I made the heart-wrenching decision to close the daytime cafe and store, which meant letting go of the staff that had toiled so valiantly the whole year. That September's newsletter was an exercise of Herculean composure, the fear and stress and doubt pounded out of the cheery copywriting:

"The Dep was created to be a place where interesting food things happen. Over the past year we experimented with a lot of different ideas. Heading into year two, The Dep will focus on the ones that worked the best. Starting in September the cafe will be closed on weekdays, and we'll be expanding our evening and weekend programs. We're going to keep doing the fun and tasty stuff that you have come to love, and put our energy into making even more interesting food things happen."

And goddammit if I didn't do just that.

2016

KABOOM CHICKEN

WHAT, AND GET OUT OF SHOW BUSINESS?

Running The Dep was now more or less a one-man show, and I focused on packing the calendar with events. The shuttering of the cafe/store managed to staunch the bleeding somewhat, and over the course of the next year a new Dep started to emerge. The Drop-In Dinners expanded to several weeknights, becoming a kind of "open mic night" for amateur culinary talent in Toronto. I started offering more Cooking Classes, the Supper Clubs became a regular weekly fixture, and I began renting out The Dep for private parties. Brunch churned through a few iterations, and I kept cooking one night a week. I had the idea to try inviting guest speakers in hopes of drawing in more people; this turned into Table Talks, an informal culinary salon and speaker series that would run for years to come.

I kept experimenting with different ways to connect people and food, and started working with several Community Supported Agriculture (CSA) programs (i.e., subscription-based produce boxes). The Dep became the biggest pickup point in the city for the then-new Fresh City Farms CSA, who offered us free produce in return for hosting their pickups. This windfall created an opportunity to "pay it forward." Helmed by Emily Zimmerman, it became the basis of a pay-what-you-can vegan night that ran for many years.

By 2013, The Dep was hosting over three hundred food events a year. It was convivial and meaningful and delicious; it was also very, very hard. I worked front of house for all the Drop-In Dinners and facilitated all the Cooking Classes and Supper Clubs. I cooked dinner for thirty once a week. I recruited all the chefs and speakers, wrote all the event write-ups, did all the marketing and promotion, ran the website and the social media, coordinated the kitchen and venue rentals, and attempted to stay on top of everything from linens to supplies to repairs to bookkeeping and taxes. The cleaning and doing dishes was the first thing I was able to gratefully delegate, but you know who was there mopping at 2 a.m. if a cleaner didn't show up . . .

It was hard, and it didn't pay well; it was stressful, and solving constant challenges filled my brain every waking hour. But amidst it all, there was something magical emerging: cooks pouring their hearts into their food, people sharing meals, and new friendships being born. It felt honest and afforded me the greatest privilege of all: to get up each day and work on something I really cared about.

I remember mopping the floor late one night, tired and contemplating my life choices: I had left a decent-paying, respectable career as a designer, but invested my life's savings, all so that I could be an unpaid dishwasher at 2 a.m. on a Saturday. It brought to mind an old joke: A guy goes to check out a visiting circus. He is sitting near one of the stage exits, and as the troop of elephants is leaving, one of them takes a gigantic, stinking crap. Someone in a clown suit rushes in to shovel up the mess. The guy asks him, "Do you ever think about getting a better job?" The clown looks up at him and replies, "What, and get out of show business?"

One of my favourite things to emerge out of my many experiments were the Table Talks. I'd invite someone to talk about something they cared about in the world of food, and I'd make a meal inspired by the topic. This informal culinary salon ended up fostering dozens of amazing conversations among authors, chefs, journalists, historians, academics, philosophers, policy-makers, activists, and entrepreneurs.

(From top to bottom)
Naomi Duguid
David Sax
Tanya Surman
Wayne Roberts

LIFE HAD OTHER PLANS

Over the next two years I slowly dragged The Dep up out of the hole I had dug. It took eighteen months or so to get the bank account out of perpetual overdraft. Eventually I repaid the loans and credit cards I had maxed out, and finally paid off the years of overdue income tax I had shamefully let pile up. **By 2015, I managed to hit my original business goal: to make it to the end of my five-year lease no poorer than when I started.** More important, I had managed to have a fun, interesting, and very tasty adventure along the way.

Nonetheless, my restless brain started cooking up more ambitious plans. I saw The Dep as a prototype, the proof of concept of a set of values and ideas at work in the food sector. I started dreaming of Dep 2.0—taking over the whole building and converting it into an urban food hub that combined production facilities, event space, and co-working office space for food organisations, all under one roof.

I spent months formalising, articulating, and pitching the concept. Along the way I discovered that The Dep occupied a peculiar category all its own, one that was not profitable enough to be of interest to investors, nor considered impactful enough to get funded as a non-profit. It seemed that the path to raising capital for Dep 2.0 was going to be a big challenge.

At the end of 2015 I sat down to negotiate the renewal of the lease with Tony, not a straightforward undertaking. Even though our signed lease clearly stated it was for five years with the option to renew for five more, Tony insisted he would only renew for three years. His health was failing, and his daughter, a real estate agent, was getting more involved in helping him with his affairs. The rent on the new, shorter lease jumped up aggressively each year, quickly arriving at double what I had started at five years earlier.

In the classic real estate paradox, the lease was now worth more because of all the work I had sunk into the space. The shortened renewal term was clearly in breach of the contract we had signed, but really, what were my options? Sue a dying man and make a sworn enemy of my landlord? I ran the new, higher numbers and felt that, with a little luck and a lot of hustle, I could still make it work. I signed on for three more years, and started working on the next chapter of The Dep.

I started off 2016 with the goal to streamline The Dep's offerings, free up more time and space for myself, and invest in more help. I tweaked pricing, cut back Drop-In Dinners to once a week, turned the Table Talks from a weekly freebie to a monthly ticketed event, expanded the roster of Cooking Classes, and hired Cara Benjamin-Pace to help with business development, focusing on private and corporate events. We had a few brainstorming sessions, filling scores of Post-it Notes with ideas. The dream was that with a bit of help I could work a bit less, pursue the dream of Dep 2.0, and maybe even make a little money.

Life, as it so often does, had other plans.

2017

DEPANNEUR
GRAND OPENING!
mazeh
LEVANTINE BRUNCH
SAT & SUN 10AM - 2:30 PM
Be the first to check it out!

A SMALL GESTURE OF HOSPITALITY

By the beginning of 2016 a global humanitarian crisis had been brewing in Syria for several years, with millions of people desperately trying to escape a deadly civil war. In response, the Canadian government offered to open its borders to 25,000 Syrian refugees. The sudden influx overwhelmed the existing settlement infrastructure, and soon hundreds of families found themselves stuck in hotel rooms, sometimes for months on end.

As this unfolded around me, **I was one of a small group of neighbours who wondered: What could we do to help?** What began as a small gesture of hospitality very suddenly snowballed into Newcomer Kitchen, an experimental non-profit social enterprise that would upend my world, put The Dep on the world stage, and forever change my life. Over the next three years we would prepare thousands of meals and put over $150,000 into the hands of more than eighty Syrian families.

The many stories and lessons of Newcomer Kitchen would easily fill an entire book of their own, and I explore a few of them later in this book. Suffice it to say, a year that started out with a goal of working less, having more free time, and making more money, turned into a whole other Dep's worth of work, done for free in my "spare" time. Yet it would become the thing The Dep would be best known for, and the ultimate validation of the values upon which it had been built.

At the same time Newcomer Kitchen was busy turning my life upside down, The Dep kept powering through hundreds of events a year. As 2018 started to draw to a close, The Dep was thriving in a steady groove with events running seven days a week. It seemed like I was actually going to get paid and maybe even contribute to my RRSPs for the first time in many years. But 2018 was also the final year of my three-year lease. Even at double what it had been when I had started, it was still a fair deal for the area. Tony had since passed away, and now his daughter and her new husband were my landlords. In late fall it became clear that they were planning another 60 percent–plus rent increase.

Much of what emerged from The Dep had sprung from taking the good deal I had and paying it forward, amplifying it into new opportunities for others. Now I had to figure out—fast—if I believed it could survive a rent hike like this. I had always meant The Dep to be small, but I was learning that smallness came with its own costs. The economics of Toronto's skyrocketing real estate market was stress-testing the viability of The Dep's model.

I was content with the modest income and vibrant community that The Dep offered, but I was getting tired, and could start to sense the shadow of burnout. I spoke about this to my mentors and advisors, explaining that while I didn't really need to make more money per se, I did need to figure out how to work less. The advice I was given was: You might need to make more money if you want to work less.

Sharing our very first meal with Syrian refugees. No one could have imagined how this small gesture of hospitality would transform all our lives.

YOU CAN'T CHANGE THE TIRES WHILE THE CAR IS MOVING

At the end of 2018, I bit the bullet and signed on to a new three-year lease—now on track to exceed 300 percent of what I was paying when I started—and began revisiting my ideas of expanding The Dep. The year 2019 represented a new set of entrepreneurial challenges: growth, rising costs, increased competition, efficiency, and scale. Even though The Dep was doing more events than ever, the higher rent put more pressure on revenue-generating activities, drawing energy away from non-profit activities like Newcomer Kitchen.

I hired more help and pushed to book even more events. We added daytime Lunch & Learn workshops, higher-priced Master Classes, more private and corporate events, and off-site classes at other kitchens. I started exploring new collaborations, like a series of outdoor communal dinners at The Bentway, a new public arts and culture space underneath the city's downtown Gardiner Expressway.

In addition to offering a lovely, convivial meal in a unique urban setting, it was an opportunity to test out a new Pay It Forward idea: people could donate a little extra money with each meal, which was passed along to the chefs and turned into additional meals for local respite centres and shelters.

Meanwhile, I began reworking the business model and looking for a bigger location. I struggled to balance the intimacy and conviviality of The Dep with the seemingly inexorable economic imperative to scale. It felt like three persons' worth of work on one and a half persons' worth of revenue; as rewarding as it was, I was in danger of burning out. After a few difficult, soul-searching conversations, I realized that I was simply stretched too thin. It is said that you can't change the tires while the car is moving. I could not conceive of, plan, and build a whole new Depanneur while running the existing Depanneur. I decided to postpone any expansion and instead take a break: after ten years, I would take a sabbatical. This would offer me the time to think carefully about what I wanted to do next, and then when I felt ready, I could thoughtfully move towards bringing it to life.

I set my sights on the end of 2020—my fiftieth birthday, The Dep's tenth anniversary, and twenty-five years since I last took time to explore the world. I closed out 2019 with the best year in the history of The Dep. After nearly a decade, I was finally making a reasonable living and the coming year was on track to be the best yet. And then, somewhere in China, someone contracted a novel coronavirus.

Photo: Wei Qi,
courtesy of The Bentway

2019

WE'RE ALL IN THIS TOGETHER

This sign, made by a local artist in the iconic Honest Ed's style, popped up in storefronts around the city.

At the beginning of 2020, the world lurched into the disorienting era of COVID-19. Suddenly whatever financial projections that had been undergirding my sabbatical plans were gone, and moreover there was nowhere to go. In the first quarter of 2020 I suspended all in-person events indefinitely, and refunded more than $25,000 worth of tickets.

Like so many other restaurateurs in the city, I frantically attempted to reconfigure The Dep to the new reality. I set up biweekly Pick-Up Dinners: prepackaged take-out meals that could be pre-ordered online and handed to customers through an open window to the street. The results were surprising. In some ways it was easier: no longer tied to the capacity of the room, I could sell two, three, or even four times as many meals as had previously been possible. Being pre-ordered meant chefs knew exactly how much food they needed to buy and cook. Having no other events meant the cooks could use the space all day to prep; a narrow pick-up window meant food stayed warm and fresh, and no dishes to do meant I was home early.

Some things didn't change: the fundamental unpredictability remained—there was no way to know which nights would be popular, and sales ricocheted from under ten meals to over one hundred. The modest Dep kitchen, which had never been designed for this kind of volume, would get overwhelmed, as would cooks unaccustomed to the logistical challenges. Despite the occasional screw-ups, apologies, and refunds, customers proved loyal, forgiving, and appreciative.

The Dep's smallness, which had

been its limiting factor, suddenly and unexpectedly became its saving grace. I had dodged a bullet: had I gone ahead with an expensive new lease on a larger space with an ambitious new build-out, and then walked into COVID, the result would have been catastrophic. Smallness offered a resilience that enabled me to sustain The Dep as a more-or-less one-man show.

Even within these constraints, I tried to find ways to innovate. I donated my basement kitchen to a short-lived project called Family Meal, which turned surplus ingredients from restaurants shuttered by the lockdown into free meals for out-of-work restaurant workers and the homeless. When a new women's shelter opened a block from The Dep, I adapted the Pay It Forward program from The Bentway events into our Pick-Up Dinners. Over the next eighteen months I would drop off hundreds of fresh homemade meals at the shelter on my way home. As in-person dining restrictions stretched into 2021, the Pick-Up Dinners re-rooted The Dep in the local community by offering the neighbourhood a welcome variety of food, a small antidote to the dreary monotony of lockdown.

It was a peculiar limbo. My sabbatical was now an indefinite write-off. I was managing to stay afloat, albeit only two days a week, but handing people takeout through the window was not really what The Dep was about. I felt a deep gratitude for all the people who continued to support the project, and felt determined to try and figure out what was possible under these strange new circumstances. I wasn't

Photo: Sandy Nicholson

going anywhere anytime soon, so was there anything else I could offer to my community of cooks and customers? How could I celebrate the amazing people, food, and stories that The Dep had been home to over the last decade? From this came the book you are holding.

COMING HOME

First and foremost, a Depanneur cookbook would need to embody the same social and entrepreneurial values as The Dep itself. But as I learned more about the economics of Canadian publishing, I began to realize that the status quo model would simply not be able to remunerate the contributors, as well as pay for the photography, interviews, and recipe testing—let alone leave anything to actually write the book. If I wanted to do this, I would need to find a different way to make it happen. **I could not do it alone, but maybe I could do it together with the community that had come together over a decade of running The Dep.**

In November 2020, I launched the book as a crowdfunded project on Kickstarter. In remembrance of the founding spirit of The Dep, I committed $5 from every book pre-sold to Kiva microloans to women food entrepreneurs around the world. It went on to become the most-funded Canadian cookbook project ever on the platform. Yet even with all the money raised, it would only just cover the costs; it wasn't enough for me to actually get paid to write the book. Fortunately, the success of the Kickstarter gave the project enough credibility to attract the interest of publishers and help secure a book deal. With the help of an incredible team of collaborators, we began to compile and test all the recipes and coordinate the photo shoots and interviews, and I sat down to write the story you are now reading.

As 2021 drew to a close, I was preparing to wind down this incarnation of The Depanneur. Behind the scenes I had been trying to negotiate a handover of The Dep's facilities and equipment to Newcomer Kitchen. I had hoped to donate the entire thing to them, so that they might continue their amazing grassroots food activism in the room where they had been born. It would have been a beautiful legacy, but it was not to be. In December, I was informed that the landlords were not open to renewing the lease; instead, they were going to make it into an office for their real estate brokerage.

The final week of The Dep was bittersweet, returning everything to the great garage sale whence it came. Many people popped by to express their well wishes, share memories, and say thanks for what The Dep had brought to our neighbourhood over the last eleven years. I was able to sell and/or give away almost everything, and as a final thank-you, on my fifty-first birthday, I put the proceeds of the liquidation towards additional Kiva microloans to female-owned food businesses.

Around this time I was talking to an old friend, processing the complicated

Photo: Sandy Nicholson

emotional exercise that shuttering The Dep entailed. He beautifully described the selling off of The Dep's pots and pans and plates and bowls as seeds blowing out into the world to take root in new places. He saw them as little relics *cathected* by the spirit of The Dep—a new word and concept for me.

Cathexis, he explained, was the opposite of catharsis. Where catharsis was the release of accumulated psychic, emotional, or spiritual energy, cathexis was the process of accumulation of that energy. It is why and how sentimental objects become sentimental, why churches are built on grounds made sacred by older temples. Those spaces, those objects have become imbued with the quality of energy and attention that had been invested in them. That was the process that made

them sacred and beautiful, and that we can still sense. **As we spoke, I realized it is through that process of investing care and attention into the things we care about that we also cathect ourselves.** I had turned a dingy old corner store into a lively place that had enriched the lives of so many people, and in doing so, had enriched my own life beyond measure.

My appetite had cunningly turned my love of travel into a kind of inverse global culinary adventure that brought the whole world into my little kitchen. It then multiplied it by allowing me to share it with thousands of people. Along the way it taught me new ways to help others, how to create connections and build community. It rekindled my curiosity and enthusiasm, and wove meaning back into my life. I followed my stomach and it led me home.

2021

Live from
The Bentway!

DEPANNEUR

STARTS

Soups

LISA KATES
ASPARAGUS AND RAMP SOUP

CHRIS DUNNE
NEWFOUNDLAND COD CHOWDER

HANNAH GRACE MEDALLA
ARROZ CALDO
Filipino Chicken Rice Congee

NATALIA "COOKIE" MARTINEZ-KECK
AJIACO SANTAFEREÑO
Colombian Chicken and Potato Soup

KERRI COOPER
IMMUNE NOURISHING SOUP

MARC KUSITOR
BOUYON AK LEGUME
Vegan Haitian Soup

CAROLE NELSON BROWN
AGUADITO DE POLLO
Peruvian Chicken Rice Soup

Starters

ROSSY EARLE
CEVICHE DE MARISCOS
Panamanian Seafood Ceviche

MICHAEL KIRKWOOD
SCOTCH EGGS

VANESHA KHADAROO
VINDAYE OURITE
Mauritian Octopus Salad

VICTOR UGWUEKE
SHRIMP SURFERS ON NIGERIAN TOSTONES

MIKIKI
SALADE DYSPÉRIGOURDINE
Not Périgord Salad, Get Over Yourself

JUSTIN FREDERIK GO
BITTERBALLEN
Beef Mini Croquettes

Snacks

ALISSA KONDOGIANNIS
LATKES
Savoury Potato Pancakes

SONBOL ZAND
KOOKOO SABZI
Persian Herb Frittata

LEO BADURIA
FOUGASSE AUX OLIVES
Olive Fougasse

PEDRO JULIO QUINTANILLA
FRITURAS DE MALANGA
Cuban Malanga Fritters

ROMAN KLIOTZKIN
ADJARURLI KHACHAPURI
Georgian Cheese Boats

SARA MELANIE LAPELL
WALNUT RAISIN CHALLAH

LISA KATES

ASPARAGUS AND RAMP SOUP

I met Lisa Kates at a food issues brainstorming session at the Centre for Social Innovation; we hit it off right away. She was exploring the possibilities of starting up a soup catering business called A Food Gypsy, and so we decided that it could operate out of The Dep's kitchen in exchange for soup. Her delicious soups became a fixture of The Dep's early menu, the colourful jars lining the retail fridge. Over time she shifted away from the physical demands of producing fifty-plus litres of soup each week towards the moral demands of addressing food insecurity in Toronto. Together with food activist Darcy Higgins, she established Building Roots, an innovative program bringing fresh food to some of the most disadvantaged and under-served communities in the city.

Ramps, also known as wild leeks, are available in early spring at local farmers' markets. They are usually available around the same time the first local asparagus appears, which makes this soup a little celebration of a new season.

Prep: 30 min
Cook: 35 min
Makes: 4 servings
Vegan

2 tbsp olive oil

1 clove garlic, minced

1 small onion, diced (1 cup/160 g)

12 ramps, chopped

1 lb/450 g bunch asparagus, woody ends trimmed

1 tsp grated lemon zest

Pinch of grated nutmeg

Salt and ground white pepper

4 to 5 cups/1 to 1.25 L water, vegetable stock, or chicken stock

In a medium pot, heat the oil over medium heat. Add the garlic and onion and cook, stirring, until soft but not browned, about 10 minutes.

Set aside ½ cup of the ramps for garnish. Add the remainder of the ramps to the pot and sauté over medium heat until soft, about 10 minutes.

Set aside 3 asparagus spears for garnish and chop the remainder. Add the chopped asparagus to the pot and sauté for 5 minutes, stirring occasionally.

Stir in the lemon zest, nutmeg, and salt and white pepper to taste. Add the water and bring to a boil. Reduce to a simmer and cook for 20 minutes.

Remove from the heat and carefully use an immersion blender to purée the ingredients. Taste the soup and adjust the seasoning. Return the pot to the stove and reheat.

To serve, top the warmed soup with the raw asparagus spears and chopped raw ramps.

TIPS:
The subtle flavours of these local vegetables are wonderful, so I prefer not to use cream.

You can experiment by adding herbs like tarragon, chopped chives, or a bit of dill. This soup is a very forgiving dish, and everyone has their favourite way of cooking it.

I moved to Ottawa and did catering there but got really tired of the cocktail party circuit and found it a little gross. So I started a food program for youth at risk: Operation Come Home. We grew food outside, we grew vegetables, and I would cook with the kids every day. They had an appreciation for what we were doing. When we went outside with scissors and cut some vegetables or some herbs, they loved that, and loved seeing how these things were transformed.

Lisa Kates is a photographer and the co-founder of Building Roots, a food security charity in Toronto. @lisa.a.kates @buildingrootsto

 ADOPT-A-RECIPE   Michael Hierlihy

Every party is a kitchen party in Newfoundland because that's where the wood stove used to be back in the day. And so everybody goes into the kitchen to be around the heat. That's what you did when you were a kid, and you went over to your uncle's or grandparents'. And when you grow up, you're having everybody over in your kitchen. And it's just never changed. This is something that's been passed down generation to generation.

Chris Dunne is a Newfoundlander who came to Toronto but wasn't about to leave his favourite foods behind. Chris has since returned to The Rock. @nlbountyhunter

CHRIS DUNNE

NEWFOUNDLAND COD CHOWDER

Prep: 20 min

Cook: 1 hr

Makes: about 2 litres (4 servings)

A born-and-bred Newfoundlander and talented self-taught cook, Chris is about as Canadian as they come. A native of St. John's, he came through The Dep a few times while he was in Toronto working for the Canadian Hockey League. Chris carried his down-home memories with him into the kitchen, and parlayed them into a thriving side-hustle doing catering gigs inspired by the cuisine of Canada's East Coast. He took his passion for Newfoundland's ingredients and flavours all the way to *Wall of Chefs* on Food Network Canada, where he got to showcase his provincial pride on the national stage. This rich and creamy chowder is a real taste of Newfoundland, filled with an abundance of fresh cod.

1 tbsp olive oil

3 to 3½ oz/75 to 100 g bacon, diced

12 oz/375 g cod

½ tsp salt

½ tsp freshly ground black pepper

4 tbsp/60 g butter

½ cup/80 g diced onion (1 small)

1 tbsp minced garlic (3 large cloves)

1 tbsp fresh summer savoury (see Tips)

1½ tsp dried thyme

½ cup/50 g diced celery (1 stalk)

½ cup/65 g diced carrot (1 small)

½ cup/70 g corn kernels (fresh, frozen, or canned)

1 cup/150 g halved baby potatoes (see Tips)

3 cups/710 mL fish or vegetable stock

1 cup/240 mL half-and-half (10% cream)

2 tbsp all-purpose flour

2 tbsp water

Minced fresh parsley, for garnish

In a large pot, heat the olive oil over medium heat. Add the bacon and fry until crispy, stirring occasionally, about 15 minutes. Using a slotted spoon, remove the bacon and place on a paper towel–lined plate to drain. Remove almost all the bacon fat from the pot, leaving a little to fry the fish.

Season both sides of the cod with the salt and pepper. Cook in the remaining bacon fat until the fish is lightly browned on both sides and flakes easily, about 3 minutes per side. Remove the fish to a plate and shred into chunks using a fork. Set aside.

Reduce the heat under the pot to medium-low and add the butter. As the butter is melting, use a spatula or spoon to scrape up browned bits from the bottom. Add the onion and garlic and sauté, stirring frequently for 2 to 3 minutes, being careful not to burn the garlic.

Stir in the savoury, thyme, celery, and carrot and cook over medium heat for about 10 minutes.

Stir in the corn and potatoes. Add the stock, cover, and bring to a boil over medium-high heat. Reduce to medium heat and cook until the potatoes can be poked with a fork yet are still firm, about 10 minutes.

Reduce the heat to low and add the half-and-half.

In a small bowl, combine the flour and water and whisk with a fork until smooth. Stir into the chowder and simmer for another 5 to 10 minutes until thickened.

Add the reserved bacon and fish. Taste and adjust the seasoning. Garnish with parsley.

TIPS:

If possible, soak the cut potatoes in a bowl of cold water for at least 1 hour before use to remove starchiness.

If summer savoury is not available, use sage.

 Ruth Gould

Prep: 15 min

Cook: 50 min to 1 hr

Makes: 4 to 6 servings

3 tbsp cooking oil

6 tbsp minced fresh ginger or galangal

1 medium yellow onion, diced

4 cloves garlic, chopped

2 lb/910 g bone-in, skinless chicken thighs (6 to 8 pieces)

2 cups/400 g jasmine rice, washed and drained

6 cups/1.4 L water, plus more as needed

¼ tsp freshly ground black pepper

2 tbsp salt (or 1 tbsp salt + 1 tbsp fish sauce)

For Garnish:

½ cup/50 g sliced green onions

Fried garlic slices, homemade (see Tips) or store-bought

4 hard-boiled eggs, quartered or sliced

6 to 10 calamansi (Philippine lime) wedges or regular lemon or lime wedges

Drizzle of chili oil (optional)

HANNAH GRACE MEDALLA

ARROZ CALDO

Filipino Chicken Rice Congee

As diverse as the cuisines of the world may be, there are some things that feel universal, like the deep satisfaction of a bowl of warm chicken soup on a chilly night. In the Philippines, this is *arroz caldo*—"rice soup"—and it is comfort food for the soul. It's a cousin of Chinese congee, loaded up with ginger and fried garlic. I love improvising variations on this soup using leftover rice and making it in a pressure cooker, which cuts the cooking time to less than 15 minutes.

In a large soup pot, heat the oil over medium heat. Add the ginger and sauté until golden, about 30 seconds. Add the onion and cook until softened, 7 to 10 minutes.

Add the garlic and cook until fragrant, about 30 seconds. Add the chicken, and cook until lightly browned all over, 3 to 5 minutes.

Add the drained rice, toss to coat, and cook for 1 minute. Pour in the water and increase the heat to bring to a boil. Cook for 10 minutes, stirring occasionally to prevent the rice from sticking to the bottom of the pot. Add the pepper and salt, reduce the heat, cover, and simmer until the meat is cooked and comes off the bone easily and the rice breaks down and the soup thickens, at least 45 minutes. Stir occasionally to prevent sticking or burning. Add water as needed to maintain the consistency of a loose porridge.

Adjust the seasoning as needed, adding more salt or fish sauce to taste. Transfer to shallow bowls and top with the garnishes.

TIPS:

My grandma's secret was to cook the ginger well before adding the onion and garlic.

If you want a bit of golden colour, you can add 1 teaspoon ground turmeric and/or 1 teaspoon dried safflower when adding the salt to the rice.

For a smoother finish, you may also use an immersion blender after cooking the rice porridge. Remove the meat and shred into large pieces, discarding the bones. Blitz the rice porridge a bit, but not completely smooth, and return the meat to the mix.

To make your own fried garlic, thinly slice 2 cloves of garlic and fry in vegetable oil over medium heat until golden brown.

ADOPT-A-RECIPE   Marnie Sohn

Back in the Philippines, my grandfather used to tell my mom and her siblings that he didn't want to see any grains of rice left on their plates, and he explained how it was harvested. At that time, they didn't have machinery for agriculture; it was hand-picked by ladies half-bent and crooked from doing it all day. I've seen the process and I salute how much work they're doing. It's heartbreaking.

Hannah Grace Medalla arrived in Toronto in 2014, studied culinary arts at George Brown College, developed her professional experience in the demanding kitchens of Casa Loma, Marriott Hotel, and The Ritz-Carlton, and now runs her own private chef and catering business. **@medallaprivatechef .catering**

In Colombia there's one region where you eat bugs. There's something called *hormigas culonas*, which is like "big ass" ants. They're fried and you have them at a certain time of the year, like April or March, and they have a nutty, nutty taste. So I even cook bugs sometimes! I like showing people different foods that maybe they never knew before. Like my husband. He's German. He didn't even know what an avocado was before he met me!

Natalia Martinez-Keck ran Colombian Street Food by Cookie Martinez in Toronto, and is now embarking on a new adventure in Germany, where she has relocated with her partner and their impossibly cute kid.
@cookiemartinezcooks

NATALIA "COOKIE" MARTINEZ-KECK

AJIACO SANTAFEREÑO

Colombian Chicken and Potato Soup

Prep: 30 min, plus marinating time

Cook: 1½ to 2 hr

Makes: about 4 litres (4 to 6 servings)

A mischievous prankster with boundless enthusiasm, Natalia (aka Cookie) hails from Colombia and would tease me about my peculiar predilection for the vintage Colombian musical style known as *cumbia*. (She was more of a classic rock fan herself.) Back in the day, when she was running her new cookie business out of The Dep's rental kitchen, I commissioned her to make ice cream sandwiches, which became one of The Dep's signature treats. After a string of popular Colombian street food pop-ups, she opened her own food stall and then parlayed that into a bricks and mortar location. Somewhere along the line she also developed a niche as one of the few chefs in Toronto seriously exploring cooking with insects.

1 medium white onion, cut into chunks

2 tbsp chopped fresh cilantro

2 cloves garlic, peeled but whole

1½ lb/680 g bone-in, skin-on chicken breast

2 tbsp/30 g butter

8 cups/1.9 L chicken stock

1½ tsp salt (if using unsalted chicken stock)

2 ears of corn (cut into 2 to 3 pieces)

1 cup/150 g big chunks peeled red potatoes

1 cup/150 g big chunks peeled yellow potatoes

1 cup/150 g papas criollas (see Tips)

1 tbsp dried guascas (see Tips), crumbled

In a food processor, combine the onion, cilantro, and garlic and chop everything together. Place the chicken in a bowl, cover with the onion mix, and refrigerate for 30 minutes.

In a large pot, combine the marinated chicken and any juices from the bowl and the butter. Stir over medium heat for about 5 minutes to melt the butter. Add the stock and the salt (if using unsalted stock) and bring to a boil. Reduce the heat to a simmer and cook until the chicken is fully cooked, 45 to 60 minutes.

When the chicken is cooked, remove it from the pot and set aside.

Add the corn pieces, all three types of potato, and the guascas to the pot. Bring to a boil, then reduce the heat, cover, and simmer until the soup starts to thicken and the potatoes are very tender, 30 to 40 minutes.

Meanwhile, shred the chicken and discard the bones and skin. Put the shredded chicken in a separate bowl.

When the soup is ready, serve in shallow bowls, making sure each bowl includes potatoes and a piece of corn. Add a portion of the shredded chicken and garnish with the crema and capers. Traditionally ajiaco is served with a side of cooked rice and slices of avocado.

For Serving:

½ cup/96 g crema, crème fraîche, or sour cream

4 tbsp capers, drained

4 cups/640 g cooked white rice

2 avocados, sliced

TIPS:

Frozen prepared papas criollas *can be found in Latin stores; whole baby white potatoes can be substituted.*

Dried guascas *is the signature herb used in* ajiaco. *In a pinch, you can substitute a mix of bay leaves, dried parsley, dried oregano, and a bit of dried mint.*

KERRI COOPER

IMMUNE NOURISHING SOUP

For the vast majority of human cultures, food and medicine are deeply interconnected, but in the industrialized world, we seem to have lost the plot somewhere in the last century or two. Only much more recently, with the growing epidemics of obesity, heart disease, diabetes, and other afflictions of overabundance, have we begun to revisit this idea in earnest. As a nutritionist, Kerri devotes herself to the healing power of food, and ran her health-focused organic meal delivery business out of The Dep's rental kitchen for many years.

I was one of those children who always had allergies and lots of ear infections; I later learned they were likely due to a dairy allergy. I've always been aware that food has powerful effects on us that maybe we don't always realize. Ironically, I started a business cooking for people, but really what I want is for people to cook for themselves, to keep those life skills and a connection to their food.

Nutritionist Kerri Cooper, together with husband and chef, Sean MacFayden, run Roots Kitchen from their home and farm in Prince Edward County. @rootskitchen.ca

Prep: 1 hr
Cook: 30 min

Makes: about 3 litres (6 to 8 servings)

Herbal Infusion:

2 inches/5 cm fresh ginger, cut into slices ¼ inch/6 mm thick

2 tbsp chopped astragalus root or 10 slices (see Tips)

2 tbsp echinacea leaf/root or mix or 3 echinacea tea bags

2 tbsp dried nettle leaf or 3 nettle tea bags (see Tips)

1 tbsp chaga mushroom nuggets (optional; see Tips)

Soup:

¾ cup/150 g lentils (preferably small brown or black lentils) rinsed and picked over

2 cups/480 mL water

3 tbsp butter or coconut oil

4 cups/460 g onions, sliced (about 3 onions)

1 tsp sea salt, plus more to taste

3 cups/250 g shiitake mushrooms, thinly sliced

3 tbsp chopped garlic

3 green onions, trimmed but left whole (optional)

8 cups/2 L chicken bone broth (homemade or store-bought; ideally homemade)

1 kabocha or other squash, peeled and cut into bite-size cubes

2 cups/85 g deribbed chopped kale leaves

2 tbsp dried wakame seaweed (optional)

⅓ cup/90 g miso, plus more to taste

⅓ cup/30 g goji berries (optional)

Prepare the herbal infusion: Cut a 6-inch/15 cm square of cheesecloth and place all of the herbal infusion ingredients in the centre and tie into a bundle. If using larger pieces of astragalus root you can put these in the soup pot separately. Set aside.

Make the soup: In a medium pot, combine the lentils and water, cover, and bring to a boil. Uncover, reduce the heat to a simmer, and cook until the lentils are tender but hold their shape, about 20 minutes, depending on the type of lentils you are using. Continue to taste as they cook to check for doneness. Set the lentils aside.

Meanwhile, in a large heavy soup pot or Dutch oven over medium heat, heat the butter or coconut oil (yes, it's a lot of oil, but trust me it's good for you and the soup)! Add the sliced onions and sea salt and sauté until the onions start to get soft and translucent, 5 to 10 minutes. Add the shiitakes and sauté for 3 to 5 minutes, stirring occasionally. Add the garlic and whole green onions (if using), stir, and cook for 1 minute or so.

Add the chicken broth and drop in the prepared herbal infusion and astragalus root (if not already in the herbal bundle). Cover and bring to a gentle boil. Reduce the heat to a simmer and cook, covered or partially covered, for at least 20 minutes to infuse the broth with the herbs.

Add the cubed squash and cook until the squash is tender but still holding its shape, 5 to 10 minutes. Drain and add the cooked lentils, kale, and wakame seaweed (if using), and cook for 2 to 3 more minutes to incorporate.

Remove from the heat. Using a slotted spoon or kitchen tongs, remove the herbal bundle, whole

ADOPT-A-RECIPE   Elizabeth Ann Howson

green onions, and/or astragalus root.

In a medium bowl, stir the miso with about ¼ cup (60 mL) of hot broth from the soup pot. Mix with a fork or whisk to melt the miso. Pour this mixture into the soup pot, stir well, and taste for seasoning. Add more salt or miso paste if needed.

Stir in the goji berries (if using). Ladle into soup bowls and enjoy!

TIPS:
Try to source the astragalus root from an Asian grocer if you can. Alternatively, you may find tea bag combinations of echinacea and astragalus root at a natural foods store.

In spring, you can substitute dried nettle leaf, for 1 cup/250 mL of fresh nettles, adding them when you add the kale.

You can find chaga mushrooms in a bark or powder form in natural foods stores.

Be creative and substitute other green herbs or vegetables you have on hand. Zucchini, fresh parsley, chard, and beet greens are also delicious additions to this soup!

Chef Marc Kusitor, a George Brown culinary grad, is interested in exploring the possibilities in the space between tradition and innovation in Afro-Caribbean cuisine. @choptimecatering

MARC KUSITOR

BOUYON AK LEGUME

Vegan Haitian Soup

Politics, identity, culture, and history all meet in the kitchen. Marc explores them all, reaching out from his own Haitian and African roots deep into a cuisine densely entangled with colonialism and slavery, resistance and revolt, creativity and celebration.

Hearty soup-stews like this *bouyon* can be found across the Caribbean, but just like its distinctive music, fashion, and lyrical Krèyol dialect, Haiti's take is infused with a style all its own.

Prep: 25 min

Cook: 35 min

Makes: 4 to 6 servings

Vegan

Epis
(see Tips):
1 medium green bell pepper, roughly chopped
1 small leek, roughly chopped
½ clove garlic, peeled
½ green onion, cut into pieces
4 tbsp chopped fresh parsley
2 tbsp vegetable oil
Salt

Soup Base:
1 tbsp olive oil
½ cup epis (see Tips)
2 bay leaves
3 sprigs thyme
2¼ tsp smoked paprika
1 tbsp tomato paste
1 tbsp liquid Maggi seasoning (see Tips), plus more to taste
10 cups/2.4 L vegetable stock
1 Scotch bonnet pepper, whole

Dumplings
(aka doumbrey):
2 cups/260 g all-purpose flour
1½ tsp salt
½ cup/125 mL water

Soup Vegetables:
1 medium cassava, peeled and finely diced
1 medium white sweet potato, peeled and medium-diced

1 green plantain, peeled and cut into 1¼-inch/3 cm rounds
1 small yellow yam, peeled and finely diced
1 chayote squash, peeled and medium-diced
½ large carrot, peeled and medium-diced
3 cups packed/90 g spinach (see Tips)
Salt and freshly ground black pepper

TIPS:
Epis *serves as the flavour base for many Haitian dishes; every Caribbean island has its own variation, so feel free to experiment. Bottled Green Seasoning, available in most West Indian grocery stores, can be substituted.*

Maggi seasoning is readily available in most Caribbean, African, or Asian grocery stores. Other bouillon liquid or cubes could be substituted, but Maggi is the Haitian choice.

The root vegetables called for in this soup are available in most West Indian grocery stores. Because they cook at different rates, it is important to add them separately.

Frozen spinach can be substituted if fresh is not available.

ADOPT-A-RECIPE   Lisa Kates

Make the epis: In a food processor, combine the bell pepper, leek, garlic, green onion, and parsley and pulse until a chunky paste forms. Pulse in the vegetable oil and salt to taste until well combined. Measure out ½ cup/125 mL to use in the soup and set aside. (Store the remaining epis in an airtight container in the refrigerator for up to 2 weeks; just add enough neutral-tasting oil to cover the top of the mixture.)

Make the soup base: In a medium soup pot, heat the olive oil over medium heat. Add the reserved ½ cup epis and sauté, stirring constantly, until fragrant, 2 to 3 minutes. Add the bay leaves, thyme, and smoked paprika. Continue to cook, while stirring, for another minute. Add the tomato paste and cook, stirring constantly, until the mixture is a deep red colour, about 5 minutes. Add the Maggi seasoning and vegetable stock. Stir well, scraping up any browned bits sticking to the bottom of the pot. Increase the heat and bring the mixture to a boil. Reduce the heat to a simmer and add the whole Scotch bonnet pepper.

Meanwhile, make the dumplings: In a medium bowl, combine the flour and salt. Add the water, 1 tablespoon at a time, and knead until it comes together and forms a smooth dough. (It should not be sticky.)

Transfer the dough to a cutting board and shape into a flat rectangle. Cut into 8 equal strips. Cut each strip in half, to get 16 pieces of dough.

With your palms, roll the dough into rough cylinders, stretching lengthwise until about the diameter of a pinky finger; they will soak up the soup and grow slightly while cooking.

Add the soup vegetables: As the soup simmers, add each of the vegetables, allowing 3 minutes between additions, starting with the cassava, followed by the sweet potato, green plantain, yellow yam, chayote, carrot, and spinach. Once all the vegetables have been added, increase the heat to medium and cook until the vegetables are softened but retain their texture, about 5 minutes.

Add the dumplings and cook until they are fluffy and cooked through, about 5 minutes.

Remove the Scotch bonnet. If you want more heat, you can burst it and leave in the soup. Taste and adjust the seasoning with salt and black pepper.

Prep: 40 min
Cook: 40 min
Makes: 4 to 6 servings

2 poblano peppers (see Tips), seeded and roughly chopped

3 green onions, roughly chopped

2 cloves garlic, smashed and peeled

2 tbsp ají amarillo paste (see Tips)

2 heaping cups/ 70 g fresh cilantro, roughly chopped

6 bone-in, skin-on chicken thighs (about 2 lb/910 g)

Kosher salt and freshly ground black pepper

2 tbsp canola oil

3 cups/710 mL water

4 cups/950 mL chicken stock

2 tsp salt (if you use salted stock, no salt is needed)

1 tbsp ground cumin

¾ cup/150 g basmati rice

1 cup/135 g frozen peas

For Serving:

1 cup/180 g black rice, cooked according to package directions

2 tbsp chopped fresh cilantro

Sliced green onions, for garnish

Crispy chicken skins (optional; see Tips)

4 to 6 lime wedges

CAROLE NELSON BROWN

AGUADITO DE POLLO

Peruvian Chicken Rice Soup

Carole is a hard-core kitchen nerd; she loves all the kitchen gadgets and the science behind how they all work. Her popular Instant Pot classes got me hooked on this game-changer of an appliance and this recipe is perfect for it, but it can easily be done on the stovetop as well. Crisping the chicken skin separately and using dramatic black rice turns this rustic comfort food into something dinner-party ready.

In a blender, combine the poblanos, green onions, garlic, ají amarillo paste, and cilantro. Add just enough water to get it going (¼ cup/60 mL should be enough, but don't worry if it's a bit more).

If you are making the crispy chicken skin (see Tips), pull the skin off the chicken and set aside. Season the chicken thighs with salt and pepper. Preheat the Instant Pot (Sauté function) and when hot, add the canola oil and chicken thighs (skin-side down if you are leaving the skin on) and brown the chicken on both sides, 8 to 10 minutes. Remove from the pot and set aside. Scrape the cilantro purée into the pot and cook, stirring frequently, until it turns a deep green, 4 to 5 minutes. Add the 3 cups /710 mL water to the blender and give it a good shake so that you don't waste any of that green purée. Add it to the pot, along with the stock, the salt (if using unsalted stock), and the cumin. Return the chicken to the pot, along with

the basmati rice. Lock the lid, set the vent to sealing, and program it for 15 minutes at High Pressure.

When the time is up, do a quick-release. With tongs, remove the chicken thighs and set aside until cool enough to handle.

Add the frozen peas to the pot and put the lid back on so the peas can heat up in the soup while you prepare the chicken.

Remove the meat from the bones (discard the bones and skin if still on) and shred roughly before adding back to the broth.

To serve, add a scoop of black rice to each bowl, ladle in the soup, and sprinkle with some cilantro and sliced green onions. If you made the crispy chicken skin, set a piece or two on top of each bowl. Serve with the lime wedges.

As Torontonians and downtown people, too many young people never learn how to cook, just order out. But to me cooking is love, and I'm like an old Italian nonna—it's how I show people I love them . . . The whole process is that you get your loved ones together and you're all in the kitchen—that's what makes food really great.

TIPS:

If you don't have an Instant Pot, you can make the soup in a pot on the stove; you will need to simmer it for about 45 minutes.

If you can't find fresh poblanos, you can use canned or substitute green peppers and 1 seeded jalapeño for some heat.

Ají amarillo paste is a Peruvian seasoning paste made from yellow chili peppers and is quite hot. It can be found in South/ Latin American grocery stores or online.

To make the crispy chicken skin: Preheat the oven to 375°F. Line a baking sheet with parchment paper.

After pulling off the chicken skin, cut each piece into 2 or 3 strips. Transfer the strips to the lined baking sheet and season generously with kosher salt and freshly ground pepper. Cover with another sheet of parchment paper. Place a second baking tray on top to weigh down the skins and keep them from curling.

Bake in the middle of the oven until the skin is totally crispy and browned, 45 to 50 minutes. Transfer to a paper towel–lined plate to drain. Allow to cool for at least 1 hour.

You can cook the crispy chicken skin up to a day before and store it covered in an airtight container.

Carole Nelson Brown wears a lot of food hats: She's a food writer, blogger, stylist, instructor, and recipe developer and tester–as well as a professional makeup artist for film and TV. @mamashack

ADOPT-A-RECIPE   Elisa Shenkier

ROSSY EARLE

CEVICHE DE MARISCOS

Panamanian Seafood Ceviche

Born and raised in Panama, at the crossroads of Latin American and Caribbean culture, Rossy delights in making those roots part of her Canadian food culture. Ceviche is a staple at pretty much every party or get-together in Panama, but one of the nicest ways to enjoy it is freshly made from any of the countless *cevicherias* near the beach.

My grandmother on my mom's side was from northern Spain. Her husband, my grandfather, was Jewish from Poland but born in Panama. Then on my dad's side, there's my grandfather, who was blond, with white skin and blue eyes. And that grandmother had African roots, even though she was white. And there's a huge Chinese influence in Panama, and I have an obsession with East and Southeast Asian food.

Born and raised in Panama, **Rossy Earle** works as a freelance chef, recipe developer, and food stylist in Toronto, with a flair for Latin American flavours. She also has a line of hot sauces, called Rossy's, including the smoky Diablo's Fuego, and the sweeter Diabla's Kiss. @pancancooks

Prep: 30 min
Cook: 4 hr

Makes: 4 to 6 servings

1 lb/450 g corvina or any firm white fish (such as sea bass, halibut, snapper, mahi mahi, tilapia), cut into ½-inch/1.3 cm cubes

½ lb/225 g bay scallops

½ lb/225 g small shrimp (51/60 count ideal; if larger, cut into ½-inch/1.3 cm pieces), peeled and deveined

Sea salt

2 cups/480 mL beer (lager or ale, not a stout or dark brown ale)

12 mussels, scrubbed and debearded

18 clams, cleaned (see Tips)

2 cups/480 mL fresh lime juice (10 to 12 limes)

1 cup/240mL fresh lemon juice (about 4 lemons)

2 tbsp apple cider vinegar

1 large white onion, finely diced (about 2 cups/320 g)

1 celery stalk, finely diced

2 cloves garlic, minced

2 tsp chopped habanero pepper (optional)

4 tbsp extra-virgin olive oil

1 tbsp honey

4 tbsp chopped fresh culantro (see Tips) or cilantro

4 tbsp chopped fresh parsley

For Serving:

1 small red onion, slivered

Chopped culantro or cilantro

Chopped parsley

4 to 6 romaine leaves

4 to 6 lemon/lime wedges

Soda crackers, plantain chips, or tortilla chips

Place the diced fish, scallops, and shrimp in a glass (or other non-reactive) bowl, season with sea salt and set aside.

In a medium pot, combine 1 cup/240 mL beer, 1 cup/240 mL water, and a generous pinch of salt and bring to a boil. Add the mussels and clams, cover, and cook until they open. Scoop them out as soon as they open and set aside to cool. (Discard any that do not open.) Remove the meat from the shells if you wish and add to the fish and seafood bowl.

In a separate glass (or other non-reactive) bowl, whisk together the lime juice, lemon juice, vinegar, and the remaining 1 cup/250 mL beer. Add the diced onion, celery, garlic, and habanero pepper (if using). Add the olive oil and honey and stir to combine well.

Pour the mixture over the seafood and stir well to make sure all the pieces are evenly coated. Cover the bowl with plastic wrap or a lid and refrigerate for 3 hours, stirring every hour or so.

When ready to serve, stir in the culantro and parsley and season with more salt if needed.

To serve: Garnish with the slivered red onion and some chopped culantro, and parsley. Serve with the romaine leaves, lemon or lime wedges, and some soda crackers, plantain chips, or tortilla chips.

TIPS:
Culantro, aka chadon beni, can be found in Asian, Latin, and Caribbean grocery stores; in a pinch, substitute cilantro.

Fish and seafood for ceviche should be sushi-grade, meaning suitable for raw consumption.

To clean clams, place them in a large bowl of cold water with a handful of sea salt or cornmeal; soak for 30 minutes, drain, and scrub.

SCOTCH EGGS

MICHAEL KIRKWOOD

Chef Michael is a lifer, an old-school kitchen pro who worked his way up through countless restaurants to head up some of the city's top fine-dining kitchens. But it is a tough grind, and between gigs Michael freelanced and graced The Dep with many fabulous meals, raising the bar as he went. His all-day, intensive pig, fowl, and whole fish butchery workshop—known as Meat Camp—was a perennial hit.

Prep: 30 min
Cook: 10 min
Makes: 4 servings

5 large eggs (free-range if possible)

½ lb/225 g ground lamb (preferably fresh, not frozen)

1 tbsp ground coriander

1 tbsp fennel seeds

1 tsp crushed chili flakes

2 tbsp dried parsley

Salt and freshly ground black pepper

¾ cup/98 g all-purpose flour

1 cup/60 g panko bread crumbs

Neutral oil, for deep-frying

Set up a bowl of ice and water. Bring a medium saucepan of water to a boil over high heat. Using a slotted spoon, carefully add 4 of the eggs, reduce the heat slightly, and cook the eggs at a gentle boil until soft-boiled, about 6 minutes. Using a slotted spoon, transfer the eggs to the bowl of ice water and cool. Carefully peel the eggs, so as not to break the yolks. Set aside.

In a large bowl, combine the lamb, coriander, fennel seeds, chili flakes, and parsley. Season with salt and black pepper. Stir to combine.

To test the seasoning, fry a small spoonful of the lamb mixture. Taste and adjust the seasoning as necessary.

Divide the lamb mixture into 4 equal portions. Roll 1 portion into a ball and flatten with the palm of your hand like a pancake. Place 1 cooked egg in the middle and gently wrap the lamb mixture around the egg. Be sure the egg is completely covered. Repeat with the remaining lamb mixture and eggs.

Set up a dredging station in three shallow bowls: Place the flour in one bowl. In the second bowl, beat the remaining raw egg. Place the panko in the third bowl. Dredge each lamb-coated egg first in the flour, then in the beaten egg, and finally in the panko.

Meanwhile, pour 3 to 4 inches/7.5 to 10 cm oil into a deep-fryer or heavy-bottomed medium pot and heat over medium-high heat to about 350°F/177°C.

Deep-fry the Scotch eggs until dark gold, 5 to 7 minutes. Allow to cool for 5 minutes. Slice each one directly down the centre and watch as the yolk oozes out. Can be served warm, at room temperature, or chilled for a picnic.

TIPS:

Serve with a nice fresh salad.

Scotch eggs can be prepped a day in advance and kept uncooked in the fridge. Allow to come to room temp (about 30 minutes) before frying.

These can also be cooked in an air-fryer: Spray well with oil and air-fry at 375°F/190°C for about 6 minutes, then turn and cook for another 6 minutes.

> *When I go to the market and I buy something, I don't know what I am going to make but I want to be creative. And then I come home or go to the restaurant and well, just give me a corner of the kitchen by myself and there's a calmness, a serenity to it. The act of creating, the act of taking those ingredients and making it something else and tasting it and then getting everyone around you to taste it. I get so excited about it—that's what food does to me.*

Chef Michael Kirkwood established his reputation in some of Toronto's top fine-dining kitchens. @chefmichaelkirkwood

Carolyn Humphreys

Mauritius is a tiny island in the Indian Ocean off the east coast of Africa. I was born and raised there and moved to Canada seventeen years ago. We are from a very middle class, modest family, a family very influenced by what we have in our backyard, and our neighbours' backyard. So, if I have mango, I'm gonna go share with my other relatives, or my neighbours. If my neighbour has a jackfruit, they'll share with us. In Mauritius, everybody is like your neighbour, everyone is like family.

Chef Vanesha Khadaroo ran
La Marmite
Mauricienne–
The Mauritian Pot–
a catering company
focusing on Mauritian
cuisine for many years,
including numerous
memorable events
at The Depanneur.
@vaneshakhadaroo

VANESHA KHADAROO
VINDAYE OURITE
Mauritian Octopus Salad

I can't say I knew anything at all about Mauritius before I met Vanesha, other than it had once been the home of the now-extinct dodo bird. From her I learned that this remote island in the Indian Ocean is a vibrant melting pot of global cultures and traditions, with a buttery French creole dialect animated by the funky tropical rhythms of *sega* music. The cuisine is a distinctive fusion of East Indian, African, and Chinese influences with French and English colonial twists. Vanesha did many events at The Dep, from street food–inspired pop-ups to the remarkable Sept Cari Ti Puri—the seven-course vegetarian banquet that is served on banana leaves at Hindu weddings on the island. This authentic Mauritian octopus salad recipe can be found at street stalls by the beaches where fishermen, known as *piqueurs d'ourite*, arrive before sunrise to fish for octopus.

Prep: 30 min
Cook: 1 hour 10 min

Makes: 4 to 6 servings

2 lb/910 g octopus, beak removed, washed

1 tbsp coarse sea salt

5 tbsp distilled white vinegar

½ cup/125 mL vegetable oil

2 tbsp crushed garlic

1 tbsp ground mustard seeds

½ tsp black mustard seeds

1 tbsp ground turmeric

½ cup/80 g roughly chopped onions (red, white, or a mix)

1 to 2 green chilies, sliced (optional, but not really)

Salt

Baguette halves, for serving

1 tbsp cilantro leaves, for garnish

Fill a large pot with water, add the octopus, coarse sea salt, and vinegar, and place on the stove over medium heat. Boil the octopus until tender enough so that you can pierce the thickest part of a tentacle with a paring knife with little resistance, about 1 hour.

Remove from the heat and rinse the boiled octopus with cold water. Cut into ¾-inch/2 cm pieces.

In a large skillet, heat the vegetable oil over medium heat. Add the garlic, ground mustard seeds, black mustard seeds, and turmeric. Cook, stirring constantly, until fragrant, about 2 minutes.

Add the octopus pieces and cook for another 3 minutes. Stir in the onions and green chilies (if using) and cook for 3 minutes. Add salt to taste.

Serve on baguette halves, topped with the cilantro leaves. Bon appétit!

TIP:
Always use a big pot to boil octopus or it may overflow.

ADOPT-A-RECIPE Marcia Ross

VICTOR UGWUEKE

SHRIMP SURFERS ON NIGERIAN TOSTONES

At over fifteen million people, Lagos is one of the largest cities in Africa, dwarfing any city in North America. Teeming with creative energy, it is a melting pot for global culinary influences that are forging a vibrant new modern African cuisine. Victor's food embodies that energy, infused with a funky Afrobeat soundtrack (one of our shared passions). Here a spicy shrimp surfs a wave of creamy avocado atop a double-cooked plantain tostone, inspired by the tradition of Nigerian "small chops," little dishes for sharing.

When I was six years old, I lost my dad, back in Nigeria. Eventually, my mom decided to start a restaurant and I started to help out there when I was eight, nine, ten years old. After school, I would go to the restaurant, and I'd help by washing the plates and stuff. From there I started doing prep in the kitchen and I worked my way up to being the kitchen manager. So, I grew up in the kitchen; I've been cooking my whole life.

Afrobeat Kitchen is Nigerian chef Victor Ugwueke's exciting New African Eats pop-up food project. Through music and food, he is sharing his *faaji* (the pleasure from having a good time) with Toronto. @afrobeatkitchen

Prep: 40 min
Cook: 15 min

Makes: 12 pieces

Marinated Shrimp:

Juice of ½ lime

1 inch/2.5 cm fresh ginger, peeled and minced

1 clove garlic, minced

½ cup/125 mL full-fat coconut milk

½ cup/125 mL pineapple juice

12 jumbo shrimp (21/25 count) about ½ lb/225 g

Salt and freshly ground black pepper

Avocado Mash:

2 medium avocados, halved and pitted

1 tbsp finely diced onion, or to taste

1 clove garlic, minced

Juice of ½ lime

Salt and freshly ground black pepper

Cayenne pepper or hot sauce (optional)

Kelewele Spice Mix:

1 tsp dried or fresh thyme

1 tsp ground ginger

½ tsp ground cinnamon

½ to 1 tsp cayenne pepper (or paprika if you prefer it mild)

Tostones:

1 yellow plantain

About 4 tbsp vegetable oil

1 cup/250 mL water

1 tsp salt

Juice of ½ lime

To Finish:

Vegetable oil, for cooking the tostones and shrimp

3 tbsp ata dindin (West African pepper sauce) or your favourite hot sauce

Lime wedges, for serving

Marinate the shrimp: In a bowl, combine the lime juice, ginger, garlic, coconut milk, and pineapple juice. Add the shrimp to the bowl, season with salt and pepper, and marinate at least 20 minutes.

Make the avocado mash: Scoop the avocado flesh into a bowl. Add the onion, garlic, and lime juice and mash the avocados into a chunky blend. Season with salt and pepper, adding some cayenne pepper or hot sauce (if using). Cover with plastic wrap touching the surface of the mix to prevent browning. Set aside.

Make the kelewele spice mix: In a small bowl, mix together the thyme, ginger, cinnamon, and cayenne. Set aside.

Make the tostones: Peel the plantain by slicing through the peel lengthwise and then prying it off. Cut crosswise into 12 slices 1 inch/2.5 cm thick.

Pour enough vegetable oil into a heavy skillet to come halfway up the sides of the plantain slices. Heat until just hot enough to bubble lightly when you add the plantain slices, about 325° to 350°F/163° to 177°C.

Line a plate with paper towels. Add the plantains slices to the hot oil and fry until soft and golden, about 4 minutes. Transfer to the paper towels to drain.

Use the bottom of a wide glass, jar, or can to gently flatten each slice.

In a small bowl, stir together the water, salt, and lime juice. Dip the flattened plantain slices into the salted lime water and set aside. Let air-dry for a few minutes. You can leave them at this stage until you're ready to fry them the second time, right before serving.

To finish: When it's time to serve, in a skillet, heat about ½ inch/1 cm of oil over medium-high heat and add the flattened plantains to the oil to briefly

crisp up, about 1 minute per side. Remove to paper towels to drain briefly, then toss with the kelewele spice.

In a separate skillet, heat some oil over medium-high heat and sear the shrimp, brushing with some of the hot sauce, until pink and cooked through, 1 to 2 minutes on each side.

(Alternatively, you could cook the shrimp on a grill over medium-high heat.)

To assemble the surfers, place a generous dollop of avocado mash on each tostone, top with a shrimp, and drizzle with some hot sauce to taste. Serve with lime wedges.

My cupboards are always, always, always stocked, to the point of overflowing. I find that I will buy, acquire, or be gifted these beautiful special foodstuffs. And I hold on to them until they're inedible because I refuse to use them. I think it's because I grew up in a part-time food insecure house that I've always been a food hoarder. This is one of the things that I have come to reckon with in terms of food security, and some of the idiosyncrasies of mental health.

Mikiki is a performance and video artist and queer community health activist. Mikiki is now dedicated to their art practice full time when not hosting their *Golden Girls* screening and queer cultural studies lecture series Rose Beef.
@mkkultra

TIPS:

Only duck gizzards will do. Rinse, pat dry, and remove extraneous fat and knobbly bits.

You need the grated zest of 2 lemons for the finished dish, so before you juice the lemons for the gizzards and the yogurt sauce, grate the zest and set aside.

Obviously 4 cups/950 mL of duck fat is not available to everyone, but even 1 cup/250 mL of duck fat plus enough olive oil to cover is better than none. You can purchase duck fat at good butchers.

You will strain and keep all the fat. It gives life and is manna from heaven and makes frying pancakes just out of this world.

MIKIKI
SALADE DYSPÉRIGOURDINE
Not Périgord Salad, Get Over Yourself

Prep: 30 min, plus 8 to 12 hr brining time
Cook: 6½ hr
Makes: 4 servings

To get some idea of what Mikiki is like in the kitchen, someone once likened them to "Julia Child on PCP." A combination provocative performance artist, committed activist, fabulous drag queen, and talented cook, Mikiki was in charge of breaking all the rules for many of The Dep's Valentine's Day Supper Clubs. You could count on a messy, joyful transgression of boundaries of genre, performance, romance, and cuisine.

This recipe is based very loosely on and inspired by one of Mikiki's favourite classic French dishes, salade périgourdine. A warm salad consisting of succulent confit duck gizzards alongside seared Chinese long beans, spiced candied walnuts, and a creamy labneh-esque schmear.

Brine the gizzards: Place the trimmed gizzards in a large metal or ceramic bowl. Rub together the thyme sprigs until the leaves become very fragrant, and add to the gizzards, along with the salt, lemon juice, and tepid water. Stir until the salt has dissolved. Ensure the gizzards are submerged in the brine, cover, and refrigerate for 8 hours or overnight.

Make the yogurt sauce: In a glass or ceramic bowl, mix together the yogurt, tahini, mustard, and lemon juice until smooth and consistent. Cover and refrigerate overnight.

Confit the gizzards: Drain the gizzards and thyme (discard the brine) and pat them dry with a clean tea towel. Line a slow cooker with the gizzards, add the thyme, garlic, shallots, and salt. Throw in some whole chilies if that's your jam. Add the duck fat (and oil if using) to cover completely and turn on low. Cook covered for 5½ to 6 hours until tender yet still firm.

To finish: In a ripping hot, well-seasoned cast-iron skillet, with as little oil as you dare, dry-fry the beans until they get charred in places and cooked through, about 5 minutes. A little water splashed off a spoon to give some steam would be fine, but these are not steamed or blanched beans. Remove from the heat and let cool to room temperature.

Thin out the harissa with a few teaspoons of water. Add it and the walnuts to a bag and toss (Shake 'n Bake style) to coat evenly. Dust the walnuts lightly with the sugar and arrange on a baking sheet set on a heatproof surface. Using a small kitchen blow torch, torch them until they caramelize. Allow to cool and harden.

Drain the gizzards in a colander over a clean pot. Reserve 1 spoonful of the fat for this recipe and the rest for another use (see Tips).

On a cutting board, pat the gizzards dry and cut into slices ½ inch/1.3 cm thick. In a skillet, melt the butter with a spoonful of duck fat over medium heat. Sear the gizzard slices quickly–*not too much*–you want to keep as much original colour as possible.

In a wide, low-rise dark oxblood-glazed ceramic bowl (or something equally pretentious), take a heaping spoon of the yogurt sauce and make a throwing motion towards off-centre of the plate. With the back of the spoon, press to the bottom of the thickest part of the sauce and drag it in a circle around the circumference of the plate. Basically, just draw a circle with the sauce.

Take the beans and lay them upon the plate wherever the heck you like.

Take a large handful of the gizzards and sprinkle them over the plate. Do the same with the walnuts.

Deglaze the skillet you seared the gizzards in with the ½ cup stock, reduce a little, and then drip that liquid lovingly and sloppily around the plate.

Sprinkle with the herbs, lemon zest, and chopped capers.

Gizzards:

1½ lb/680 g duck gizzards (see Tips)

1 bunch thyme sprigs

4 tbsp salt

Juice of 1 lemon (see Tips)

2 cups/480 mL water

2 heads garlic, halved horizontally

3 shallots, sliced widthwise

2 tbsp salt

Whole chilies (optional)

4 cups/950 mL duck fat plus olive oil (see Tips)

Yogurt Sauce:

1 cup/225 g full-fat plain yogurt

1 cup/240 g tahini

2 tbsp whole-grain mustard

Juice of 1 lemon

To Finish:

Vegetable oil

2 bunches long beans, trimmed

4 tbsp harissa paste

1 cup/100 g walnuts

4 tbsp sugar

4 tbsp/60 g salted butter

½ cup/125 mL stock, white wine, or water

A fistful of herbs

Zest of 2 lemons (see Tips)

½ cup/68 g capers, roughly chopped

 ADOPT-A-RECIPE   Salimah Y. Ebrahim

MIKIKI

Going out for dinner on Valentine's Day, that saccharine celebration of heteronormativity, feels like an ideal occasion for a bit of subversion. I had some fun with it over the years, with Kalmplex's gender-fluid, vegan Ital Valentines, Paula Costa's 7 Deadly Sins, and my own attempt at a provocative Secret Heart Supper Club. So, when Mikiki approached me about doing some events, Valentine's Day seemed like the perfect place to shake things up.

Towering at over six foot five in huge heels, with 4-inch eyelashes and full kabuki-esque paint, Mikiki combined a wicked, transgressive sense of humour, ambitious culinary ideas, and a sophisticated conceptual and artistic sensibility that were all integral to the performance that was the meal. It was drag on a plate. The inaugural 2017 dinner, My Funny Valentine, tested the waters with dishes like Street Meat Urchin: an amuse-bouche of crispy pork skin, a light sparkling gel of sauerkraut juice, and a mustard/sea urchin crema. Or Any Port in a Storm: confit of salt cod with preserved

Roses are red
Gender is performative
Let's make Valentine's Day
Less heteronormative

Jax Ruggiero/@simply.jax

quail egg crumble and pickled blueberries on a disc of grilled potato. Dishes were served interspersed with raunchy banter, cabaret songs, and personal storytelling around the inspiration of the dishes. It was literally and figuratively and colloquially fabulous. I was delighted that someone was taking full advantage of the freedom The Dep could offer to reimagine what a night at a "restaurant" could mean.

Emboldened by their success, **Mikiki went on to host a string of fantastic events, each facing the non-trivial challenge of how to outdo the previous one.** In 2018, the dinner was My Bloody Valentine, themed on the Saint Valentine's Day Massacre, the mob assassination of seven men on Chicago's North Side in 1929. Blood was the star ingredient, and each course was dedicated to one of the slain mobsters. Challenging the outer limits of food, art, and social convention, guests were given lancets and invited to garnish their digestif with a single drop of their own blood, or to exchange drinks in a ritual evoking the "blood brother" pacts of schoolyard boys.

The iconic image of the night was that of a glamorous Mikiki, in a magenta wig and gold lamé evening gown, delicately touching up their lipstick from a litre container of duck blood. Mikiki would host several more Valentine's Day Supper Clubs, with themes ranging from Tentacle Porn to Hot Garbage, each one fearless, funny, and truly provocative— in both the sexy and confrontational sense.

Prep: 45 min, plus at least 5 hr refrigeration (ideally overnight)

Cook: 3½ hr

Makes: 30 to 35 bitterballen

Bitterballen:

3 cups/710 mL water

1 lb/450 g stewing beef

1 vegetable stock cube

Salt

5 tbsp/75 g salted butter

½ tbsp finely chopped onion

¾ cup/97 g all-purpose flour

1 tbsp white wine or cooking wine

¾ tsp nutmeg

1 tsp ground mace

½ tsp ground white pepper

1 tsp dried parsley

For Deep-Frying:

½ cup/65 g all-purpose flour

2 large eggs

1 cup/60 g panko bread crumbs

Oil, for deep-frying

JUSTIN FREDERIK GO

BITTERBALLEN

Beef Mini Croquettes

The Dep was a fertile testing ground for entrepreneurial ideas, a safe, low-stakes way to try out an idea and work out the kinks before undertaking the much riskier endeavour of launching a new business. Around 2014, Justin, with the help of his partner, Alison Broverman, started a roving pop-up featuring hard-to-find-classic Dutch snacks like these *bitterballen*. They did a string of popular Drop-In Dinners at The Dep, and the confidence and experience gained paved the way to them opening Borrel, their own Dutch-themed restaurant and bar inspired by old-fashioned Amsterdam pubs known as "brown cafés."

Make the bitterballen: In a medium pot, bring the water to a boil. Reduce the heat to a simmer and add the stewing beef, cover, and simmer until very tender so it falls apart easily, about 3 hours. (Alternatively, do this in a standard or electric pressure cooker, where it will take 45 minutes.) Reserving the cooking liquid in the pot, remove the beef with a slotted spoon. Pull the beef apart with two forks and chop into 30 to 35 small pieces. (You can also dice it finely in a food processor.)

Heat the reserved cooking liquid (if it evaporated too much, add water to have about 3 cups/710 mL) in the pot. Add the vegetable stock cube and combine, adding salt if the broth tastes a bit bland. Remove from the heat.

In a medium pot, heat the butter over low heat. Add the onion and allow to soften, about 10 minutes. Don't burn it! Sprinkle on the flour and mix until the butter is absorbed. Increase the heat slightly and gradually add the broth to the roux, about ½ cup/125 mL at a time, stirring constantly. You are looking for a consistency of thick gravy. Don't add all the broth if the roux is getting too thin. (Adding the shredded beef later will help thicken it more.)

Cook the roux for 2 to 3 minutes to get rid of the raw flour taste. Add the white wine and season with the nutmeg, mace, white pepper, and dried parsley.

Add the beef to the roux and stir it all together. The roux should stick to a spoon fairly well. If it feels too thin, you can continue to cook it on low heat a bit longer; too thick and you can add a bit more broth.

Transfer the roux to a container and allow it to cool and solidify before covering. Place in the fridge to chill, ideally overnight.

To deep-fry: Set up a breading station in three shallow bowls: Place the flour in one bowl. Whisk the eggs in the second bowl. Spread the panko in the third. Use a small scoop or spoon to make little balls of the beef roux, about 1 inch/2.5 cm in diameter. Coat each beef ball first in the flour, then in the eggs (a slotted spoon helps), and finally in the panko, placing them on a tray as you work.

Refrigerate the tray of bitterballen for 30 minutes. (They also freeze well at this stage, just thaw them fully overnight before you fry them.)

Preheat 3 to 4 inches/7.5 to 10 cm of oil in a deep-fryer or Dutch oven and heat to 350°F/177°C.

Working in batches of about 5 at a time, fry the bitterballen for 2 to 2½ minutes. Keep an eye on them, if they are still a bit frozen or if there's a leak in the breading, they can come apart in the fryer. They are done when golden brown and they float to the top.

Serve with your favourite mustard and a drink!

ALISSA KONDOGIANNIS

LATKES

Savoury Potato Pancakes

Alissa has the Jewish instinct for comfort food: tender challah fresh from the oven, gooey chocolatey babkas, and, of course, crispy potato latkes. Latkes are emblematic of Hanukkah, the Jewish Festival of Lights, which features fried foods to signify the miraculous lamp oil that lasted eight days under siege. Potatoes, being from the New World, are a relatively recent addition to Jewish cooking; more ancient versions included buckwheat or cheese pancakes.

The first meal I ever made on my own was for my husband when we first moved in together. It was morogo, a spinach and potato dish. And I remember feeling very proud of myself. We were meant to be the new South Africans, we were meant to be multicultural, the first white people to have black friends. We were moving towards this whole new progressive South Africa. And I was making an African dish. I don't even remember if it tasted any good. I just remember that I made it and I was just thrilled.

Alissa Kondogiannis began her cooking career in Johannesburg in the early '90s. Today, you'll find her running a small catering company. @barnstarkitchen

Prep: 15 to 20 min
Cook: 20 to 30 min
Makes: 6 servings

6 medium white potatoes (2 lb/ 900 g), peeled

1 large onion, finely chopped or grated (about 1½ cups/ 240 g)

3 large eggs, lightly beaten

1 tsp salt

½ tsp freshly ground black pepper

4 tbsp all-purpose flour

2 tsp baking powder

1 tbsp vegetable or canola oil, plus more for frying

With a box grater or food processor, grate the potatoes. Transfer to a large bowl lined with a tea towel. Add the onion to the potatoes. Gather the ends of the towel and twist, over a sink, to remove as much liquid as possible.

Return the potatoes and onion to the bowl. Add the eggs, salt, pepper, flour, baking powder, and 1 tablespoon oil. Stir well to combine.

Line a baking sheet with paper towels. Pour ½ inch/1.3 cm oil into a large skillet and heat over medium heat. Slowly drop heaped tablespoons of the potato mixture into the oil, flattening slightly into a 2-inch/5 cm round. Fry until golden, 2 to 3 minutes per side. Transfer to the paper towels to drain and continue with the next batch.

TIPS:

Be sure to thoroughly wring out the potato mixture or the latkes won't crisp as well.

Traditionally topped with applesauce or sour cream, latkes can be eaten hot, right out of the pan, or at room temperature.

Cooked latkes can be frozen, flat on baking sheets, and then stored in freezer bags. Reheat from frozen in a 450°F/230°C oven for 5 minutes.

ADOPT-A-RECIPE   Gale Rubenstein

We make this for the Persian New Year, Nowruz. (Now means "new" and ruz means "day.") So it's the first spring day and the dish is filled with the new things that are in the world. I always have a very good memory of this, of Persian New Year that gathers all the families together, sitting there at one table. My mom used to make it when I was a kid and she still actually does that. It brings me very good memories.

Sonbol Zand's passion for cooking has become a sanctuary after long hours at work as an IT manager. Growing up in an Iranian home, Persian dishes are among her favourites to prepare and share with others.
@sonbijoon

SONBOL ZAND

KOOKOO SABZI

Persian Herb Frittata

Prep: 30 min
Cook: 30 min
Makes: 6 to 8 servings

Persian culture's breadth and depth makes it one of the most historically influential in the world, and one can taste its legacy from the Balkans all the way to the Indian subcontinent. This herb-packed, frittata-like omelette is also a deeply symbolic dish—fresh green fronds of rebirth and renewal, bound by the fertility of eggs—that is traditionally served on the spring equinox at the start of the Persian solar year.

Working in batches, either by hand or in a food processor, finely chop or pulse the parsley, cilantro, dill, and chives. Make sure not to overdo it. Place the chopped herbs in a large bowl. Pulse the green onions and garlic and add to the bowl of herbs. The key is to ensure everything is finely chopped but not mushy. Add the barberries and walnuts (if using).

In a large bowl, whisk together the salt, cinnamon, turmeric, saffron (if using), and pepper. Add 6 eggs and whisk until blended.

Add the herbs and stir to combine well; you want the mixture to have the consistency of thick yogurt. If it's too thick, stir in the remaining 2 eggs.

In a 10- or 12-inch/25 or 30 cm nonstick skillet, heat the oil over low heat. Pour in the herb/egg mixture and spread it out evenly. (You don't want it to be much deeper than 2 inches/5 cm; if it is, use a larger pan). Cover and let it cook gently for 10 to 15 minutes over low heat.

Uncover, reduce the heat to very low, and flip the omelette (see Tips). Let the other side cook gently uncovered for another 15 minutes.

When both sides are firm and dark green, remove from the heat, turn out onto a cutting board, and cut into squares or triangles. Serve with Persian bread.

TIPS

Barberries can be purchased from Persian or Middle Eastern grocery stores; if they can't be found, substitute ⅓ cup/50 g dried cranberries, roughly chopped.

To flip, cover the pan with a large plate and carefully invert, then slide the omelette back into the pan. (Alternatively, you can use a spatula to cut the omelette into quarters and flip each one individually.)

You can also bake the kookoo in the oven: Preheat the oven to 350°F/180°C; use ⅓ cup/175 mL oil to generously grease a 1 quart/1 L baking dish. Pour in the mixture and bake for about 30 minutes. Remove from the oven, cut into 6 pieces, and flip each piece over. Drizzle 2 tablespoons oil between the slices, and bake 15 to 20 minutes more.

2 cups/150 g roughly chopped fresh parsley

2 cups/80 g roughly chopped fresh cilantro, leaves and tender stems

1 cup/45 g roughly chopped fresh dill

1 bunch of chives, roughly chopped

6 small green onions, finely chopped

1 clove garlic, chopped

⅓ cup/32 g dried barberries (see Tips)

½ cup/50 g walnuts, roughly chopped (optional)

½ tsp kosher salt

¼ tsp ground cinnamon

½ tsp ground turmeric

¼ tsp ground saffron (optional)

¼ tsp freshly ground black pepper

6 to 8 large eggs

⅓ cup/75 mL vegetable or olive oil

Persian bread, for serving

LEO BADURIA
FOUGASSE AUX OLIVES
Olive Fougasse

Leo lived in Montreal from 1977 to 1988, where the city's many fine boulangeries first got him excited about artisanal bread. Over time, Leo pursued this passion, assisting bakers in Montreal, France, and Italy, accumulating techniques and experience that would become the foundation of his own baking. At The Dep, his baking classes became so popular we ended up running additional ones out of a second kitchen across town.

Fougasse is the French Provençal version of the Italian focaccia, this one made with chopped olives and sprinkled with coarse salt, though you can change it up by substituting walnuts, dried apricots, or fresh herbs for the olives.

Prep: 30 min, plus 2 hr for proofing

Cook: 30 min

Makes: 1 fougasse (4 servings)

Vegan

1 cup/130 g unbleached flour

1 cup/140 g whole wheat flour

1 tbsp /9 g quick-rise (instant) yeast

1 cup/240 g spring water, at room temperature

1 tbsp extra-virgin olive oil, plus more for brushing

1 tsp fine sea salt

½ cup/75 g Kalamata or Niçoise olives, pitted and chopped

1 tsp coarse sea salt

In a large bowl, combine the flours and yeast. Add the water and mix thoroughly until all the dry ingredients are incorporated. Cover the bowl with a damp cloth or plastic wrap and let rest for 20 minutes.

Add the olive oil and fine sea salt and knead until smooth. Shape into a ball and place it back into the bowl. Cover and let rest in a warm, draft-free location until the dough has more than doubled in size, about 1 hour.

Line a baking sheet with parchment paper and generously brush the paper with oil. Knead the olives into the dough and transfer to the lined baking sheet. Lightly flatten the dough and shape into an 8 × 5-inch/20 × 13 cm oval.

Using a knife or pizza cutter, cut 2½-inch/6.5 cm slits in the dough. Stretch the slits, widening the holes to about 2 inches/5 cm. (Brush the dough generously with olive oil to make it easier to handle.) Cover loosely with a tea towel and let rise at room temperature for 30 minutes.

Meanwhile, position a rack in the centre of the oven and preheat the oven to 425°F/220°C.

Just before baking, sprinkle the dough with the coarse salt. Bake until the fougasse is golden brown, about 30 minutes.

Transfer to a wire rack and let cool for 15 minutes before serving.

 Marna Yates

> *I'm a baker but my background is Filipino. Filipinos never use bread as part of the actual meal. Back home, bread is mostly for breakfast or things like empanadas, influenced by the Spanish. But when I was growing up—we grew up right in the middle of the city —my father had a catering business, and beside us was a bakery, so I grew up really liking bread.*

Leo Baduria is a professional wine geek, as well as a painter, cook, and deeply committed baker and instructor who has taught hundreds of people about the mysteries and delights of freshly baked bread. **@mywindowtotheworld**

Cuban-born chef Pedro Quintanilla started at an early age, inspired by his *abuela*, who shared with him the secrets of the Cuban kitchen. After training as a chef, he worked in some of Havana's best restaurants and spent a few years as head chef at the French Embassy in Havana. He arrived in Toronto in the '90s and has been pioneering his personal brand of Nuevo Latino cuisine ever since.
@chezpedrin

PEDRO JULIO QUINTANILLA

FRITURAS DE MALANGA
Cuban Malanga Fritters

Malanga—also known as eddoes—are a smaller, slightly hairy relative of taro (which they are also sometimes called, depending where you are and who you ask). They are one of the many root vegetables popular in Caribbean cooking. I have great memories of eating these in Cuba, and was delighted to find a Cuban chef who would make them here.

Prep: 10 min

Cook: 3 min

Makes: 16 to 18 fritters

Vegan

4 small malanga roots (about 4.4 oz/ 125 g each)

6 cloves garlic, crushed to a paste

2 tbsp finely chopped fresh parsley or cilantro

2 green onions, finely chopped

Salt and freshly ground black pepper

Neutral oil, for shallow-frying

Chipotle mayo, aioli, or salsa, for serving

Peel the malanga roots and grate them using the grating disc of a food processor or the fine holes of a box grater. Try to work quickly as they will start to darken with exposure to air. (You should end up with about 3 cups/750 mL.)

Stir in the garlic paste, parsley, and green onions. Season with a good pinch each of salt and pepper.

Pour at least 1 inch/2.5 cm oil into a medium skillet and heat the oil over medium-high heat to around 350°F/177°C. Line a plate with paper towels.

Take one heaping tablespoon of malanga mix and carefully drop it into the skillet. There should be enough oil in the skillet to fully submerge the fritters. Only add a few at a time, do not overcrowd the skillet. Cook the fritters until golden brown, 2 to 3 minutes. Remove with a slotted spoon and place on the paper towels to drain any excess oil. Sprinkle with salt to taste.

Serve with chipotle mayo, aioli, or your favourite salsa.

TIP:
Malanga fritters are usually eaten as a starter or snack, but unseasoned fritters are also a great dessert, drizzled with honey or maple syrup, or dusted with powdered sugar.

ADJARURLI KHACHAPURI

Georgian Cheese Boats

Prep: 30 min, plus 2 to 6+ hr rising time (depending on room temperature)

Cook: 10 min

Makes: 4 boats

½ cup/118 g warm water

½ cup/118 g 2% milk, warm

1 tsp sugar

1 (7 g) envelope instant dry yeast

6 large eggs

2 tbsp vegetable oil, plus more for oiling the bowl

2 tsp salt

3 cups/390 g all-purpose flour, plus more as needed

2 cups/200 to 250 g grated mozzarella cheese

2 cups/200 to 250 g crumbled good-quality feta cheese

8 tsp/40 g butter, 4 tsp melted and 4 tsp cut into 4 small slices

1 tbsp chopped fresh parsley or dill, for garnish

Back when The Dep was still just an idea, Roman was the kind of person I thought of when I imagined who might be interested in cooking here. He has a completely separate career as a software developer, but off the clock is simply obsessed with food. The Dep was the perfect place to do a few pop-ups a year as a combination creative outlet, technical challenge, shot of adrenaline, and healthy dose of personal satisfaction.

Khachapuri is a general term for Georgian bread pastry filled with melted cheese and topped with butter and a raw egg. The Adjaruli-style *khachapuri* are made in the shape of a boat, thought to represent the sailors who navigated the Black Sea from the Adjara region. The original recipe uses sulguni cheese, a brined cheese that is hard to find outside Georgia, but can be substituted by a mix of sheep's feta and mozzarella.

In the bowl of a stand mixer (or in a large bowl), mix the water, milk, sugar, and yeast. Set aside for 10 minutes to activate and start to bubble.

Add 1 beaten egg, 2 tbsp of vegetable oil, and salt. Slowly add 3 cups of flour, mixing by hand until completely incorporated.

Set the bowl on the stand mixer, snap on the dough hook, and mix on medium speed until the dough is elastic and pulls away easily from the bowl, 8 to 10 minutes. (Or turn the dough out of the bowl onto a flat surface and knead for at least 10 minutes until the dough is shiny, elastic, and can be shaped into a ball.) If you find the dough is too sticky, you can add 1 to 2 tablespoons of flour in small increments.

Transfer the dough to a lightly oiled bowl and cover with plastic wrap. Set the dough aside until doubled in size, at least 2 hours (see Tips).

While the dough is rising, in a bowl, toss together the mozzarella and feta. Add 1 beaten egg.

Preheat the oven to 500°F/260°C.

Turn the dough out onto a flat surface and divide into 4 equal balls. Working with one at a time (and keeping the remaining balls covered), roll a dough ball out into a flat, oval shape about 12 × 9 inches/30 × 23 cm. A small wooden rolling pin is the best tool for this task. Carefully start folding/rolling in each of the sides of the oval to create the sides of the boat. Once there is about 4 inches/

10 cm left between the sides, pinch the two ends together, creating the bow and stern of the "boat."

Fill the boat with enough cheese mixture to come up to the sides but not over–you need to leave some room for the egg you'll be adding later. Cover and set aside as you work on the other boats. Brush the sides of the boats with the melted butter.

Carefully transfer the boats to a baking sheet. Bake until the bread is light brown and the cheese is bubbling and browning in spots, about 15 minutes.

Meanwhile, crack the remaining 4 eggs into four separate small bowls.

Take the boats out of the oven, make a well in the middle of the hot cheese with a spoon, and slide an egg in. Return the boats to the oven and bake until the whites of the eggs are half-set, about 5 minutes more.

Remove the boats from the oven and put a slice of butter into each one. Garnish with the parsley or dill. To eat, break off a piece of bread from the side of the boat, mix it in the half-set egg and the melted cheese–and try not to burn yourself!

 Lisa Singer

Roman Kliotzkin dreams of doing something cool with food one day. Born in Kaliningrad, Roman blends Eastern European cuisine with modern techniques and seasonal ingredients. @romankliotzkin

TIPS:

You can let the dough rise overnight–it even makes it taste better. However, if you put the dough in the fridge to pause rising, let it come to room temperature (at least 30 minutes) before continuing to work with it.

If you assemble individual boats on precut pieces of parchment paper, you can lift the paper and place it on the baking sheet.

One non-traditional variation: Brush the sides of the boats with butter and sprinkle sesame seeds for an extra-fancy look.

> For Passover we rid our homes and bodies of anything leavened ... On a spiritual level, we're sort of acknowledging that we don't create independently; it's always through the help of our community and our Creator. So that's what I think about when I think about leavened bread: None of us are totally independent—we're interconnected with other humans and with other life forms, such as these wee yeasties that make the bread rise.

Sara Melanie Lapell ran her bakery, Nice Buns, out of The Dep for several years. Now she works supporting autistic youth, but still bakes for fun. @lapellsara

TIPS:

The turmeric provides a nice colour to the dough. Omit if desired.

Substitute your choice of dried fruit and nuts for the raisins and walnuts.

Up to half of the all-purpose flour can be swapped out for whole wheat.

Using weight measurements for baking is recommended as it yields more consistent results. Many factors can impact dough hydration, such as the flour used, and ambient humidity. This is a relatively soft, sticky dough and you can add a little more flour if/as necessary while kneading to keep it from sticking too much.

This recipe can also be made as 12 buns, or 1 loaf and 6 buns. You can find many videos online with different ways to shape the buns after rolling the dough into a ball and then into a snake shape. The ones in the photo are simple knots. The buns take 15 to 20 minutes to bake.

There are many great online tutorials showing other methods of braiding challah.

A large, clear plastic bag (like the ones from bulk goods) can be cut along one side and the bottom to make a sheet to cover rising bread.

SARA MELANIE LAPELL

WALNUT RAISIN CHALLAH

The smell of Sara Lapell's freshly baked breads is a special Depanneur memory. In the very earliest days of The Dep she would make her delicious sourdoughs, fougasse, and to-die-for cinnamon buns in our little kitchen. Later on, as her freelance bakery business, Nice Buns, expanded, she would become one of the first tenants of the rental kitchen I built in the basement, where her warmth and genuine smile helped make it a welcoming place for new food entrepreneurs. This slightly sweet, nutty, and vegan bread is ideal for special occasions and perfect for plant-based diets.

Prep: 1 to 1½ hr, plus 2½ hr rising and resting time

Cook: 30 min

Makes: 2 loaves; 10 to 12 servings (see Tips)

Vegan

½ cup/80 g raisins

⅔ cup/80 g chopped walnuts

5¼ cups/680 g all-purpose flour, plus more for dusting

2 tsp fine salt

1 (7 g) envelope quick-rise (instant) yeast

½ tsp ground turmeric (optional)

2 cups/500 g water, at room temperature

5 tbsp maple syrup

4 tbsp vegetable oil

1 tbsp plant-based milk (almond, soy, etc.)

In a small bowl, cover the raisins with warm water and soak until softened, about 20 minutes. Drain and set aside.

In a small, dry skillet over low heat, toast the walnuts until fragrant, 4 to 8 minutes. Remove from the pan and set aside to cool.

In a large bowl, mix together the flour, salt, yeast, and turmeric (if using).

In a medium bowl, mix together the water, 4 tablespoons of maple syrup, and the oil. Add the wet ingredients to the flour mixture and mix with a fork or spoon until too stiff to mix further, about 2 minutes. Then mix by hand in the bowl until fully incorporated (bring the bottom of one side to the top, push down into the centre, turn the bowl, and repeat). This should take 5 to 10 minutes at the most.

Cover the bowl with a damp cloth or plastic wrap and let the dough rest for 20 to 30 minutes to allow the flour to hydrate.

Add the walnuts and drained raisins and knead for 5 to 10 minutes, until the additions are evenly distributed and the dough is smooth and elastic. Cover the bowl and let the dough rise until almost doubled in volume, about 1 hour.

Line a baking sheet with parchment paper. Using lightly floured hands and a knife or bench scraper, divide the dough in half. Divide each half into 3 equal portions, rounding each to form a ball.

Using your hands or a rolling pin, flatten each ball into a disc. Using your hands, roll each disc to form a rope, pressing gently to close the seam. Gently elongate each rope, rolling with your hands to stretch it out.

Pinch one end of the 3 ropes together to secure and braid the strands (left-over-centre and right-over-centre). Tuck the ends under at the end of the loaf and place on the lined baking sheet. Repeat with the second half of the dough to make a second loaf and place several inches apart from the other loaf.

Cover loosely with a damp cloth or plastic wrap and let rise at least ½ hour, until a gentle finger poke doesn't bounce back quickly.

Meanwhile, preheat the oven to 375°F/190°C.

In a small bowl, whisk together the plant milk and remaining 1 tablespoon maple syrup. With a pastry brush, gently apply the milk mixture to the tops and sides of the loaves.

Place the baking sheet into the oven and immediately reduce the oven temperature to 350°F/180°C. Bake until the loaves are evenly browned and sound hollow when tapped on the bottom, 20 to 30 minutes, rotating the baking sheet front to back about halfway through.

Use the leftover milk mixture to brush the loaves again after removing them from the oven for extra shine and sweetness (optional).

Let cool completely on a wire rack before slicing.

ADOPT-A-RECIPE   Kevin Kelly

SIDES

Salads

JIVA MacKAY
ZESTY GREEK SALAD

SANA MAHMOUD
SALATET SHMANDAR
Beet Salad

ERIKA ARAUJO
ENSALADA DE NOPALES
Mexican Cactus Salad

ERWIN JOAQUIN
BEET POKE

CAROL MARK
LAHPET
Burmese Fermented Tea Salad

SEEMA AND AMREEN OMAR
BHAIYA CHANNA CHAAT
Tangy Mumbai Chickpea Salad

MARGRET HEFNER
WARM WHITE BEAN AND
TOMATO SALAD WITH
DRY-ROASTED VEGETABLES

CINDY FUNG
CURRIED CAULIFLOWER
BUDDHA BOWL

Schmears

MIRA BERLIN
HUMMUS WITH CONFIT MUSHROOMS

HAJAR JAMAL EDDINE
ZAALOUK
Moroccan Ratatouille

EMILY ZIMMERMAN
GEHAKTE ZONROYZ ZOYMEN
Vegan Chopped Liver

NAJIB NASR
FASULYA
Yemeni Kidney Bean Dip

Side Dishes

CANDACE ESQUIMAUX
MANOOMIN
Wild Rice and Cranberries

SHELDON HOLDER
FRY BODI
Trini-Style Sautéed Long Beans

AN NGUYEN
BIBIM GUKSU
Korean Spicy Buckwheat Noodles

MARIA POLOTAN
KALABASA SA GATA
Squash in Coconut Milk

CAMILLA WYNNE
FALL HARVEST PICKLES

KETAN DONGRE
NASHIK MISAL
Curried Moth Beans

REBEKKA HUTTON
FERMENTED HOT SAUCE

JIVA MACKAY

ZESTY GREEK SALAD

Jiva was there when The Dep was born, perhaps one could even consider her its doula. She had recently returned from a *stage* at Chez Panisse in California, and I tapped her to help me figure out our very first menus. An artist in a chef's jacket, her ideas were often lyrical and romantic, but she came with the skills to back them up. Years later, she would work at a nearby coffee shop while pursuing her degree in holistic nutrition, giving us a hundred little chances to kindle our friendship, a few minutes at a time.

This dish really shines at the end of summer, with a variety of local tomatoes.

Prep: 25 min

Makes: 4 servings

½ cup/125 mL extra-virgin olive oil, plus more for drizzling

Grated zest of 2 lemons

1 tsp freshly ground black pepper, plus more for serving

6 drops oregano oil (see Tip)

1 tsp dried oregano

3 cloves garlic, peeled

½ lb/225 g goat feta

1 small red onion (or ½ large)

¼ cup/60 mL fresh lemon juice

2 medium or 3 small field cucumbers

3 handfuls cherry or 3 medium salad or 2 beefsteak tomatoes (or a combo)

1 (generous) handful sun-dried olives, pitted

Sea salt

Warm bread, for serving

In a large salad bowl, combine the olive oil, lemon zest, black pepper, oregano oil, and dried oregano. Using a Microplane, grate the garlic into the oil mixture and mix. Cut the feta into 4 pieces and place in the bowl, covering each piece with the seasoned oil.

Cut the red onion into rings or half-rings, whichever you like, and put in a small bowl. Pour the lemon juice over the onion to acidulate it.

Peel the cucumbers almost completely, leaving just little strips of green. Cut in half lengthwise and then crosswise into ½-inch/1.3 cm pieces.

Carefully remove the feta from the oil (set aside on a plate) and put the cucumbers in the bowl with the remaining oil. Cut the tomatoes into large bite-size pieces and add to the large bowl on top of the cucumber. Add the olives and a sprinkle of sea salt. Add the onion with its juice.

Only when you're ready to serve, toss the salad and plate, placing a piece of feta on top of each plated salad. Finish with a final drizzle of olive oil and a turn of fresh ground pepper.

Serve with warm bread; everyone loves soaking up the delicious juices at the end!

TIP:
Oregano oil is often sold as a medicinal oil at natural foods stores.

> *I grew up on Queen Street [in downtown Toronto] ... I didn't even know what an eggplant looked like! So I was really curious, and it blew my mind. I think everyone should see what food looks like growing. It's been abstracted for a long time, for generations. People need to be re-educated about what actually happens on farms, and exactly how much work it is. And the food chain; there's so many people involved.*

Jiva MacKay is a holistic nutritionist and plant-based chef who has been exploring the intersection of food, art, nature, and well-being for more than twenty years. @medicine_bread

ADOPT-A-RECIPE   Constance Dykun

Prep: 20 min
Cook: 40 min
Makes: 4 servings
Vegan

Dressing:

4 tbsp olive oil

Juice of 1 medium lemon

1 tbsp apple cider vinegar

1 tsp minced garlic

1 tsp ground cumin

Salt and freshly ground black pepper

Salad:

3 large beets

5 medium carrots, peeled and cut into ½-inch/1.3 cm cubes

1½ cups/245 g cooked chickpeas (see Tips)

2 medium tomatoes, cut into ½-inch/ 1.3 cm cubes

1 medium onion, cut into ½-inch/1.3 cm cubes

1 cup/250 mL ½-inch/1 cm cubed dill pickles

1 cup/75 g chopped fresh flat-leaf parsley

SANA MAHMOUD

SALATET SHMANDAR

Beet Salad

Some people became regular fixtures in The Dep's constellations of cooks, perennial favourites who did events year after year. Others were more like shooting stars, that shone brightly for a brief moment, never to appear again. A retired Lebanese school teacher, Sana was interested in exploring the possibility of getting into catering. Together with her husband she cooked two fabulous Middle Eastern meals in late 2020, and then I never heard from her again. So it goes.

Make the dressing: In a screw-top glass jar, combine the olive oil, lemon juice, vinegar, garlic, and cumin. Add salt and pepper to taste and mix well. Set aside.

Make the salad: Bring a medium pot of water to a boil. Add the beets and cook until tender, about 40 minutes. Drain and set aside.

In a separate medium pot of boiling water, cook the carrots until tender, 8 to 10 minutes. Drain and rinse under cold water. Set aside.

Once the beets are cool enough to handle, peel and cut into ½-inch/1.3 cm cubes.

To assemble the salad, in a large bowl, combine the carrots, chickpeas, tomatoes, onion, and pickles. Drizzle with the dressing and mix to combine. Add the beets (see Tips) and mix again lightly. Sprinkle generously with parsley and serve.

TIPS:

Chickpeas that have been cooked from dried have a firmer texture, but 1 can (15 oz/425 g) of chickpeas, drained, can be substituted.

Since beets tend to colour everything, mix the other ingredients with the dressing first, then add the beets just before serving and toss again lightly.

You can prep this salad 2 to 3 days ahead. Boil, peel, and dice the beets and carrots and store in separate containers in the fridge so the colours don't bleed.

Make the dressing ahead but don't mix with the salad until ready to serve.

Sana Mahmoud believes that food is a common language that brings people together. Throughout a twenty-plus-year career in academic teaching, some of her favourite moments were sharing food with her students.

ADOPT-A-RECIPE   Lesley Ciarula Taylor

Erika Araujo
found her passion for cooking after emigrating to Canada. She has been tirelessly promoting Mexican culture and cuisine at workshops and culinary events through her brand Ixiim.
@ixiimtoronto

ERIKA ARAUJO

ENSALADA DE NOPALES

Mexican Cactus Salad

The markets of Mexico are some of my favourite places on Earth. Even with all the trendy tacos crowding Toronto's restaurant scene, finding authentic Mexican food can still be challenging. Erika's dinners and popular Mexican Street Food classes introduced many people to these fabulous flavours.

Nopales are the flat paddles or leaves of the same cactus that produces the prickly pear fruit. Somewhere between a salsa and salad, you might find this served on top of a *tlacoyo*: a thick oval corn masa cake stuffed with beans or cheese, served up from countless street stalls in Mexico City.

Prep: 30 min
Cook: 20 min
Makes: 4 servings

3 or 4 medium nopales (cactus paddles)

2 cups/360 g diced tomatoes (2 to 3 medium)

1 cup/40 g chopped fresh cilantro

1 cup/160 g chopped white onion

¼ tsp dried Mexican oregano

Salt and freshly ground black pepper

¼ cup/35 g crumbled queso añejo, queso Cotija, or feta (optional)

If the nopales still have spines, you'll need to remove them carefully. Wearing gloves or using a tea towel, hold the pad by the stem end. With a sharp knife, cut against the grain to remove the bumps that house the spines. Rinse well.

Slice the nopales widthwise into strips ¼ inch/6 mm wide. Place in a medium pot and cover with water. Bring to a boil, reduce to a simmer, and cook until tender, about 20 minutes. They should have the texture of a cooked green bean, not too soft, with a little bit of bite.

Drain and rinse the nopales under cold water until cool. (Alternatively, you can do this by placing them in a bowl of ice water for a few minutes.)

In a large salad bowl, combine the cooled nopales, tomatoes, cilantro, onion, and oregano. Season with salt and pepper to taste. Sprinkle with the cheese.

TIPS:

This is a very refreshing salad for the summer and goes well with grilled meats, scrambled eggs, stews, or piled on tacos or tlacoyos.

Fresh cactus paddles (nopales) and Mexican cheeses can be purchased in Latin stores. If you opt for canned or bottled nopales, rinse them very well.

You can boil the cactus paddles ahead of time and store them in a plastic bag in the fridge for up to 1 week.

For a different presentation, use julienned red onion instead of the chopped white onion.

"You have to have an open mind with the food that you eat . . . Food is a central place of interactions, where you can grow relationships. I'm in sales, and if I'm invited to a Moroccan restaurant and I'm not gonna eat what's in the tagine, that might offend the potential client or impact the deal that we'll be making. In a sense, having an open palate affects your relationships, either in your career, or your personal life."

Inspired by the culture and food Hawai'i has to offer, **Erwin Joaquin's** Big E Hawaiian Grinds aims to re-create the most-loved traditional Hawaiian dishes with a modern spin. @bigegrinds

BEET POKE

Hawai'i may technically be a US state, but its long, complex history and culture is very distinct from the rest of America, reflecting its deep Polynesian roots and strong Japanese and Filipino influences. Fish-based poke bowls became a hot food trend in the low-fat, gluten-free 2010s, and with it came an opportunity for Erwin to introduce more people to Hawaiian culture and cuisine. This plant-base beet poke represents another evolution of the dish, a mirror reflecting the ever-changing landscape of food and culture.

Prep: 25 min, plus 1 hr marinating time

Cook: 25 min

Makes: 4 to 6 servings

Vegan (if modified)

Beet Poke:

4 to 5 large beets, peeled and cut into ½-inch/1.3 cm cubes (about 3 cups/400 g)

1 tbsp olive oil

1 cup/250 mL soy sauce (preferably Japanese shoyu)

1 tbsp sesame oil

½ large sweet onion, thinly sliced

Dressing:

1 avocado, halved and pitted

1 clove garlic, grated

2 tbsp finely chopped green onions

2 tbsp chopped fresh cilantro

¼ cup/60 mL water

Juice of 1 lemon

1 tsp Worcestershire sauce (or Bragg Coconut Aminos for a vegan dish)

¼ tsp salt

½ tsp freshly ground black pepper

Assembly:

1 cup/110 g shredded carrots (about 2 carrots)

1 cup/95 g shredded red cabbage

1 cup/130 g diced cucumber

Shredded toasted nori, for garnish

Prepare the beet poke: Preheat the oven to 350°F/180°C. Line a baking sheet with parchment paper.

In a bowl, toss the cubed beets with the olive oil and arrange on the lined baking sheet. Bake until fork-tender, 25 to 35 minutes. Start testing beets after 25 minutes; they should be fork-tender. Remove from the oven and set aside to cool.

When the beets have cooled down, place them back in the bowl, and add the soy sauce, sesame oil, and sweet onion. Set aside to marinate for at least 1 hour.

Make the dressing: Scoop the avocado into a food processor or blender. Add the garlic, green onions, cilantro, water, lemon juice, Worcestershire sauce (or coconut aminos), salt, and pepper and purée until smooth. Add more water to thin if needed.

To assemble: Divide the beets onto serving dishes. Top each with the shredded carrots, cabbage, and cucumber. Add a dollop of the dressing on top and garnish with shredded toasted nori.

TIP:
Serve as a starter or salad, or on top of a mound of sushi rice as a meal.

CAROL MARK

LAHPET

Burmese Fermented Tea Salad

Carol is a fascinating person, whose wild biography could fill a book of its own. She was the first tea sommelier I ever met, and once did a fabulous Supper Club with different teas used in every course. This is her modern take on a distinctive Burmese dish that utilises fermented tea leaves and that Carol developed to showcase Ontario garlic for the Toronto Garlic Festival.

Prep: 30 min, plus 2 days for fermenting the tea

Cook: 20 min

Makes: 4 servings

½ cup/125 mL distilled white vinegar

About ⅓ cup/20 g organic green tea leaves

½ cup/125 mL water

2 tbsp fish sauce

2 to 3 cloves local organic garlic, chopped

2 tbsp fresh lemon juice

3 tbsp vegetable oil

3 tbsp sesame oil

4 cups/300 g chopped napa cabbage

Topping Suggestions (see Tips):

3 green onions, chopped

4 to 5 lychees

4 to 6 cherry tomatoes, sliced

1 small cucumber, sliced

6 to 8 cherries, pitted and sliced

½ bell pepper, chopped

2 tbsp goji berries

½ cup/20 g fried split mung beans (see Tips)

3 tbsp toasted pumpkin seeds

2 tbsp toasted sesame seeds

2 tbsp toasted coconut

½ cup/75 g roasted peanuts, chopped

For Garnish:

3 to 4 lime wedges

3 cloves garlic, chopped and fried (see Tips)

In a medium saucepan, combine the vinegar, tea leaves, and water and bring to a boil. Reduce the heat and simmer for 20 minutes. Let cool and then squeeze the water out of the tea leaves.

In a medium stainless steel bowl, combine the tea leaves, fish sauce, garlic, lemon juice, vegetable oil, and sesame oil. Using an immersion blender (or food processor), blitz the tea leaves mix into a chunky paste. Store it in the refrigerator for 2 days to allow the flavours to develop.

In a medium bowl, toss the napa cabbage and the fermented tea dressing. Serve on a platter with your choice of toppings. Garnish with the wedges of lime and fried garlic.

TIPS:

Be adventurous and try different toppings! The toppings used here are just a suggestion. You want an interesting mix of crunchy (nuts, seeds, fried beans, etc.), juicy (tomatoes, cucumbers, etc.), and chewy (coconut, goji, etc.);

the garlic and lime are a must though.

Fried split mung beans can be found in Asian or Indian supermarkets. Ask for tua thong *(Thai) or* moong dal *(Hindi).*

You can buy already fried garlic at Asian grocers, or make your own: Slice the cloves thinly and fry in vegetable oil for 3 to 4 minutes until lightly golden. Remove with a slotted spoon and place on paper towels to drain and crisp up. Sprinkle with salt.

ADOPT-A-RECIPE   Jacqueline Tam

Seema Omar was born and brought up in Mumbai, but after moving to Toronto she really missed the exciting flavours of traditional Mumbai-style street food snacks. Together with her sister-in-law, Amreen Omar, they decided to start Bombay Street Food. Starting from a Dep pop-up, they became a fixture at the East York Farmers Market, before opening it as a restaurant on Bay Street in downtown Toronto. @seemapaniwala @amreenomar1

We began this cooking journey as a healing process after a huge loss. We started at the farmers' markets and then we ended up jaywalking into The Depanneur to do a pop-up. We had no idea what we were doing. We just showed up with bags of rice and a lot of produce.

SEEMA AND AMREEN OMAR

BHAIYA CHANNA CHAAT

Tangy Mumbai Chickpea Salad

The first time sisters-in-law Seema and Amreen ever cooked for strangers was at The Depanneur. That little experiment was the first step on a remarkable journey that over the next few years would lead them through farmers' markets and pop-ups to a beautiful new restaurant in downtown Toronto. Along the way they would discover how food could open doors, heal wounds, and transform lives.

Chaat is a kind of anytime Indian street snack, a lively blend of contrasting textures and salty, sour, sweet, and spicy flavours seasoned with a distinctive spice mix called *chaat masala*.

1 cup green chickpeas (chholia; see Tips)

1 tsp kosher salt

2 tbsp/30 g butter

2 tsp finely chopped green chilies (about 3 small chilies)

⅔ cup/80 g finely chopped red onions

⅓ cup/50 g diced boiled potatoes

½ tsp chili powder

⅓ cup/60 g finely chopped tomatoes

¼ tsp amchur powder (see Tips)

2 tsp chaat masala (see Tips)

4 tsp fresh lemon juice

Green (unripe) mango, very finely diced (optional)

2 tbsp finely chopped fresh cilantro, plus more for garnish

Lime or lemon wedges, for garnish

Papdi (see Tips) or crackers, for serving

Prep: 20 min, plus overnight soak

Cook: 1½ hr

Makes: about 1½ cups/375 mL (4 servings)

Vegan (if modified)

Soak the chickpeas in water to cover overnight. Drain, rinse, and place in a pot. Cover with water by 2 inches/5 cm and add the kosher salt. Bring to a boil, then reduce the heat to a bare simmer and cook until tender, 1 to 1½ hours, checking for doneness after 1 hour. Drain and cool.

In a skillet, heat the butter over medium heat. Add the green chilies and sauté for a few seconds. Add the onions and sauté until the onions turn translucent, 1 to 2 minutes. Add the drained chickpeas, potatoes, and chili powder and stir until well mixed. Add the tomatoes, amchur powder, and chaat masala. Taste for salt and add more if needed. Remove the pan from the heat and add the lemon juice, green mango (if using), and cilantro and mix well.

Garnish with more cilantro and wedges of lime or lemon on the side. Serve as a side dish with a meal, with tea, or on its own as a nutritious snack with some crispy papdi or crackers to scoop it up. It can be served warm or at room temperature.

TIPS

Green chickpeas (ccholia), also called channa or hare chaney, are popular in Desi cooking and can be found dried at Indian grocers. Regular chickpeas could be substituted in a pinch.

Amchur (dried mango) powder and chaat masala (chaat spice mix) can be found at Indian groceries.

Papdi are little crispy fried discs of dough that are like a cross between a chip and a cracker.

You can also substitute vegan butter alternative to make this recipe vegan.

ADOPT A RECIPE   Graeme Couture

SEEMA AND AMREEN OMAR

Like art and music, food also offers a way to share and process emotions, and in so doing, transforms pain into beauty. Sisters-in-law Seema and Amreen Omar had started cooking together as a way to cope with the pain, grief, and confusion that followed the sudden, unexpected death of Seema's husband. Coming from corporate backgrounds, neither had ever really cooked for anyone beyond immediate family, but somehow, they found their way to The Dep's kitchen, and their nights were an immediate success.

They found a kind of focus and purpose in the creativity, challenge, and intensity that the cooking demanded, and they slowly built a food business based around weekly stalls at some local farmers' markets. They shored up their skills and confidence as food entrepreneurs for a few years, then in 2016 they opened a beautiful, modern, fast-casual restaurant—Bombay Street Food—on Bay Street in downtown Toronto.

I attended the grand opening, and over the door hung a poster: *"Every Exit Is An Entry To Somewhere Else."* When I saw it, I could feel a swell of emotion as **I thought about the journey from despair to pride that their love of food had taken them on.** It was an ambitious, well-funded, elegantly designed, and professionally marketed restaurant concept, well suited to upscale food halls and fast-casual business lunches. But they now had to make it in one of the most competitive industries out there—approximately 60 percent of restaurants fail within the first year of operation and 80 percent fail within the first five years.

Even though they did everything right, they were only able to hold down the fort until the end of 2018 when Bombay Street Food closed its doors, joining the constellations of thousands of culinary dreams that twinkle in and out of existence every year, in every city.

This food is an important connection to our families and childhood experiences and memories cooking with our mothers in both Bombay and New Brunswick. And the best part of this journey was working together. Our relationship as sisters-in-law deepened, and the process of opening and running our business gave us a sense of purpose when it was really needed.

Seema and Amreen at the grand opening of Bombay Street Food

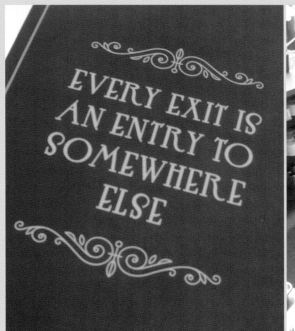

Margret Hefner has worked in restaurant kitchens, as a private chef, and culinary tours in San Miguel de Allende in Mexico. In 2013 she devoted herself to work on *Frutas y Verduras*, an interactive English field guide to the markets of Mexico.
@fyvmexico

MARGRET HEFNER

WARM WHITE BEAN AND TOMATILLO SALAD WITH DRY-ROASTED VEGETABLES

I met Margret in the early days of The Dep, when she had a fledgling tamale business. She did a handful of dinners and workshops that illuminated a complex and subtle side of Mexican cuisine I had not encountered in restaurants here. An impassioned advocate of Mexican foodways, she returned to Mexico to author a comprehensive guide to the fruits and vegetables of the local *mercados* and *tianguis* (farmers' markets).

Make the pickled red onion: Put the onion slices in a bowl and sprinkle with the coarse salt. Add the citrus juices, stir around to distribute the salt, and let sit for about 20 minutes, after which they are ready to use. You can refrigerate the leftovers in a jar for up to 1 week.

Make the sauce: In a small skillet, briefly toast the coriander seeds and anise (if using) over medium heat, then grind with a mortar and pestle or in a spice grinder.

If using fresh tomatillos, peel off the husks, rinse the fruits to remove the sticky coating, and set aside. If using canned tomatillos, drain and put 10 into a blender, food processor, or container appropriate for an immersion blender and give them a quick whirr to break them down. You want about 1½ cups/ 360 mL, so add more if needed. Or, if using bottled salsa verde, measure 1½ cups/360 mL into the blender.

In a large heavy skillet, place the whole tomatillos (if using), the white onion slices, and garlic in the skillet and set over medium-high heat. Leave each of these undisturbed for a few minutes until they start to blister and brown. Turn them so that all sides brown and each ingredient gets soft. Once softened, remove and discard the peel from the garlic and add all the ingredients to the blender.

Add the toasted spices, the tarragon (if you didn't use anise seeds), cilantro, and parsley. If not using jarred salsa, add the chili pepper. Pulse until well blended, leaving some texture. Taste and add salt to your liking. Measure out 1 cup/250 mL of the tomatillo sauce and set aside for the vegetables and garnish.

Prepare the beans: Reserving the liquid (either the cooking liquid or the liquid from the cans), drain the beans. In a bowl, combine the tomatillo sauce with the drained beans. Do not refrigerate if you are planning to serve it the same day; this dish is best at room temperature.

Dry-roast the vegetables: Preheat a well-seasoned comal, griddle, or cast-iron skillet over medium-high heat. (Or preheat an outdoor grill and lightly oil the grates.) Do not oil the vegetables. Lightly salt the vegetables and place on the hot surface. Don't disturb for 4 to 5 minutes, turning when browned and slightly blistered. (Alternatively, you can dry-roast them in the oven: Preheat to 375°F/190°C, and roast until softened, about 15 minutes.)

Put the roasted vegetables in a bowl and toss with about ½ cup/125 mL of the reserved tomatillo sauce. Taste and add salt as needed. This may be served thick (see Tips), or you can loosen it up by adding some of the cooking liquid from the beans.

To serve: In a dry skillet over medium heat, toast the pumpkin seeds until some of them swell and turn light golden-brown. Remove to a bowl and crush the mint (if using) into the pumpkin seeds either with the back of a spoon or with a mortar and pestle to combine. Set aside.

To plate, portion out about 1 cup of the bean mixture into the centre of a soup plate. Place the roasted vegetables over the beans. Drizzle the remaining tomatillo sauce around the plate or encircle the beans with it for a pretty effect. Sprinkle the crushed pumpkin seeds and mint over the whole dish. Garnish with sprigs of watercress and the pickled red onion.

Prep: 45 min

Cook: 40 min

Makes: 4 servings

Vegan

Pickled Red Onion:

1 small red onion, thinly sliced

½ tsp coarse salt

3 to 4 tbsp fresh lime juice (preferably Mexican or Key lime)

1 tbsp fresh orange juice (optional, but recommended)

Sauce:

1½ tsp coriander seeds

1 tbsp fresh tarragon leaves or ½ tsp ground anise seeds

1 lb 10 oz/750 g tomatillos (10 to 12 medium), fresh or canned; or 2 cups/ 480 ml jarred salsa verde (see Tips)

2 slices white onion, ½ inch/1.3 cm thick

2 to 3 cloves garlic, unpeeled

4 tbsp roughly chopped cilantro (including soft stems)

4 tbsp roughly chopped fresh Italian parsley

1 small serrano or medium jalapeño pepper, stem end cut off, sliced lengthwise, and seeds removed (omit if using jarred salsa)

Salt

3 cups/750 mL cooked white beans (white kidney/ cannellini or Great Northern), cooked or 2 (14 oz/398 mL) cans

Dry-Roasted Vegetables:

Salt

1 medium chayote squash (see Tips), cut into slim wedges

4 to 6 radishes, quartered lengthwise

6 to 8 thin young carrots, halved lengthwise and/or 2 small beets, cut into slim wedges

For Serving:

4 tbsp raw hulled pumpkin seeds (pepitas)

4 tbsp chopped fresh mint or 1 tbsp dried mint leaves, crumbled (optional)

Watercress sprigs, for garnish

TIPS:

If using jarred salsa, I like Herdez Salsa Verde.

You can substitute zucchini for the chayote.

If you have used fresh tomatillos, you will find the natural pectins make the sauce gel after sitting for a while; thin it with a bit of water or cooking liquid from the beans.

Margret goofing around in the kitchen

CINDY FUNG

CURRIED CAULIFLOWER BUDDHA BOWL

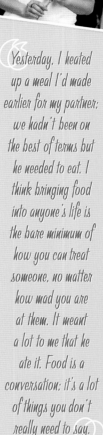

Cindy is a little bit fancy; she likes to take things up a notch. She did a few pop-up events at The Dep that were considerably more sophisticated than the kind of home cooking–inspired meals that I was accustomed to. Her impressive skills, ambition, and culinary curiosity really stood out.

This recipe is pretty cheffy and relies heavily on mise en place—meaning having all the ingredients organized and ready to go; but with a little planning it can come together pretty easily. All the parts can be made in advance, or in stages, and assembled at room temperature when you're ready to eat.

Prep: 2 hr
Cook: 45 min
Makes: 4 to 6 servings

Chili-Tofu Crumble

½ lb/225g firm tofu

Marinade:

1 mushroom bouillon cube, crumbled

1 tbsp garlic powder

1 tbsp onion powder

1 tbsp cayenne pepper

1 tbsp chili powder

1 tbsp ground white pepper

¼ tsp ground turmeric

¼ tsp salt

1 tbsp sesame oil

½ cup/120 mL cold water, plus more as needed

Dredge:

4 tbsp corn starch

1 tbsp salt

1 tbsp ground white pepper

¼ tsp curry powder

1 tbsp neutral oil

Quinoa

2 cups/480 mL water

Pinch of salt

1 cup/170 g quinoa (multi-coloured if possible)

Lemon Potato and Curried Cauliflower

3 large Yukon Gold potatoes, peeled and cut into long wedges

1 vegetable or chicken bouillon cube

½ tsp curry powder

½ tsp garlic powder

½ tsp smoked paprika

½ tsp ground turmeric

1 tsp salt

3 cups/400 g cauliflower florets

Olive oil, for drizzling

3 cloves garlic, crushed

Juice of ½ lemon

Truffled Mushroom Medley

¼ cup/60 mL extra-virgin olive oil

2 tbsp chopped garlic

2 tbsp fresh thyme

8 cups/2 L mixed Asian mushrooms (oyster, cremini, shimeji, king oyster, enoki, shiitake, etc.), roughly chopped

1 tbsp/15 g unsalted butter

1 tsp salt

1 tsp truffle oil

Green Goddess Dressing

1 avocado, halved and pitted

¼ cup/60 mL fresh lemon juice

4 tbsp chopped fresh dill

4 tbsp roughly chopped fresh parsley

4 tbsp roughly chopped fresh tarragon

4 tbsp roughly chopped green onions

6 cloves garlic, peeled but whole

½ cup/125 mL Greek yogurt

½ cup/120 mL sour cream

1 tsp salt

Up to 4 tbsp vegetable oil

Final Assembly

2½ cups/100 g mixed greens

Microgreens and/or radish slices, for garnish (optional)

Yesterday, I heated up a meal I'd made earlier for my partner; we hadn't been on the best of terms but he needed to eat. I think bringing food into anyone's life is the bare minimum of how you can treat someone, no matter how mad you are at them. It meant a lot to me that he ate it. Food is a conversation; it's a lot of things you don't really need to say.

Cindy Fung is part of a creative team behind a range of innovative lifestyle, event, and hospitality brands like Preserve Indulgence, Pray Tell Bar, Sixteen Ounce prepared meals, and Caviar Citizen.
@preserveindulge
@caviarcitizen
@praytellbar
@sixteenoz_

Here's the plan:

Organize all your ingredients.

Heat water for the quinoa.

Prep the tofu marinade, the dredge, and the cauliflower spice mix.

Marinate the tofu (this can be done the day before).

Start cooking the quinoa. Heat the water for the potatoes/ cauliflower.

While the quinoa's cooking, prep the cauliflower, mushrooms, and potatoes.

When the quinoa's done, fluff, cover, and set aside.

Boil the potatoes, steaming the cauliflower over them.

While the veg are cooking, preheat the oven. Crumble and dredge the tofu.

Season the potatoes and cauliflower.

Bake the veg and tofu to crisp.

Sauté the mushrooms and blend the dressing.

Let things cool down a bit until you're ready to serve.

Assemble the bowls and garnish.

Chili-Tofu Crumble

Cut the tofu into bite-size slices.

Make the marinade: In a shallow bowl, whisk together the bouillon cube, all the spices, the salt, and sesame oil. Add ½ cup/120 mL cold water or more as needed to cover the tofu. Add the tofu and marinate for a minimum of 30 minutes. (Overnight is better.)

Preheat the oven to 400°F/200°C. Line a baking sheet with parchment paper. Drain, pat dry, and crumble the tofu.

Dredge and bake: In a bowl, combine the corn starch, salt, white pepper, and curry powder. Add the tofu and toss. Using your hands, a colander, or a spider strainer, remove the tofu, leaving extra dredge behind, and place on the prepared baking sheet. Drizzle with the oil and bake until a bit crispy, 20 to 30 minutes.

Quinoa

In a saucepan, bring the water and salt to a boil. Add the quinoa and return to a boil. Reduce the heat to medium, cover, and cook until tender, 12 to 15 minutes. Remove from the heat and fluff with a fork. Cover and let stand for 15 minutes.

Lemon Potato and Curried Cauliflower

Preheat the oven to 400°F/200°C. Line two baking sheets with parchment paper.

In a large pot that can accommodate a steamer basket, cover the potatoes with cold water and add the bouillon cube. Bring the water to a boil, then reduce the heat to medium.

Meanwhile, in a bowl large enough to hold the cauliflower florets, combine the curry powder, garlic powder, smoked paprika, turmeric, and ½ teaspoon of salt.

Once the water has started to boil, place a steamer basket over the potatoes (or separately), add the cauliflower, cover, and steam until lightly cooked, 5 to 7 minutes. Remove the cauliflower, toss with the curry mixture, and place on one of the prepared baking sheets. Drizzle with olive oil.

Continue to simmer the potatoes, covered, until tender, another 7 to 10 minutes (20 minutes total). Drain and toss with a drizzle of oil, the garlic, lemon juice, and remaining ½ teaspoon salt. Arrange on the second prepared baking sheet.

Bake the cauliflower and potatoes until a bit crispy, 20 to 30 minutes.

Truffled Mushroom Medley

In a very large skillet or wok, heat the olive oil over medium-high heat. Stir in the garlic and thyme and then add all the mushrooms. Cook, stirring occasionally, until the liquid has been released and evaporated and the mushrooms start to brown, 12 to 15 minutes. (If you don't have a big pan, do this in two batches).

Add the butter and season with the salt. Toss with the truffle oil.

Green Goddess Dressing

Scoop the avocado into a food processor. Add the lemon juice, herbs, green onions, garlic, yogurt, sour cream, and salt and mix everything on high speed until combined and almost smooth. With the machine running, drizzle in the vegetable oil as needed to thin out to a thick cream consistency. Store covered in the fridge.

Final Assembly

Following the plan above make the tofu, quinoa, potatoes and cauliflower, mushrooms, and dressing. Let all the components cool to warm or room temperature.

To assemble the Buddha bowls, make a base of mixed greens in each of four to six large bowls. Sprinkle with the quinoa, mushrooms, cauliflower, and tofu. Set some potatoes on the side. Generously drizzle with the dressing. If desired, garnish with microgreens and/or radish slices.

> *My mom's from Montreal, and my dad was born in Palestine-Israel, but I don't know if he would call himself Israeli or not. One of the things I should say right away about my family is that there's a huge amount of politics around the word "Israel" . . . . It's such a complicated identity to have. It's very interesting that the food that I'm drawn to is from that region, and that brings up some pretty complicated political stuff.*

Many of **Mira Berlin's** earliest memories are of licking spoons and stirring pots in her mother's kitchen. Over the years, notepad in hand, Mira has collected recipes from her family and a few very kind and willing chefs she met along the way.
@mira.berlin

TIPS:

When soaking, the chickpeas will double in volume, so use more water than you think you need.

Save the chickpea cooking liquid and use it to store any remaining cooked chickpeas.

The secret to creamy hummus is overcooking the chickpeas: Don't worry if they are mushy and falling apart a little when you cook them.

For the mushrooms, canola or another neutral oil is preferable, but olive oil works as well. The oil left from cooking the mushrooms can be strained and saved for later use in stews, omelettes, or meat dishes.

If scaling the hummus recipe up or down, it is important to respect the 2:1 ratio of cooked chickpeas to tahini sauce.

You can top this recipe with any kind of meat. I've done slow-cooked lamb, as well as braised chicken with pomegranate molasses. They're both wonderful!

HUMMUS WITH CONFIT MUSHROOMS

Mira's obsession with hummus started in one of the many little *hummusiyas* in the old city of Jaffa near Tel Aviv. Light-years away from the pasty supermarket stuff she knew from Canada, the hummus here was luxuriously smooth and creamy, nutty and slightly bittersweet. Her infatuation with this dish led to countless hours experimenting with recipes, which she then brought to The Depanneur to much acclaim.

Prep: 20 min, plus 12 hr soaking time

Cook: 1½ hr

Makes: 2 cups/ 480 mL

Vegan

Make the hummus: Place the chickpeas into a large bowl with 1 teaspoon of baking soda. Cover with water (see Tips) and soak overnight at room temperature.

Drain and rinse the chickpeas under cold water and place into a large pot with the remaining 1 teaspoon baking soda. Add cold water to cover by at least 4 inches/10 cm. Bring to a boil over high heat, skimming off any scum that rises to the surface. Reduce the heat to medium, cover, and simmer until the chickpeas are very tender, about 1 hour. Drain and set aside (see Tips).

Measure out 2 cups/330 g of the chickpeas and transfer to a food processor. Reserve the remainder for garnish (see Tips). Add the tahini sauce and purée for several minutes, until extremely smooth and uber-creamy. Taste, adding salt to your liking, blending well to incorporate.

Make the confit mushrooms: Wipe the mushrooms with a dry kitchen towel to remove any dirt. Remove woody ends of stems. If heads are very large, cut in half. Place the cleaned mushrooms in a large heavy-bottomed pot and add enough oil to fully submerge them. Add the garlic cloves, thyme, lemon peel, and 1½ to 2 tablespoons salt. Simmer over low heat until the mushrooms are fully cooked and the oil smells fragrant, 20 to 30 minutes.

Let the mushrooms cool slightly in the oil.

To serve, mound the hummus in a shallow bowl. Create a well in the centre using the back of a spoon. Top with the reserved chickpeas, the tahini sauce, and the warm mushrooms. Drizzle with the fragrant oil from the mushrooms and garnish with paprika, parsley, and sea salt to taste. Add a squeeze of lemon, if desired.

Tahini Sauce

In a blender or food processor, combine the garlic, lemon juice, and ¼ teaspoon of the salt and process on high for a few seconds until you have a coarse purée. Let the mixture stand for 10 minutes to allow the garlic to mellow.

Pour the mixture through a fine-mesh sieve set over a large bowl, pressing to extract as much liquid as possible. Discard the solids.

Stir the tahini, cumin, and remaining ¼ teaspoon salt into the lemon mixture. Add ¼ cup/60 mL of the ice water and whisk together until smooth (you can also use a food processor). Continue adding ice water, a few tablespoons at a time, until you have a perfectly smooth, creamy, thick sauce. The sauce will lighten in colour as you whisk. Taste and adjust the seasoning.

The tahini sauce will keep for up to 1 week refrigerated, or it can be frozen for up to a month. If the tahini sauce has been stored, you may need to whisk in a few more tablespoons of water, as it will thicken with refrigeration or freezing.

Hummus:

1 cup/200 g dried chickpeas

2 tsp baking soda

1 cup/250 mL tahini sauce (recipe follows), plus more for garnish

1 tsp kosher salt

Confit Mushrooms:

1 lb/450 g button mushrooms

4 cups/1 L oil (see Tips), plus more as needed

1 head garlic, separated into cloves but unpeeled

2 sprigs thyme

Peel from 1 lemon

Kosher salt

For Garnish:

Paprika

Chopped parsley

Sea salt

Lemon juice (optional)

Tahini Sauce

Makes: 2 cups/ 480 mL

1 head garlic, separated into cloves but unpeeled

6 tbsp fresh lemon juice

½ tsp kosher salt

1 cup/240 g tahini

¼ tsp ground cumin

¾ cup/175 mL ice water

ADOPT-A-RECIPE Alicia Peres

ZAALOUK
Moroccan Ratatouille

Visiting the Djemaa el-Fna, the spectacular night market in Marrakech, made an indelible impression on me. A vast, teeming bazaar of sweets and spices, exotic (to me at least) flavours, and vibrant colours that somehow impossibly sprang into existence each night, only to magically disappear again each day. This warm and luscious eggplant mezze (small dish) evokes those memories, layered with spices and the elusive citrus note of preserved lemon.

2 large eggplants (about 1 lb/450 g), halved lengthwise

4 tbsp olive oil

2 medium tomatoes, peeled and finely diced

3 cloves garlic, finely chopped

1 tsp ground cumin

1 tsp freshly ground black pepper

1 tsp paprika

½ tsp ground chili pepper, such as Espellete or Aleppo

2 tbsp minced fresh cilantro, plus 1 tbsp cilantro leaves for garnish

½ preserved lemon (preferably Moroccan), finely chopped (see Tip)

1 tsp salt

2 tbsp green olives, sliced (optional)

Flatbread or sliced baguette, for serving

Prep: 30 min
Cook: 50 min

Makes: 4 servings
Vegan

Preheat the oven to 400°F/200°C. Line a baking sheet with foil.

Place the eggplants, cut-side down, on the foil-lined sheet and roast until softened, about 30 minutes. When cool enough to handle, remove the eggplant flesh and chop it into small pieces.

Meanwhile, in a large skillet, heat the olive oil over medium heat. Add the tomatoes, garlic, and spices and sauté until the tomatoes are softened and the liquid has evaporated, 5 to 7 minutes.

Add the chopped eggplant and continue cooking for another 5 minutes.

Add the cilantro, preserved lemon, salt, and olives (if using). Cook for another 4 to 5 minutes to allow the flavours to blend.

Let the ratatouille cool slightly before serving with flatbread or sliced baguette. Garnish with the cilantro leaves.

TIP:
Preserved lemons can be purchased at Middle Eastern markets.

I used to help my mother cook when I was a kid. She'd be cooking, and I'd be helping her, and chopping things. The smell of the things she used to cook in the kitchen made me travel, somehow. So when she died, I didn't know all the recipes, but I tried to recall the smell of the things she used to cook and I'd try to make this smell how she did. And this is how I ended up cooking my recipes.

Hajar Jamal Eddine is the manager of Moroccan Way, a start-up aimed at bringing the best of Moroccan handmade products to Canada. She's a food lover and passionate cook who loves to share her know-how with others—because food speaks all languages.
@moroccan_ way_canada

EMILY ZIMMERMAN

GEHAKTE ZONROYZ ZOYMEN

Vegan Chopped Liver

Emily has been a Depanneer since the very beginning. There isn't a facet of The Dep that she has not had a hand in, from her creative vegan Supper Clubs to her multi-year stint running a weekly PWYC Drop-In Dinner. She taught some of our most popular workshops like vegan cheesemaking and holiday chocolates. For me, it was a years-long apprenticeship in the versatility of plant-based cooking. Beyond just food, Emily introduced me to new ideas in music, culinary history, social justice, and Judaism, and all the interesting places where they intersect and overlap.

Chef's Note: This is a deliciously rich, vegan version of a classic Ashkenazi Jewish appetizer. There were elements of chopped liver that I missed when I officially became vegetarian as a teen. So I worked on re-creating it in vegan form. It was important that it be an affordable dish, and I also wanted to use ingredients that are already staples of my cultural kitchen: vegetable oils and agar-agar are used in mainstream Jewish cooking as kosher substitutes for lard and gelatin, respectively.

When I've done seder at The Depanneur, I talk a lot about the act of food as a healing ritual, which is what a seder is. Like, "Hey, my ancestors presumably went through an experience that was so dehumanizing that 5,000 years later, we still have to do this healing ritual to remember what that was like and to reconfirm our humanity." . . . When I'm making community meals, that's part of my mindset, that this is a healing ritual because eating a shared meal is incredibly good for you, spiritually and socially.

Emily Zimmerman is a chef, community worker, and food justice activist. She currently works as a community kitchen facilitator in Hamilton.
@pearandpepper

Prep: 20 min, plus 1 hr to chill

Cook: 1½ hr of hanging out in the kitchen while the onions cook

Makes: 4 as an appetizer to 8 for light grazing

Vegan

½ cup/125 mL coconut oil (see Tips), plus more as needed

6 medium onions, sliced

2 cups/280 g sunflower seeds

⅓ cup/75 mL water

2 tbsp agar-agar powder or 4 tbsp agar-agar flakes

1 tsp salt (use smoked or truffle salt for extra umami)

Freshly ground black pepper

Bonus Garnish:

Vegan Gribenes (recipe follows; optional)

Crackers or rye bread, for serving

Pickles, for serving

Chutney, for serving (optional)

Vegan Gribenes

1 to 2 tbsp neutral oil

1 medium onion, chopped

A handful of yuba (dried tofu skins)

Salt

Generously coat the bottom of a skillet (ideally cast-iron) with the coconut oil and toss in the onions. Put the pan over low heat. Like, very, very low (1.5 out of 10 low). Do not give in to the temptation to turn up the heat.

Go about your regular kitchen business, stirring the onions every 20 minutes or so, for about 1½ hours. Add more oil if necessary. Don't turn up the heat because we want to slowly, thoroughly caramelize the onions to a golden brown, without burning them at all. Don't add salt because salt will cause the onions to release their water content, diluting the oil, and the onions will just sauté instead of caramelizing.

While this is going on, in another skillet, lightly toast the sunflower seeds over very low heat, for about 5 minutes, until toasty and lightly browned. (Alternatively, spread out on a baking sheet in a 300°F/150°C oven for about 10 minutes.)

In a small saucepan, bring the water to a simmer on the stovetop. Whisk in the agar-agar and continue to whisk for 2 minutes, then remove from the heat. Proceed immediately with the rest of the steps while the agar is still hot.

Once the onions are a lovely soft golden brown and your whole house smells like Bubbe's kitchen, scoop the onions out of the pan. Reserve about 4 table-spoons of the onions for topping the pâté. (Hold on to the pan if making the Vegan Gribenes; see recipe below.)

Place half the onions in a food processor with the sunflower seeds and the warm agar-agar mixture. Pulse until it's a smooth, buttery consistency. (Add more warm water, a tablespoon at a time, if it's too grainy.) Add the salt and pepper to taste and pulse again.

Transfer the pâté to a bowl and fold in the other half of the onions. (If desired, press the pâté into small, oiled moulds.) Refrigerate for at least 1 hour.

To serve, unmould or scoop the pâté into a small, ideally very decorative, dish and top with the reserved caramelized onions. If desired, top with vegan gribenes.

Serve with crackers or rye bread, pickles, and maybe chutney.

Vegan Gribenes

Pronounced *gree-bins*, these are originally chicken skins that are fried until crispy.

So you just made the legit, proper, caramelized onions for your pâté, right? And you still have an oniony, oily pan. Don't wash it yet.

Add the oil to the pan and turn the heat way up. Add the onion and the yuba and fry the heck out of the onion until everything's crispy and maybe a little black around the edges. Drain and season with salt.

TIPS:

Grapeseed oil works as a lighter substitute, but it won't have the same meaty/fatty texture.

Quick and dirty cheaters' version: Preheat the oven to 400°F/200°C. Mix the onions, sunflower seeds, and oil in a baking dish. Bake for 15 minutes. Purée with salt and pepper and proceed as above. Don't bother with the agar-agar because cheaters don't deserve authentic mouthfeel.

 Michael Zimmerman

FASULYA

Yemeni Kidney Bean Dip

***Fasulya* is a traditional Yemeni bean stew,** a cousin to the Levantine *foul*, a popular breakfast or brunch dish to be scooped up with soft, fresh flatbread. It makes an interesting, equally healthy alternative to hummus.

Prep: 10 min
Cook: 20 min
Makes: 4 servings
Vegan

2 tbsp olive oil

1 medium red onion, finely chopped

2 green chilies or jalapeños, seeded and finely chopped

3 cloves garlic, minced

2 tomatoes, diced

1 tsp kosher salt

2 tbsp tomato paste

½ cup/125 mL water

1 (19 fl oz/540 mL) can kidney beans (see Tips), drained

½ tsp ground cumin

1½ tbsp/22 g olive oil (or ghee or butter, melted; optional)

Chopped fresh cilantro, for garnish (optional)

Tahini sauce (see Tips) or yogurt, for serving

Warm flatbread, for serving

In a skillet, heat the oil over medium heat. Add the onion, chilies, and garlic and sauté until the onion is golden brown, 8 to 10 minutes.

Add the tomatoes and ½ teaspoon of kosher salt and wait for them to soften, about 2 minutes.

Add the tomato paste and water. Let the sauce thicken for a minute or two. Add the beans, cumin, and remaining ½ teaspoon kosher salt. You can add some more water if you like, but we Yemenis like it nice and thick. Let it simmer for about 10 minutes.

Use a potato masher to mash it a bit but not too much—just until it's nice and thick, but still chunky.

Pour the olive oil on top and sprinkle with cilantro (if using). A drizzle of tahini sauce or a dollop of yogurt is a nice addition.

Serve with warm flatbread for scooping it up.

TIPS

You can use 1 cup/185 g dried kidney beans soaked overnight and cooked until done; a mix of fava and kidney beans is also popular.

To make a simple tahini sauce, thin some tahini with lemon juice and cold water, then add a little minced garlic and salt and pepper to taste.

I learned to cook from my mother. When I was fifteen, I went from my village in Yemen to the big city and started working in a bakery. From there I learned how to make authentic Yemeni cuisine while working in other restaurants. I went from Yemen to Turkey, then to Cuba, then Ecuador, then Colombia. Then to New York, Los Angeles, Texas. But it was impossible to get any work papers in America. . . . So I came to Canada and now I am going to become a permanent resident.

Najib Nasr was born and raised in Yemen, and currently works as a full-time chef at a Middle Eastern restaurant in Toronto. His biggest inspiration is his mother, whose recipes he loves to re-create.

CANDACE ESQUIMAUX

MANOOMIN

Wild Rice and Cranberries

Chef Candace—whose name is Nawatiin Kwe, meaning Calm Water Woman—is an Anishinaabe entrepreneur from Aundeck-Omni-Kaning on Manitoulin Island. After ten years as a frontline worker, she developed an interest in wellness and nutrition inspired by the traditional foods and connection to the land of her First Nation family.

Manoomin—also known as wild rice, good berry, or harvest berry—is one of the very few traditional First Nation foods that can be readily found in Canadian supermarkets. It is gathered from lakes and waterways by canoe in late August and early September, during the wild rice moon (*manoominike giizis*). It is highly nutritious, with twice the protein of brown rice.

Prep: 10 min
Cook: 45 to 50 min
Makes: 6 servings
Vegan

Rinse the wild rice well before putting it into a pot. Add 3 cups/710 mL water and the cranberries. Bring to a boil. Reduce the heat to low, cover, and cook at a low simmer for 45 minutes. Add a bit more water towards the end if it's looking dry. The rice should not be crunchy or tough. If you see the grains beginning to split along the sides, the rice is done. If you have leftover liquid in the pot, drain off the water in a fine sieve. Fluff with a fork and serve!

1 cup/180 g wild rice
3 to 4 cups/710 to 950 mL water
½ cup/80 g dried cranberries

TIPS:
For a more savoury dish, substitute stock for water.
Feel free to add any herbs or seasonings at the end.

For a delicious hot or cold dessert, add maple syrup and wild blueberries at the end.

Chef Candace Esquimaux
is an Indigenous entrepreneur who has worked as a frontline worker over the last fifteen years. Candace's Catering was born out of a lifelong passion for food and another way to serve her community.
@candace_catering_

ADOPT-A-RECIPE Gordon Goldschleger

FRY BODI

Trini-Style Sautéed Long Beans

A talented musician and charismatic performer, Sheldon ran The Dep's brunch in the very early days. He had just recently returned to Toronto after a few years of combining food, music, and culture at Alice Yard, an arts and culture space in Port of Spain, Trinidad. When I invited him back to The Dep in 2021 for a Pick-Up Dinner, and to contribute to the book, he brought his now-adult son along to help out. Through the waft of curry steam and staccato chop of knives, memories and stories, tradition and culture moved invisibly across time, borders, and generations.

Prep: 15 min

Cook: 30 min

Makes: 4 to 6 servings

Vegan

---

3 tbsp vegetable oil

4 cloves garlic, thinly sliced

½ cup/80 g finely diced onion

1 cup/115 g diced squash (such as butternut or Jamaican pumpkin)

1 lb/450 g Chinese long beans (bodi), cut into 1-inch/ 2.5 cm lengths

1 medium tomato, diced

1 tbsp amchar masala (see Tips; preferably Chief brand)

1 tsp salt

1 tsp freshly ground black pepper

Tomato slices, for garnish (optional)

In a heavy pot, heat the oil over medium-high heat. Add the garlic and cook until lightly browned, about 2 to 3 minutes. Add the onion, reduce the heat to medium, and cook until the onion is translucent, about 5 minutes. Add the squash and cook until soft, about 10 minutes.

Add the beans, cover the pot, and allow the beans to steam for 5 to 10 minutes (see Tips). You can add up to 4 tablespoons water if needed to keep things moist.

Stir in the diced tomato and amchar masala and allow it to cook for another 5 minutes. Season with the salt and pepper. If desired, garnish with tomato slices.

TIPS:

You can get Chinese long beans (aka bodi, yardlong bean, or snake bean) and amchar masala at most Asian, East Indian, or West Indian grocery stores.

You can keep the beans a bit crunchy, or cook them until they are soft, up to you. Taste them while you cook it to set your preference.

Growing up in Canada in the 1970s and living in Mississauga was a bit difficult because we were maybe the only black kids that were going to my school at the time. My father told me "Hey, you know, when we go back to Trinidad, there's no racism." But that was not the case. People do mix, but it is a myth that every creed and race find an equal place. People struggle to maintain connection across racial lines. But one good thing is that we mix up our food.

Sheldon Holder (right, with his eldest son) is a musician, singer, songwriter, and lead singer of the Toronto band Avenue for Outrage (AFO). He is also a Gestalt psychotherapist in training. @SheldonHolderTO

AN NGUYEN

BIBIM GUKSU

Korean Spicy Buckwheat Noodles

A longing for the flavours of her homeland led An Nguyen to pursue the ideal Vietnamese banh mi sandwich (including a hundred attempts to perfect her own homemade baguettes). Along the way she discovered Korean cold buckwheat noodles (*bibim guksu*), which reminded her of Vietnamese vermicelli (*bún*). She makes this cool noodle salad with crispy fried tofu nuggets, shredded vegetables, and a sweet-spicy gochujang dressing. Some recipes use honey, agave, brown sugar, and/or mirin for sweetness, but this one gets a resourceful Canadian spin with maple syrup and strawberry jam.

How did I start cooking? I was a cheap kind of person and when I went out to eat I enjoyed the food so much, but they only gave me a small portion. So I said, "Okay, why don't I make it at home and eat as much as I want?" I studied ingredients, watched YouTube, and then I learned by myself.

An Nguyen has been in Canada for two years, and after working in a few food service jobs, she launched her own Vietnamese Street Food project, Saigon Meals, specializing in a variety of banh mi–style sandwiches and sides.
@saigonmeal

Prep: 35 min
Cook: 10 min

Makes: 4 to 6 servings
Vegan

Dressing:

4 tbsp gochujang (Korean mild red pepper paste; see Tips)

6 tbsp soy sauce

6 tbsp maple syrup

4 tbsp sesame oil

8 tbsp gochugaru (Korean red pepper flakes; see Tips)

8 tbsp strawberry jam

8 cloves garlic, minced

6 tbsp fresh lemon juice

Vegetables:

3 cups/285 g thinly sliced red cabbage

3 cups/750 mL sliced kimchi

3 cups/330 g julienned carrot, or a combination of carrot and daikon (see Tips)

2 cups/260 g julienned cucumber

Noodles:

1 cup/250 mL vegetable oil

1 lb/450 g medium-firm tofu, cut into ½-inch/1.3 cm slices

1 lb /450 g naengmyeon (Korean buckwheat noodles; see Tips)

4 tbsp sesame oil

6 tbsp sesame seeds

4 tbsp chopped fresh cilantro

Make the dressing: In a medium bowl, mix together the gochujang, soy sauce, maple syrup, sesame oil, gochugaru, strawberry jam, garlic, and lemon juice. Refrigerate.

Prep the vegetables: Put them in the fridge to chill.

Make the noodles: In a large skillet, heat the vegetable oil over medium-high heat until shimmering. Add the tofu slices and fry, turning until very crispy and golden brown on both sides, at least 5 minutes per side. Set aside on paper towels.

Bring a large pot of water to a boil. Add the noodles and cook according to the package directions. Drain and immediately rinse the noodles well under very cold running water until they are completely cold.

In a bowl, toss the cold noodles with the sesame oil. Refrigerate until ready to serve.

To assemble: In a large bowl, combine the chilled vegetables, 4 tablespoons of sesame seeds, and the dressing, reserving a small amount of each vegetable for garnish. Mix well.

Chop the fried tofu slices into cubes.

Divide the noodles among bowls. Top with the veggies and fried tofu cubes. Garnish with the reserved veggies, the remaining 2 tablespoons sesame seeds, and the cilantro.

ADOPT-A-RECIPE

Gochujang, gochugaru, and kimchi can be found in any Korean grocery.

If you can't find the chewier Korean-style buckwheat noodles, use soba, the Japanese-style buckwheat noodles that are often easier to find.

You can also use store-bought Vietnamese-style pickled julienned carrot and daikon (đồ chua) and/or Korean pickled daikon (spicy musaengchae or sweet, yellow danmuji).

MARIA POLOTAN

KALABASA SA GATA

Squash in Coconut Milk

Maria probably did more to transform my appreciation of Filipino food than anyone. Prior to starting The Dep, I hadn't really had a memorable experience with this cuisine. I then hosted a few *kamayan* Supper Clubs—lavish multi-course spreads served on banana leaves and eaten with one's hands—and became a die-hard fan. Maria brought these amazing flavours to her Brunch residency at The Dep, and all I can say is if you have not had the chance to try a Filipino brunch, you want to get on that ASAP.

This dish is traditionally prepared with the addition of shrimp or pork, but this vegan version is equally satisfying.

My mother was the cook of the house, and she was an intuitive cook. She would make something really tasty from whatever she could get in the market. And I learned to cook by smells. I would know when the adobo was just at the right moment that I needed to turn off the heat because the smell would turn a little bit sweet while the sour note was still there. No recipe can tell you when that is.

Maria Lourdes Polotan grew up in a kitchen where the family congregated and her mother presided. After many years working in documentary film, Maria began to share her passion for food through Mama Linda's, offering traditional Filipino home cooking with quality local ingredients.
@mamalindasto

Prep: 10 to 15 min
Cook: 25 to 30 min
Makes: 4 servings
Vegan

¾ lb/340 g squash (preferably kabocha)

1 stalk lemongrass

1 tbsp neutral oil

½ medium onion, minced

1 tbsp minced garlic

1 tbsp minced fresh ginger

2 to 2½ cups/480 to 590 mL coconut milk, depending on how dry the squash is

1 tsp vegetarian bouillon powder

Salt and freshly ground black pepper

1 to 2 green chilies, roughly chopped

4 tbsp chopped fresh cilantro, including stems

Peel the squash and remove the seeds. Cut into 1½-inch/4 cm cubes. Set aside.

Remove the tough outer layers of the lemongrass. Slice the pale inner stalk into three parts (2 to 3 inches/5 to 7.5 cm each). Bruise the lemongrass pieces by crushing them gently with a rolling pin, meat mallet, or side of a heavy knife.

In a heavy-bottomed sauté pan, heat the oil over low to medium-low heat. Add the lemongrass, onion, garlic, and ginger and sauté until softened and fragrant, about 5 minutes. Add 2 cups /480 mL of the coconut milk, increase the heat to high, and bring to a boil. Reduce the heat to low and simmer for 5 minutes.

Add the squash, increase the heat to high and bring to a boil. Reduce the heat to low again, add the bouillon powder, and season with salt and pepper. Simmer until the squash is tender, 10 to 15 minutes. Add the chilies and cook for 2 more minutes.

Taste and adjust the seasoning and add a bit more coconut milk if it seems too dry. Stir in the chopped cilantro.

TIPS:

The best squash to use is the kabocha variety, although other hard squashes work too.

You can cut the squash into larger pieces but cooking time will be lengthened.

I recommend Thai Kitchen (organic) or Aroy-D coconut milk.

ADOPT-A-RECIPE   Mess Hall

Prep: 15 min

Cook: 15 min

Makes: six
1-pint/500 mL jars

Vegan

4 cups/1 L trimmed
and halved Brussels
sprouts

4 cups/1 L
cauliflower and/or
Romanesco florets

4 cups/1 L green
cherry tomatoes (see
Tips), halved if large
and pricked if whole

4 shallots, peeled
and thinly sliced

3 tbsp pickling salt
(see Tips)

6 sprigs thyme or
rosemary

6 cloves garlic,
peeled

1 tbsp peppercorns

1 tbsp mustard
seeds

1 tbsp crushed
chili flakes or a few
slices of hot pepper
(optional)

1½ heaping tsp
calcium chloride
(see Tips)

3 cups/710 mL apple
cider vinegar

3 cups/710 mL water

CAMILLA WYNNE

FALL HARVEST PICKLES

Camilla is a kindred Montreal soul in Toronto. One of Canada's only Master Preservers, she took over as The Dep's go-to canning maven and makes a damn fine pickle. This recipe makes great use of the last of any garden vegetables, like the green tomatoes left over at the end of summer.

Fill a large pot with about 6 inches/15 cm of water. Place a round cake rack or tea towel on the bottom to protect the jars from the hot metal. Cover and bring to a boil, then turn off the heat.

Place the vegetables and shallots in a large bowl and stir to combine. Set aside.

Wash six 1-pint/500 mL canning jars with new snap lids.

In each jar, place 1½ teaspoons pickling salt, 1 sprig thyme or rosemary, 1 clove garlic, ½ teaspoon peppercorns, ½ teaspoon mustard seeds, ½ teaspoon chili flakes (if using), and a heaping ¼ teaspoon calcium chloride.

Pack the vegetables into the jars, leaving a generous ½-inch/1 cm headspace.

In a medium saucepan, combine the vinegar and water and bring to boil.

Pour the hot brine over the vegetables, leaving a ½-inch/1 cm headspace. Remove air bubbles and add more brine if necessary to maintain the ½-inch/1 cm headspace. Seal fingertip tight with new snap lids.

Place the jars in the prepared pot (the water should be hot but not boiling), making sure they are covered by at least 2 inches/5 cm of water (top up if necessary). Cover and bring to a boil, then reduce the heat to medium and set a timer for 10 minutes. When the time is up, turn off the heat, uncover, and let sit for 5 minutes before carefully removing the jars to a wire rack or tea towel set on the counter.

Allow the jars to cool for 24 hours. Check the seal before storing somewhere cool, dark, and dry. Allow the pickles to cure at least 3 weeks before eating. Pickles will keep at least 1 year.

At the end of summer I start to put jars of preserves in weird places, because I run out of room. I just jam them in corners or hutches. I should write myself a note that says, "I put all the tomatoes in the bottom of this hutch," because I'll forget I have them. Preserving is like you're investing in your future. You're like, "This is not for me today. This is for me when I'm sad in the winter and I need some raspberries."

TIPS:

It pays off aesthetically to use both white cauliflower and Romanesco (if you can get it), as its green colour and fractal shapes contribute much interest.

Instead of green cherry tomatoes, use green tomatoes cut into ½-inch/1.3 cm wedges.

Pickling salt is a pure salt with no iodine or anti-caking agents, and as its name suggests, the best choice for making pickles. Kosher or sea salt can be substituted in a pinch, but avoid iodized table salt.

Calcium chloride is a type of salt that helps keep pickles crunchy. It is commonly sold with the canning supplies, under the brand name Pickle Crisp.

Camilla Wynne is a writer, home preserving teacher, and the founder of Preservation Society, a small-batch canning company. She is one of Canada's only Master Preservers and is the author of two cookbooks: *Preservation Society Home Preserves*, and *Jam Bake*. **@camillawynne**

KETAN DONGRE

NASHIK MISAL

Curried Moth Beans

> *I just like thinking about food. If my head is a pie chart, more than half of it is filled with cooking, food, and meals I ate a couple of years back.*

Ketan does a kind of kitchen jujitsu, taking traditional dishes from rural India and flipping them through the skills and techniques he has honed working in fine-dining and hotel kitchens around the world. This simple vegetarian breakfast dish from Maharashtra, in western India—traditionally eaten with *pav*, a soft, brioche-like bread roll—shows off the complexity and nuance of Indian spices.

Prep: 30 min, plus overnight soaking
Cook: 25 to 30 min

Makes: 4 to 6 servings

Vegan

½ lb/225 g moth beans (see Tips)

8 to 10 dried Kashmiri or Byadagi chilies (see Tips)

3½ tbsp coriander seeds

½ tsp black peppercorns

½ tsp cumin seeds

¼ tsp whole cloves

¼ tsp ground cinnamon

8 to 10 cloves garlic, peeled

½-inch/1.3 cm piece fresh ginger, peeled and chopped

1 tsp ground turmeric

½ tsp kosher salt, plus more to taste

6½ tbsp neutral oil

4 medium onions (red or white), 2 sliced and 2 chopped

⅓ cup/25 g unsweetened shredded coconut

1 tsp mustard seeds

1 to 2 cups/5 to 10 g fresh curry leaves (see Tips)

2 tsp red chili flakes

Juice of 1 lemon (optional)

Chopped cilantro

For Serving:

1 small onion (preferably red), finely chopped

½ bunch fresh cilantro

2 tbsp per portion nylon sev (see Tips) or crushed potato chips

Rinse the beans well and soak them at room temperature in water to cover overnight.

Soak the chilies in hot water for 10 minutes, then drain.

In a blender, combine the chilies, coriander seeds, black peppercorns, cumin seeds, cloves, cinnamon, garlic, and ginger. Add 1 to 2 tablespoons water and blend to a smooth paste.

Drain the beans and add them to a large pot. Add water to cover, 3 to 4 cups/710 to 950 ml. Add the turmeric and kosher salt and let the beans come to a boil for about 5 minutes. Check them frequently and once they are al dente, strain them and save the cooking water. You should be left with about 3 cups/710 mL of liquid.

In a skillet, heat 1½ tablespoons of oil over medium heat. Add the sliced onions and sauté until lightly browned, about 10 minutes. Remove from the heat and set aside to cool.

To the same skillet, add the shredded coconut and sauté until golden, about 5 minutes. (Keep a close eye on it as it can burn very quickly.) Remove from the heat and let cool a bit. Place the cooled sliced onions and coconut in a blender and blend to a smooth paste, adding a little water if necessary.

In a heavy-bottomed pot, heat the remaining 5 tablespoons oil over medium heat and add the mustard seeds. Once they start popping, add the curry leaves. When the leaves sizzle, add the chopped onions and sauté them until they are translucent, about 8 minutes. Add the chili flakes, cover, and fry for 2 to 3 minutes. Add the blended spice mix and fry for about 3 minutes, stirring constantly.

Ketan Dongre hails from Nagpur, a small city situated near the centre of India. He became interested in cooking through his first job as a cook at The Grand Hyatt in Mumbai. Since then, he has worked at O&B, The Ritz-Carlton, and The St. Regis Hotel.
@091_indianfood

Add the blended onion and coconut paste and fry for another 3 minutes, stirring to prevent sticking. If the mix gets too dry, splash in some water.

Add the cooked beans and mix them in the curry base for 2 to 3 minutes. Add the reserved cooking liquid and bring to a boil, stirring gently. Cook for 4 to 5 minutes, adding salt to taste.

Finish the dish with some lemon juice (if using) and chopped cilantro.

To serve: Spoon into bowls and top with the finely chopped onion, cilantro, and nylon sev or crushed chips.

TIPS:

All ingredients are readily available at Indian grocery stores.

Instead of moth beans (aka matki*), whole mung beans can be substituted.*

Kashmiri chilies have a vibrant red colour, but not a lot of heat; dried guajillo chilies can be used instead.

Fresh curry leaves are best, but dried can be used.

Nylon sev are thin, fried chickpea noodles eaten as a snack or used to garnish dishes.

Prep: 30 min

Fermentation:
2 weeks
to 2 months

Makes: about
4 cups/1 litre

Vegan

13 oz/380 g washed
and stemmed sweet
red peppers

3½ oz/100 g peeled
garlic (about 2 large
heads; preferably
organic)

1.3 oz/36 g sea salt
or any unrefined or
kosher salt (do not
use iodized table
salt)

1 lb 9 oz/
720 g washed and
stemmed chili
peppers

Optional additions:
fruit (stone fruit,
berries), vegetables
(such as carrots,
onions, shallots—raw,
roasted, or grilled),
herbs

Filtered water, as
needed (optional)

IMPORTANT NOTE:
*For reliable fermenting,
the ratio of vegetables
to salt is crucial, so it
is better to work by
weight than volume
(see more in Tips). All of
the vegetable weights
given here are after
they have been cleaned
and trimmed.*

FERMENTED HOT SAUCE

Rebekka is another alumna from the early days of The Dep's rental kitchen. She had just returned from California where artisanal fermenting was much further developed than in Toronto. She set about establishing a new company, Alchemy Pickle, which continues to thrive more than a decade later. When she outgrew our space, she took a bit of The Dep DNA with her, sharing her kitchen with other fledgling food entrepreneurs.

In a food processor, purée the sweet peppers, garlic, and salt. Add the chili peppers and any optional fruits/veggies and blend until fairly smooth. A little filtered or boiled and cooled water can be added to help with blending or if the pepper mix is looking rather dry. You will have roughly 5 cups/1.25 litres.

Wash a 2-quart/2-litre jar or two 1-quart/1-litre jars well in hot soapy water and rinse well. Place the jar(s) in an empty sink and sanitize by carefully pouring just boiled water inside. Discard the water and wait for the jar(s) to cool.

Pour the pepper purée into the jar(s). Only fill the jar(s) 70 to 75 percent full to allow for expansion during active fermentation. Stirring often in the first week will help keep it from bubbling up too much. Loosely lid and label the jar(s) with the date and ingredients and place in a cool spot. The ideal temperature is 64° to 68°F/18° to 20°C, but anywhere between 61° and 79°F/16° and 26°C will work (see Tips).

For the first 3 to 7 days, stir carefully each day with a super-clean utensil. Make sure not to close the lid tightly as pressure will build up inside the jar(s). If you see any white film on the surface forming, this should be skimmed off. It is still safe! After the first week, you can stir less often–maybe once a week. Try to taste how the flavour is changing each time you stir. You will notice as time passes that the pepper mash will take longer to separate and will taste more sour. After a few weeks it will be more cohesive. I like to ferment mine for about 2 months, but you can put it into the fridge once it has stopped separating and tastes great after a minimum of 2 weeks.

At this stage, you could blend further for a smoother hot sauce, or even run through a sieve to remove the seeds. Sterilize and label/date some smaller jars or bottles and decant your hot sauce into them before lidding and storing in the fridge. This should be safe to enjoy for a year or more.

TIPS:
The ratio of salt to vegetables by weight is crucial: The salt should be 3 percent of the weight of the vegetables. So, for example, for 1,000 g of peppers plus vegetables you need 30 g salt (3 percent by weight).

On the other hand, the ratio of garlic to peppers, hot peppers to sweet peppers, or other additions can be adjusted according to your flavour preferences and what you have available.

The hotter the peppers, the hotter the sauce! For this recipe I used 30 medium-hot chilies (1½ lb/690 g) and about 18 hot Thai bird's eye chilies (1 oz/30 g).

The spice level can be reduced somewhat by removing the seeds from the chilies.

The warmer the ambient temperature, the faster the fermentation will be, and you'll have to keep a closer eye on it and stir it more often.

You can always add a little water after fermenting if the sauce is too thick.

Given the time and labour involved, and the longevity of the finished product, it's worth making a large batch; it also helps for more reliable fermentation.

Wear gloves and work in a well-ventilated area when dealing with hot peppers.

When washing the food processor bowl or any jars that had chili pepper purée in them, rinse in cold water first so you don't inhale spicy steam. Then wash with hot soapy water very well, and then do it again to remove all residual oil from the hot peppers.

Growing up, there wasn't a lot of money. . . . My grandmother was always cooking and sharing food with everyone. She always made it seem kind of effortless. Her garden was huge, and she was producing huge amounts of food and just giving it to neighbours. So, there were these feelings, feelings of abundance. That's how we were rich, you know, rich like we have too many beans.

Rebekka Hutton is the pickle maker and owner of Alchemy Pickle Company, with seasonal fermented vegetable pickles, sauerkraut, and kimchi, and naturally carbonated kombucha all made with produce purchased directly from certified organic Southern Ontario farmers. @alchemypicklecompany

ADOPT-A-RECIPE   Joe and Veronika

STARS

Veggies

GREG COUILLARD
VIETNAMESE "KRAFT DINNER"

LUCIANO SCHIPANO
RISOTTO AL TARTUFO NERO E BURRATA

Black Truffle Risotto with Burrata

PAOLA SOLORZANO
CAULIFLOWER TACOS WITH HABANERO PINEAPPLE SALSA AND CREAMY COLESLAW

REBECCA PEREIRA
BAINGAN BHARTA

Roasted Eggplant Curry

IVÁN WADGYMAR
TLACOYOS DE MAÍZ AZUL

Blue Corn Tlacoyos

ABEDA OTURKAR
KOFTAT ALNIKHI

Khaleeji Chickpea and Sweet Potato Kofta with Tamarind Sauce

KALMPLEX
ROYALTY PROVISIONS

NICOLE DI NARDO
PASTA RIPIENA CON CECI E FUNGHI

Chickpea Ravioli Filled with Mushrooms

Seafood

STUART SAKAI
TUNA AND TOFU

RHOMA AKOSUA SPENCER
SALTFISH RUNDUNG

Salt Cod and Coconut Braise

PAULA COSTA
CALDEIRADA DE MARISCO

Portuguese Seafood Stew

DALI CHEHIMI
TAGINE HOUT

Fish Chermoula Tagine

JOSÉ ARATO
PAELLA DE CAMARÓN

Spanish Shrimp Paella

MARY FREIJ
SAYADIEH

Lebanese Fish and Rice

NANTHA KUMAR
KETAM CILI SINGAPURA

Singapore-Style Chili Crab

LAURA GUANTI
GNOCCHI AL NERO DI SEPPIE CON CALAMARI, POMODORINI, E RUCOLA

Squid Ink Gnocchi with Calamari, Cherry Tomatoes, and Arugula

Chicken

AVERY BILLY
JAMAICAN JERK CHICKEN

CHANTAL VÉCHAMBRE
POULET BASQUAISE
Basque Country Chicken

MONIQUE MULOMBO
POULET À LA MOAMBE
Congolese Chicken in Peanut Sauce

NASIR ZUBERI
MURGH HARA MASALA
Pakistani Green Curry Chicken

ELITA ROCKA
AYAM GULAI PADANG
Padang-Style Chicken Curry

TSEWANG AND LHUNDUP CHODON
KOTEY MOMOS
Tibetan Dumplings

Pork

ALEXANDER CHEN
HÓNG SHĀO RÒU
Crispy Skin Red-Braised Pork Belly

NIKY SENATER
VARZĂ CĂLITĂ
Romanian Braised Pork
Hocks with Sauerkraut

LEO MONCEL
DANDAN MIAN
Dan Dan Noodles

JASON REES
BBQ PULLED PORK

CHENG FENG
LAOYOUFEN
Old Friend Noodles

KATIE KRELOVE
TORTA AHOGADA
Mexican "Drowned" Sandwich

SONYA GAMMAL
TOURTIÈRE
Québécois Pork and Beef Pie

Beef, Lamb, and Game

ROBERT YEE
XĪNJIÁNG KǍO CHUÀN
Xinjiang Spicy Lamb Skewers

SELAM TECLU
DUBA BAMIA
Eritrean Pumpkin, Okra, and Beef Stew

KSENIJA HOTIC
SARME
Bosnian Cabbage Rolls

RIDHIMA KALRA
GOSHT DO PYAZA
Goat Curry

FRISHTA GHAFOORI
KOFTE ALOO BOKHARA
Lamb Meatballs with Sour Plum Sauce

TUBA TUNÇ
HÜNKAR BEĞENDI
Sultan's Delight (Turkish Eggplant
Purée with Braised Beef)

ZHANAR KHAMITOVA
MANTI
Kazakh Lamb and Squash Dumplings

FATIMA KHLIFI AND ZEYNEB BEN REJEB
KOSKSI
Tunisian Couscous

TAYLOR PARKER
VENISON IN THE WOODS

Pete Forde, Janet Polivy, and Jane French

VIETNAMESE "KRAFT DINNER"

Prep: 45 min, plus 1 hr soaking time
Cook: 30 min
Makes: 4 servings
Vegan (if modified)

In Toronto, Chef Greg Couillard forged a lifelong reputation as a fearless culinary innovator, a kind of supercollider of food ideas, smashing them together to produce novel and exotic new dishes. After more than five decades in the kitchen, it would not be hyperbole to suggest that he has been one of the most influential chefs in the evolution of this city's food scene. Through groundbreaking restaurants like The Parrot, Stelle, Avec, Sarkis, The Spice Room, and others, his prescient embrace of this city's multicultural flavours and ingredients helped revolutionize fine dining in Toronto. This signature dish of comfort food noodles in a vibrant, creamy sauce, embodies Greg's sophisticated, international palate and cheeky sense of humour.

1 (1-lb/450-g) package rice stick noodles (preferably fettuccine-size)

Green Sauce:

1 (14-oz/400-ml) can coconut milk

1 (14-oz/400-ml) can coconut cream

2 cups/57 g baby spinach

2 cups/60 g cilantro, leaves and stems, tightly packed

2 tbsp minced fresh ginger

2 tbsp Thai green curry paste

4 tbsp honey

1 tbsp kosher salt

1 cup/250 mL chicken or vegetable broth, plus more as needed

Stir-Fry:

6 baby bok choy, quartered lengthwise

24 sugar snap peas

1 small carrot, julienned

1 (8 oz/225 g) container shimeji mushrooms

2 tbsp sesame oil

2 tbsp canola oil

4 tbsp minced garlic

4 tbsp minced fresh ginger

4 tbsp minced shallots

1 small yellow bell pepper, julienned

1 small red bell pepper, julienned

2 tbsp Chinese-style "light" soy sauce

1 tbsp oyster sauce (use vegetarian oyster sauce for a vegan dish)

2 tbsp hoisin sauce

1 cup/57 g baby spinach

For Garnish:

2 cups/225 g bean sprouts

½ bunch Thai basil

¼ bunch garlic chives

2 tbsp store-bought crispy fried shallots or onions

Soak the rice noodles in a bowl of tepid water for 1 hour. Drain and set aside.

Meanwhile, make the green sauce: In a blender, in batches if necessary, combine the coconut milk, coconut cream, spinach, cilantro, ginger, green curry paste, honey, salt, and broth. Purée until smooth. Set aside.

Prepare the stir-fry: Bring a large pot of water to a boil over high heat. Fill a large bowl with ice water on the side.

Blanch the bok choy in the boiling water for 2 minutes. Remove with a slotted spoon and plunge into the ice water. Remove with a slotted spoon and dry on a paper towel.

Repeat with the sugar snap peas, blanching for 2 minutes, and the carrot, blanching for 3 minutes.

Remove the bottom ½ inch/1.3 cm of the mushrooms so the clumps separate.

In a large deep saucepan, bring the green sauce to a simmer over medium heat. Add the soaked rice noodles and cook until al dente, about 2 minutes, but taste to your liking. Thin with more broth, if needed, to keep the noodles from becoming gluey.

Heat a wok over high heat. Add the sesame and canola oils. Once hot, quickly add the garlic, followed by the ginger, and then the shallots. Add the bok choy, sugar snap peas, carrot, bell peppers, and mushrooms, stirring constantly, to heat through.

Add the soy sauce, oyster sauce, and hoisin, tossing to coat. Fold in the spinach leaves just before serving.

To serve: Place the noodles in a bowl and top with the vegetables. Garnish with the bean sprouts, Thai basil, and garlic chives. Finish with the crispy shallots.

> *Every time I cook something, it startles me. It's kind of a religious thing, not about churches or anything, but small 'n' religious. It's certainly a happier experience now than it's ever been before.*

Greg Couillard has his hands in a few pies at the moment, splitting his time among Chemong Lodge in the Kawartha Lakes region northeast of Toronto, Boca de Iguanas in La Manzanita, Mexico, and his signature line of No Refund hot sauces. **@couillardgreg**

GREG COUILLARD

Greg Couillard's entry into the orbit of The Depanneur was a bit of serendipity. If I recall correctly, Sandy Stagg, a grand dame of Toronto's fashion and culture scene, popped by one day accompanied by Greg's sister, Gaye Couillard. Gaye had run the beloved Vienna Home Bakery on Queen Street W back in the '80s and '90s, a place that, in addition to serving fabulous pies and coffee, quietly did farm-to-table long before it was a "thing." They adopted some wilting hydrangeas that had been an opening day gift and returned with Greg in tow. Now, as much as I loved food, I knew next to nothing about the world of fine dining or celebrity chefs. But Greg Couillard was one of a handful of elite Toronto chefs whose outsize reputation had penetrated even my sheltered consciousness.

I was a bit starstruck, stunned that a chef of this calibre would be up for hosting a $40 dinner party in my little corner store. Having a "big name" chef on The Dep's roster was validating and exciting and drew a crowd of his longtime fans. Over the next ten years, working with Greg would become one of the culinary highlights of The Dep.

In the '80s and '90s he blazed a trail through Toronto's restaurant scene, equally famous for his spectacular talent and his *enfant terrible* reputation. He was one of a handful of chefs who transformed fine dining in Toronto from a provincial enclave of old French fare and stuffy steakhouses into an explosion of colours, flavours, and spices that reflected the energy and diversity of a rapidly changing city. He brought a subversive, glam, and punk sensibility that shook up fine dining; similarly, his wild-child personality left chaos in its wake.

By the late '80s his Jump Up Soup was arguably Toronto's most famous, sought-after dish. Inspired by the first Caribana Parade in 1967 (which would go on to become the largest Caribbean festival in the world outside the Caribbean), it was a riot of colour, music, and tropical heat that crashed through the stolid grey of downtown Toronto much like Greg's cooking would do to the City's uptight restaurant scene in the decades that followed.

Despite being such a diverse food city, in reality Toronto has next to nothing in the way of unique, signature dishes—I can't think of a "Toronto-style" anything. **This soup, its vibrant mix of colours and textures, sweet, rich, spicy, and alive— a post-modern Caribbean fever dream in the mind of a punk queen from Manitoba, served up to an impressionable generation of newly minted yuppies— remains to me the quintessential Torontonian dish.**

The Dep became a playground for Greg's borderless culinary imagination. With his trademark approach to global fusion, he could playfully pull flavours, spices, and ideas from a dozen different cultures and masterfully combine them into something new, delicious, and uniquely his own. Like a master jazz improviser, he knew how to quote flavours and reference familiar dishes while creating something both original and cohesive. He knew the rules, and he had the skill to break them beautifully.

Greg would go on to do more than seventy events at The Dep, and along the way, undergo a quiet but profound transformation. He spent his winters cooking at a tiny boutique hotel in Mexico, where he absorbed the kaleidoscope of Mexican cuisine and ingredients and helped apprentice aspiring young Mexican chefs into the world of the professional kitchen. Back in Toronto, he kick-started a program to bring wholesome food to a busy addiction rehab centre, perhaps the payment of a kind of karmic debt, an act of gratitude for surviving a lifestyle that devoured so many of his friends. He remains to this day the most remarkably talented chef I have ever encountered, with an ability to make any dish indelibly his own.

LUCIANO SCHIPANO

RISOTTO AL TARTUFO NERO E BURRATA

Black Truffle Risotto with Burrata

Luciano is a one-man ambassador of Italian cuisine, whether he is teaching at Culinarium, his Toronto cooking studio, leading culinary tours in Calabria, or cooking risotto for two hundred in his gigantic, metre-wide *pentolo*, the largest pan of its kind in North America. He first made this fabulous dish at The Dep as part of a burrata-making Master Class; utterly simple but also incredibly luxurious.

Prep: 15 min
Cook: 25 min
Makes: 4 servings

6½ cups/1.5 L vegetable stock

2 tbsp extra-virgin olive oil

2 cups/400 g Italian short-grain rice (see Tips)

4 tbsp black truffle paste (see Tips)

7 oz/200 g burrata, torn into chunks

Salt and freshly ground black pepper

1 cup/20 g arugula, for garnish (optional)

In a medium saucepan, bring the vegetable stock to a boil over medium-high heat. Reduce the heat to low and keep the stock warm while you prepare the rice (see Tips).

In a large sauté pan, heat the olive oil over medium-low heat. Add the rice, mix well, and cook until the rice becomes translucent, 1 to 2 minutes.

Add enough stock to cover the rice, about ½ cup/125 mL. Cook, stirring occasionally, until the liquid is almost absorbed and then add another ½ cup/ 125 mL of stock. Repeat until the rice is cooked, 20 to 25 minutes.

Remove from the heat and gently stir in the truffle paste. Add the burrata (including the cream) and stir until the rice becomes creamy. If the risotto is too dry, add 1 to 2 tablespoons additional hot stock.

Taste and adjust the seasoning with salt and pepper. Garnish with the arugula, if desired.

TIPS:

Although Arborio rice is the most common short-grain Italian rice in Canada, it isn't the ideal rice for risotto. Look for Carnaroli, Vialone Nano, or Baldo instead.

*Pure truffles (*tartufi*) and truffle paste are very, very expensive. More common and affordable is* tartufata, *a blend of truffles, mushrooms, and seasonings. Be aware that most truffle pastes, along with almost anything labeled "truffle oil," rely on artificial truffle flavouring.*

Look for Italian rice, truffle paste, and burrata at an Italian grocery store or gourmet food shop.

The vegetable stock has to be kept hot so that the rice temperature does not drop when you add the liquid.

You can add white or oyster mushrooms, sliced ¼-inch/6-mm thick, when you toast the rice for extra flavour and an earthy tone.

Your risotto should be moist and creamy (or, as we say, all'onda, which means "wavy"), not sticky.

For a different presentation, top each individual plate with burrata instead of mixing it into the risotto.

I'm a historian, I like to go back to old, old books, like nineteenth-century books, and cook old recipes. Those books are more authentic than nowadays because there are no preservatives. Very seasonal, very local, and focused on the flavours and tastes. Believe it or not, I cooked up a panettone recipe that was from 1879. It was great to give it life again.

Luciano Schipano is a Red Seal–certified chef, teacher, and food consultant, as well as the co-president of Slow Food Toronto, and the director of the Italian Federation of Chefs. Luciano also owns and runs Culinarium, an Italian cooking studio in Toronto.
@Lucianoschipano
@culinarium.to

ADOPT-A-RECIPE   Carl Bloom

Born and raised in Mexico, **Chef Paola Solorzano** (right) comes from a large family of passionate cooks. Paola joined forces with Adriana Rubio (left) to found Santo Pecado Mexican Catering, a catering company specializing in authentic Mexican flavours. @santopecadoto

PAOLA SOLORZANO

CAULIFLOWER TACOS WITH HABANERO PINEAPPLE SALSA AND CREAMY COLESLAW

Santo Pecado Mexican Catering, founded by Paola Solorzano and Adriana Rubio, is one of the many successful small businesses to emerge from The Dep's basement incubator kitchen. Over the years they showcased a huge range of Mexican cooking at The Dep, from popular street foods like tacos and tortas, to unique pre-Columbian recipes, to sophisticated modern fusion menus. Now with their own bricks and mortar space and line of seven fabulous hot sauces (one for every cardinal sin!), they are making their mark on the city's food scene.

Fried Cauliflower:

1 cauliflower, cut into florets (3 to 4 cups/400 to 540 g)

¾ cup/50 g Tajín seasoning (see Tips)

2 cups/255 g corn starch

2 cups/480 mL carbonated water

1 tsp salt

Freshly ground black pepper

Canola oil, for deep-frying

Creamy Slaw:

3.5 cups/250 g shredded napa cabbage

1 cup/160 g shredded carrot

¾ cup/75 g shredded red cabbage

2 tbsp vegan mayonnaise

½ tbsp apple cider vinegar

Salt and freshly ground black pepper

Tacos:

1 cup/250 mL water

2 to 3 tbsp neutral oil

10 to 12 corn tortillas

Habanero Pineapple Salsa (recipe follows)

Habanero Pineapple Salsa

4 habanero peppers (this will make it pretty spicy, so use less if you prefer)

1 thick (1- to 1½-inch) slice fresh pineapple, peeled, cored, and cut into large pieces

¼ medium white onion

1 clove garlic, peeled but whole

Salt and freshly ground black pepper

3 tbsp plus 1 tsp fresh lime juice

Prep: 30 min
Cook: 30 min

Makes: 10 to 12 tacos
Vegan

Prepare the cauliflower: In a medium bowl, toss the cauliflower florets with the Tajín. In a separate bowl, mix the corn starch, carbonated water, and salt. Season with some black pepper and whisk until combined and smooth.

Line a tray with paper towels. Pour 2 inches/ 5 cm canola oil into a large deep skillet or heavy-bottomed Dutch oven; heat oil over medium heat.

Working in batches or a few at a time, carefully dip the cauliflower pieces into the corn starch batter and drop them into the oil with the aid of a long fork or tongs. Fry until golden and crisp, about 5 minutes. Remove to the paper towels.

Make the creamy slaw: In a bowl, mix the shredded napa cabbage, carrot, and red cabbage with the mayonnaise and vinegar. Season with salt and pepper to taste.

Assemble the tacos: In a bowl, whisk together the water and oil. Using a pastry brush, brush the mix onto the tortillas to get them hydrated before heating them up. Place the tortillas one by one on a hot skillet or griddle for 30 to 40 seconds per side. Put aside, wrapped in foil to keep them warm.

Place a few pieces of cauliflower in each tortilla, then top with some slaw and a splash of the habanero pineapple salsa. Serve and enjoy!

Habanero Pineapple Salsa

Heat a cast-iron skillet over medium-high heat. Add the habanero peppers, pineapple, onion, and garlic and sear for about 5 minutes, turning once. Transfer to a blender and blend until you have a chunky purée. Season with salt and black pepper to taste. Add the lime juice. Store in an airtight container in the refrigerator for a few days until ready to use.

TIPS:
Tajín is a brand of popular chili-lime-salt seasoning that is often dusted on vegetables and fruits; it is available in some large supermarkets and anywhere Mexican products are sold.

This recipe also works really well with fish instead of cauliflower.

REBECCA PEREIRA

BAINGAN BHARTA

Roasted Eggplant Curry

Becca is another alumna of The Dep's shared rental kitchen, where her media-darling food pop-up, Spice Girl Eats, started under the tutelage of her best friend: her mom. Together they're blazing a trail through Toronto's food scene with a trendy Instagram presence and cool new products like her artisanal Chai Concentrate.

Prep: 15 to 30 min
Cook: 45 to 90 min
Makes: 4 servings
Vegan

1 large eggplant

6 cloves garlic, peeled but whole

3 tbsp netural oil

½ tsp cumin seeds

1 large onion, finely diced

2 green chilies, finely chopped

2 medium tomatoes, finely diced

1 tbsp ground coriander

1 to 2 tsp cayenne pepper

½ tsp ground turmeric

1¼ tsp garam masala

Salt and freshly ground black pepper

Pinch of sugar

Juice of ½ lemon, or to taste

Handful of fresh cilantro leaves, chopped

Roti, naan, or cooked rice, for serving

Make 6 deep slits on the eggplant and insert a garlic clove into each one. Poke a skewer into the eggplant and place it directly over the flame of either the gas burner of your stove or barbecue, turning it around from time to time so that the skin blisters and gets charred and the eggplant flesh gets soft. Set aside to cool. (Alternatively, place the eggplant and garlic in a roasting pan, rub a little oil over the eggplant and bake at 350°F/180°C for about 1 hour or until it feels soft when pressed lightly with your finger. At this point place it under the broiler for a minute or two, turning it over to char the skin. Remove and set aside to cool.)

In a medium skillet, heat the oil over medium heat and add the cumin seeds. When they splutter, add the onion and cook, stirring, until translucent but not browned, 6 to 8 minutes.

Add the green chilies and sauté for a few minutes more. Add the tomatoes and cook until they soften, 3 to 4 minutes. Add the coriander, cayenne, turmeric, and 1 teaspoon of garam masala, and stir well. If too dry, add a splash of water. Continue to cook the mixture for a few minutes until the oil starts to separate. Season with salt and black pepper to taste. Set aside.

Cut the eggplant in half lengthwise and scoop out the flesh and roasted garlic into a small bowl. Use a fork or potato masher to mash the soft flesh into a pulp.

Return the sauce to the stove over medium heat, add the mashed eggplant, and mix well, cooking for another few minutes. Taste and adjust with a little salt, the sugar, lemon juice, and remaining ¼ teaspoon garam masala to finish off the dish.

Sprinkle the chopped cilantro on top and serve hot with roti, naan, or rice.

I was sixteen or something when I started modelling. So that's a really impressionable age. Till then, it didn't click to me that what you ate affected your body. I never thought that way. . . . Now that I have stopped modelling, it's blowing my mind because for the first time I'm free. I've probably gained like twenty-five to thirty pounds but I'm okay with it. I actually feel quite comfortable and happy with my body.

Becca Pereira started cooking at a young age, inspired by her mother's and grandmother's recipes from Mumbai and Goa. After a successful modelling career, Becca channelled her passion into a new food business, Spice Girl Eats. @spice.girl.eats

 Derek Ruth

Restaurants are suddenly really into "farm to table," but I think we also need the reverse: instead of making it just farm to table, it's also a table-to-farm kind of project, linking restaurants back to farms. I still do it with our tortilla business—although the quantity is less. I treat all organic waste as compostable material, and farm using that compost.

Iván Wadgymar is a *tortillero* and *molinero* who runs Maizal, a business that evolved from a Mexican restaurant into an end-to-end producer of artisanal corn masa, tortillas, and totopos. He grows heritage corn locally and nixtamalizes it in the traditional manner, producing products that seek to reconnect to centuries of cultural tradition and wisdom. **@maizalto**

IVÁN WADGYMAR

TLACOYOS DE MAÍZ AZUL

Blue Corn Tlacoyos

Prep: 40 min

Cook: 30 min (depending of the size of cooking surface)

Makes: 4 servings

I knew Ivan's food before I knew Ivan. I had eaten at a then-new Mexican restaurant and was impressed by how much better their tortillas were than what I was accustomed to finding in Toronto. I started reaching out to them when I needed some for my own Drop-In Dinners. Eventually I got to meet Ivan and learn more about his multi-faceted engagement in the complex relationship between Mexican ingredients, agriculture, sustainability, flavour, tradition, and culture.

The *tlacoyos* he makes are thick, oval-shaped, stuffed corn cakes that date back to Mexico's pre-Hispanic cultures. While they can be made with yellow or white corn, they are often made with blue corn, which gives them a distinct flavour and colour.

3 nopales (cactus paddles; see Tips)

1 tbsp vegetable oil

1¾ lb/800 g fresh blue, white, or yellow corn masa (or prepared masa harina; see Tips)

1¾ cups/400 g refried black beans (see Tips)

½ to 1 cup/120 to 250 mL salsa roja or salsa verde

5 oz/150 g Cotija cheese or queso fresco, grated or crumbled by hand

With a knife, carefully peel the spines off the nopales. Rinse well and dry.

Heat a skillet over medium heat. Add the oil and sear the nopales on both sides so that they lose their fresh green colour. (You can grill them as well.) Cut into strips ½ inch/1.3 cm wide and set aside.

In a large bowl, knead the masa for a few minutes, while hydrating with water. There is no exact measurement of water, so knead and add a little at a time until the masa feels like Play-Doh. It should be soft and moist, not wet. If it is too dry, it crumbles in your hand, and if it is too wet it sticks to your hand. Form into balls the size of a large lime or small lemon (about 3 oz/80 to 100g) and cover with a towel.

On a flat surface, lay out a sheet of plastic (a large zip-seal plastic storage bag cut open along both sides works great). Grab one ball of masa and flatten it out slightly with the palms of your hands. In the centre, place about 2 tablespoons of refried beans, then close the masa up around it to make a sphere. Place this stuffed ball on the plastic sheet and place another plastic sheet on top. Now carefully flatten out the ball between the two sheets, making sure there is no breakage. The typical shape to flatten out to is oval, but if you want to make rounds or a funkier shape, that is totally fine. The flatter you can get them, the better.

Place a skillet or griddle over medium heat. Carefully transfer a tlacoyo to the hot pan or griddle. Cook on one side until it starts getting some darker patches, about 3 minutes, then flip over with a spatula or with your hand. Cook for about the same time on the other side. Repeat with the other masa balls.

To serve, spread the salsa of your choice on the surface, then top with the cactus strips and crumbled cheese. Eat with your hands!

TIPS:

Cactus paddle slices (nopalitos) are also available jarred or canned, but I strongly encourage you to use fresh ones, which can be found at Latin grocers.

You can cook fresh cactus paddles in boiling water with 1 teaspoon baking soda for about 10 minutes before frying or grilling if you wish to remove their slightly viscous texture.

If at all possible, find somewhere that grinds fresh masa. If fresh masa is not available, replace it with masa harina and follow the package directions to get 800 g masa dough.

Refried beans can be bought in a can, but I much prefer to make my own from scratch.

ADOPT-A-RECIPE   Niky Senater

ABEDA OTURKAR

KOFTAT ALNIKHI

Khaleeji Chickpea and Sweet Potato Kofta with Tamarind Sauce

Like the spices and recipes she has spent years studying, Abeda herself reflects the restless movement of people, ingredients, and ideas. Originally from India, she worked extensively in food in Dubai, and becoming intimately familiar with the distinctive Khaleeji cuisine of the Gulf states—a mix of Arabic, Persian, Indian, and Asian influences that is the product of centuries of global spice trading. It was something I had never encountered in Toronto, so was delighted that she would share it with the folks at The Dep.

> I used to think chilies were Indian or Asian, and as I got deep into learning about herbs and spices, something dropped, not a penny, not a coin, but a boulder! We [in South Asia] never even had chilies until the 1600s after the Spanish had reached the South American coast. . . . It took me many nights, and many sleeps, to come to terms with the fact that chilies weren't Indian, that they came from somewhere else. To learn this was a shocker, a shocker!

Prep: 45 to 55 min

Cook: 35 to 40 min

Makes: 4 to 5 servings (about 20 kofta)

Vegan

Abeda Bihari Oturkar spent more than a decade as a food entrepreneur in Dubai. Abeda also runs PaperSpree, a website that offers eco-friendly paper products and personal accessories.
@Abedaskitchen
@paperspree

Preheat the oven to 400°F/200°C.

Wash the chana dal under running water until the water is clear. In a large pot, combine the chana dal with water to cover by 2 inches/5 cm. Bring to a boil and cook for 10 to 15 minutes until half done (i.e., rehydrated but not tender). Alternatively, you can soak them for 2 hours instead of cooking. Drain and set aside.

Poke the sweet potato a few times and bake whole until half done and still firm, about 20 minutes. When cool enough to handle, peel, roughly chop, and set aside.

Make the tamarind sauce: In a measuring cup, stir the tamarind paste with enough water to make 2 cups/480 mL tamarind juice.

In a saucepan, heat the oil over medium heat. Add the onion and sauté until light golden brown, about 5 minutes. Reduce the heat, add the tomato paste, and fry for a minute. Add the water, brown sugar, and tamarind juice and bring to a boil. Reduce the heat and add the spices and salt (go light on the salt as the sauce will concentrate a bit; you can always add more later). Continue cooking, stirring and checking that it does not stick to the bottom, until it reduces by around one-third. Cook the sauce until it is smooth and you see a glaze on top. The consistency of the sauce should be similar to a thin gravy. Add the lemon juice and rose water before taking it off the heat. Taste the sauce and adjust as needed for the right sweet-sour-spicy balance.

Make the kofta: In a large bowl, combine the drained dal and sweet potato. Add the fried onions, cilantro, parsley, ginger, garlic, green chili, ibzaar, paprika, black pepper, turmeric, and salt. Mix well. In a food processor, pulse the mix into a fine mince, but not a paste. Pulse in the raisins (if using).

To make the balls, rub a little oil on your palms, take a tablespoon or so of the mix, and roll it into a ball shape, 1½ inches/4 cm in diameter. You should get at least 20 kofta.

Pour several inches of oil into a heavy-bottomed pot or wok and heat until hot but not smoking. Working in batches of 2 to 4 kofta (depending on the size of the pot), cook until browned and crisp, 3 to 4 minutes. (Alternatively, you can place the koftas on a baking sheet lined with parchment paper and bake in the oven at 350° to 400°F/180° to 200°C for 15 to 20 minutes until they form a crust.)

Serve over hot basmati rice and drizzle generously with the tamarind sauce.

Ibzaar

In a dry skillet, lightly toast the peppercorns, cumin seeds, coriander seeds, cinnamon stick, whole cloves, and cardamom pods just until fragrant, being very careful not to burn them. Let cool, then combine with the nutmeg and chilies. Roughly pound in a mortar and a pestle, or grind in a spice or coffee grinder. Store in an airtight container.

1½ cups/250 g dried chana dal (split black chickpeas; see Tips)

1 medium sweet potato

4 tbsp/20 g crispy fried onions (store-bought)

½ cup/20 g chopped fresh cilantro leaves

½ cup/35 g chopped fresh parsley leaves

1-inch/2.5 cm piece fresh ginger, grated

4 cloves garlic, crushed or chopped

1 green chili, finely chopped

1 tsp Ibzaar (recipe follows; also see Tips)

½ tsp paprika

¼ tsp freshly ground black pepper

¼ tsp ground turmeric

1 tsp salt

2 tbsp raisins, roughly chopped (optional)

Oil, for deep-frying

Tamarind Sauce:

4 tbsp tamarind paste

2 tbsp cooking oil

1 small onion, finely chopped

3 tbsp tomato paste

1 cup/250 mL water

4 tbsp brown sugar or Indian palm sugar (jaggery)

¾ tsp roasted cumin powder

¾ tsp ground ginger

½ tsp chili powder, or to taste

1 tsp salt, or to taste

2 tbsp fresh lemon juice

1 tbsp rose water

Hot basmati rice, for serving

Ibzaar

1 tbsp black peppercorns

1 tbsp cumin seeds

1 tbsp coriander seeds

2-inch/5 cm cinnamon stick (preferably cassia)

3 to 4 whole cloves

3 to 4 cardamom pods

½ to 1 whole nutmeg, depending on size, grated

1 to 2 dried red chilies (preferably Kashmiri)

TIPS:

Chana dal is one of several kinds of Indian chickpea that has been split and hulled, and is available at any South Asian grocer. You could substitute regular dried chickpeas, but not canned chickpeas, since the recipe requires them to be uncooked to make the kofta.

Ibzaar is another name for the spice mix known as baharat, *or* baharat al Khaleeji, *"spice of the Gulf."*

KALMPLEX

ROYALTY PROVISIONS

Kalmplex defies categorization; a multi-disciplinary artist, photographer, filmmaker, performer, activist, and vegan chef whose unique dishes draw from African and Caribbean traditions like Ital, the religious vegetarianism practiced by Rastafarians. This dish builds on "provisions," a broad category of starchy tubers and vegetables that are a foundational part of Jamaican cooking. Kalmplex's food embodies how food, identity, and cultural, artistic, and spiritual practices can be all woven together.

Prep: 1 hr, add 2½ hr if using dried beans

Makes: 4 to 6 servings

Vegan

Chayote:
1 cho cho (chayote), peeled, pitted, and cut into matchsticks or thinly sliced

4 tbsp lemon juice (fresh or bottled)

Beans:
⅔ cup/130 g dried beans, soaked overnight, or 2 cups/520 g canned beans

2 tbsp coconut oil

½ bunch fresh thyme, leaves only

4 tbsp chopped fresh rosemary leaves

1 Scotch bonnet pepper, whole

2 cloves garlic, chopped

1 tbsp chopped sun-dried tomatoes

Ground Provisions:
1 tsp salt

1 breadfruit (about 1¾ lb/800 g), peeled (see Tips), halved, cored, and cut into slices ½ inch/1.3 cm thick

1 large chunk Jamaican yellow yam, chopped into 6 to 8 pieces (about 1 lb/450 g)

1 large chunk calabaza (aka Jamaican pumpkin), chopped into 6 to 8 pieces, about 1½ lb/700 g

4 green (cooking) bananas, peeled

Plantains:
1 large or 2 small ripe plantains

3 tbsp coconut oil

Greens and Mushrooms:
1 cup/60 g sliced mushrooms (any varieties you like)

1 clove garlic, chopped

1 Scotch bonnet pepper, seeded and finely chopped

½ bunch callaloo, discarding any tough stalks, greens chopped

1 bunch asparagus (optional; see Tips)

Cabbage Salad:
¼ small head green cabbage, very thinly sliced (about 2 cups/190 g)

¼ small red cabbage, very thinly sliced (about 2 cups/190 g)

3 tbsp fresh lemon juice

1 clove garlic, finely chopped

4 tbsp chopped sun-dried tomato

¼ tsp kala namak (black salt)

Assembly:
1 large avocado, sliced

Agave or maple syrup

1 naseberry, aka sapodilla or sapote, sliced (optional)

 Francine Freeman

Prepare the chayote: Put the sliced cho cho in a jar with a lid and add enough lemon juice to cover. Refrigerate until ready to use. (Can be done the day before.)

Cook the beans: For soaked dried beans, place them in a large pot with 2 quarts/2 litres water. Cook over medium heat until tender, about 2½ hours. Drain. For canned beans, simply drain and rinse.

Heat the coconut oil in a large pan over medium heat and add the drained beans, thyme, rosemary, Scotch bonnet, garlic, and sun-dried tomatoes. Cook, stirring occasionally, for about 15 minutes. Discard the Scotch bonnet.

Make the ground provisions: Fill a large pot with water and add the salt. Bring to a boil over medium heat. Add the cut breadfruit and yellow yam, return to a boil, and cook for 10 minutes. Add the chopped calabaza and green bananas. Let cook until everything is fork-tender, another 20 minutes. Drain and set aside.

Cook the plantain(s): Peel the plantain(s) by cutting off both ends and cutting a slit down the middle. Remove the peel by peeling side to side rather than lengthwise. Cut on a bias into slices ¼ inch/6 mm thick.

Line a plate with paper towels. In a skillet, heat the coconut oil over medium heat. Add the plantain slices and fry until crisp and golden on both sides, about 5 minutes per side. Remove the plantain slices to the paper towels. Reserve the skillet with the oil.

Cook the greens and mushrooms: In the reserved skillet, over medium heat, fry the mushrooms, garlic, and Scotch bonnet for a minute or two. Add the chopped callaloo and asparagus (if using). Sauté the vegetables for about 10 minutes over medium heat and transfer to a plate.

Make the cabbage salad: Place both cabbages in a bowl. Add the lemon juice, garlic, sun-dried tomatoes, kala namak, and pickled cho cho together to create your salad.

To assemble: On each serving plate, dividing evenly, arrange the provisions and spoon beans over them. Top with the greens and mushrooms. On the side, place the fried plantain, top with the avocado slices, and drizzle with some agave or maple syrup. Garnish with a slice of naseberry (if using). Serve with the cabbage salad.

TIPS:

You can find provisions and callaloo at Caribbean grocers. Look for kala namak at South Asian grocers.

To peel the breadfruit, cut a slice off the bottom so it can sit flat and use a sharp knife to slice off the rough skin. Remember to cut out the middle (core) of the breadfruit as that can't be eaten.

Keep chopped yellow yam in a bowl of water to prevent browning.

Wash the callaloo well and discard any tough stalks.

When sautéing the greens and mushrooms, you can add or sub other vegetables, such as corn, sliced carrots, red bell peppers, broccoli, etc.—though you may need to add a bit more coconut oil.

PASTA RIPIENA CON CECCI E FUNGHI

Chickpea Ravioli Filled with Mushrooms

Pasta-making classes were some of The Dep's most popular, and Nicole taught a lot of them. They were her connection to her Italian roots, and the soulful *cucina povera* (literally "poor cooking") of the Sicilian countryside. When an autoimmune illness threatened to take her beloved pasta away, Nicole fought back with her skills as a holistic nutritionist and creative cook; the result is this fabulous gluten-free chickpea ravioli.

I like to spread my love of Italian food, but I'm also a holistic nutritionist and I came to it from a place of illness. The doctors were like, "Yeah, you have an autoimmune disease. Might go away, might not." I was like, "I can't really deal with that." I started looking into alternatives and I looked at food as a way of healing. I believe that we can eat very delicious food that's good for our gut, can lower inflammation, and can actually be healing.

Make the chickpea dough: Mix the chickpea flour, xanthan gum, and salt together on a clean work surface. Make a well in the centre. In a small bowl, whisk the eggs, then slowly add to the well while mixing flour from the edges of the well to combine. Continue to add the egg bit by bit, incorporating until it's all combined.

Using a bench scraper, scrape everything from the surface and form into a ball. Knead well for 5 to 10 minutes, using more chickpea flour for dusting. Wrap in plastic wrap and let rest while you make the filling.

Make the filling: In a nonstick saucepan, melt 2 tablespoons of butter over medium heat. Add the onion and cook, stirring, until lightly caramelized, 15 to 20 minutes.

Add the garlic, rosemary, and nutmeg and cook until aromatic (don't let the garlic brown), 2 to 3 minutes. Set aside to cool.

In a separate pan, melt the remaining 1 tbsp butter over medium-high heat. Add the mushrooms, working in batches if necessary to minimize overlapping, and cook until they have a golden-brown colour, 2 to 3 minutes. Set aside to cool.

In a food processor, combine the onion mixture, mushrooms, lemon zest, and goat cheese and pulse, slowly adding almond milk or milk to loosen if needed, until smooth. Taste and adjust the seasoning.

To stuff the ravioli, cut the dough into 8 equal portions. Working with one piece at a time, flatten and pass through a pasta machine. Keep the remaining pieces covered with a damp tea towel. Dust lightly with chickpea flour between each pass through the machine. Start on the biggest setting and go down, incrementally, until you reach the #4 setting. Repeat with the rest of the dough. Dust finished sheets generously with chickpea flour,

stacking them in a sheet pan covered with a damp tea towel.

On a clean surface dusted with chickpea flour, place one rolled sheet of pasta. Put the filling into a piping bag (or use a zip-seal plastic bag with a corner cut off). Pipe a dollop of filling (about 1 tsp) onto the pasta sheet every 3 inches/7.5 cm.

Dip a clean finger into a bowl of warm water and trace around each dollop of filling with water. Place another pasta sheet, about the same length as the bottom one, on top of the pasta and filling. Gently but firmly press down on the top sheet, circling the filling to remove air bubbles and seal.

Using a 3-inch/7.5 cm cookie cutter or ravioli stamp, cut out each ravioli. Press all around the perimeter to ensure a tight seal and set aside on a dusted surface.

Bring a large pot of salted water to a boil. Drop the ravioli in the boiling water and boil 5 to 6 minutes.

Make the butter sauce: In a large skillet, melt the butter over medium-low heat, swirling often. Continue to cook the butter for 2 to 3 minutes, stirring often with a heatproof spatula. Keep cooking and stirring until the butter solids are browned, 3 to 4 minutes longer.

Add the sage leaves and cook (still over medium-low heat), stirring constantly, until the sage is dark green and crisp, about 1 minute. (If you think things are getting too dark, add a splash or two of pasta cooking liquid to the hot pan; this will halt the browning process.) Remove the skillet from the heat and season with the salt and pepper.

Use a slotted spoon or spider to carefully move the ravioli from the water into the butter sauce and swirl for a minute to coat the pasta.

Serve and enjoy!

Nicole Di Nardo is a holistic nutritionist, teacher, and therapeutic chef who hosts cooking classes, conducts corporate wellness seminars, and teaches at The Institute of Holistic Nutrition. **@nicole.nutrition**

Prep: 2 hr
Cook: 25 min
Makes: 4 servings

Chickpea Dough:

2¼ cups/270 g chickpea flour, plus more for dusting

1 tsp xanthan gum

½ tsp kosher salt

4 large eggs

Filling:

3 tbsp/45 g unsalted butter, divided

1 yellow onion, finely chopped

2 cloves garlic, finely chopped

2 sprigs rosemary, leaves finely chopped

⅛ tsp freshly grated nutmeg

1¼ lb/560g mixed mushrooms, sliced

Grated zest of ½ lemon

3.5 oz/100 g goat cheese

Almond milk or milk, if needed

Salt

Butter Sauce:

16 tablespoons/ 240 g unsalted butter, cut into 8 pieces

16 fresh sage leaves

1½ tsp salt

½ tsp freshly ground black pepper

TIPS:
Fresh organic eggs at room temp are best.
Look for fine organic chickpea flour.
Your sauce will be as good as the quality of your butter.

STUART SAKAI
TUNA AND TOFU

Stu is probably the most knowledgeable person I know when it comes to traditional Japanese foods—something that became clear in his fun workshops on how to make *tsukemono* (Japanese pickled and fermented vegetables) from scratch. I loved the story of this humble dish that his father came up with to fill a yearning for Japanese comfort food using what he could find in Canada in the '70s.

Prep: 10 min
Cook: 10 min
Makes: 4 servings

2 (5 oz/142 g) cans tuna packed in oil (see Tips)

1 tsp funyu (fermented tofu; see Tips)

1 tsp grated fresh ginger

2 (12.3 oz/349 g) cartons silken tofu (see Tips), cut into 1-inch/2.5 cm cubes

4 tbsp shoyu (Japanese soy sauce)

2 tbsp mirin (Japanese sweet wine)

2 tsp dashi no moto (dashi broth powder)

4 green onions, thinly sliced

Juice of ½ lemon

Cooked rice, for serving

Tōgarashi (Japanese chili powder; optional)

Open both cans of tuna and discard about half the oil. Place a 10- to 12-inch/25 to 30 cm nonstick skillet on a burner, but don't turn it on yet. Empty both cans of tuna into the pan. Add the funyu and ginger over the tuna, then add the cubes of tofu over the top. Add the shoyu, mirin, and dashi no moto.

Turn the heat to medium, cover the skillet, and cook until it begins to boil, 5 to 7 minutes.

Add the green onions and lemon juice, remove from the heat, and cover for 1 minute.

Serve alongside or over rice, with a sprinkle of tōgarashi, if desired.

TIPS:

If you can't find tuna packed in oil, use water-packed and add 1 tablespoon of neutral oil to the pan.

Funyu can be found at most Asian grocery stores. The dish still tastes great without it, but you could substitute (or just add) kimchi.

Silken tofu works best here. If using a firmer tofu, add a splash of water to the pan.

Feel free to add additional vegetables to amp it up, such as carrots, napa cabbage, and mustard greens.

> I grew up in a Japanese home and spent a lot of time in my grandparents' house, where we ate a lot of food. When I went to university, like when I was nineteen or twenty years old, my grandmother had a stroke. It occurred to me that no one else in the family knew how to make all the stuff she made. And all that tradition, which we have all been taking for granted, perhaps just disappeared. At that point is when I started to cook and started to try to re-create foods my grandmother made.

Stuart Sakai is a fourth-generation Japanese-Canadian. He is the owner/operator of Sakai Bar, an intimate sake-focused restaurant offering Japanese country cuisine through a contemporary lens. @sakaibarto

ADOPT-A-RECIPE   John Hanna

Rhoma Akosua Spencer is an award-winning actor and director, playwright, acting coach, comedienne, and cultural critic. When not performing or directing, Rhoma runs Sweethand Delights, serving up traditional dishes from Trinidad and Tobago. @sweethanddelights

SALTFISH RUNDUNG

Salt Cod and Coconut Braise

Rhoma is more than a great cook, she is a historian and ambassador, champion and critic of the diverse culture of Trinidad and Tobago. Her plays, her sharp comedy, and her encyclopaedic knowledge of calypso and Carnival all tell the complex, layered stories of the people, but you can taste it in her food.

Prep: 2 hr
Cook: 20 to 25 min
Makes: 6 servings

1 lb/450 g boneless salt cod

4 tbsp fresh lime juice

4 tbsp vegetable oil

Just a smidge chopped Scotch bonnet pepper (optional)

1 large onion, roughly chopped

6 to 8 cloves garlic, finely chopped

3 sprigs thyme

4 sprigs chive, thinly sliced

1½ cups/360 mL canned coconut milk

1 large red bell pepper, sliced

1 large green bell pepper, sliced

4 cups/380 g shredded green cabbage

½ cup/20 g chopped fresh cilantro

In a medium pot, combine the salt cod with water to cover, filling so the pot is three-quarters full. Bring to a boil over high heat, then reduce the heat to medium and boil for 20 minutes. Drain and rinse with cold water. Repeat the process if the cod is still too salty.

Shred the salt cod by pulling it apart, similar to pulling pork. Sprinkle with the lime juice and set aside.

In a medium skillet or heavy-bottomed Dutch oven, heat the oil over medium heat. Test how warm the oil is by putting a piece of onion in it. If it sizzles, then it's ready. Add the Scotch bonnet (if using), followed by the onion and sauté until translucent, about 2 minutes. Add the garlic and sauté for another 2 minutes, being careful not to let it burn.

Add the thyme and chives, stirring for 2 minutes to allow the flavours to combine. Throw in the pulled salt cod and cook for 2 more minutes while continuing to stir.

Reduce the heat to medium-low, add the coconut milk, and simmer for 3 minutes. Add the bell peppers and cabbage, cover, and allow to cook down for another 5 to 7 minutes, making sure the liquid doesn't evaporate completely.

Serve garnished with the fresh cilantro.

TIPS:

Salted cod is available at many supermarkets, as well as most West Indian or Portuguese grocers.

If you are on a low-sodium diet, do a second boil of the saltfish by throwing out the first water and boiling again in fresh water.

Some cooks like to add ½ cup/125 mL tomato ketchup to the recipe to give the stew some colour and sweetness.

This dish is best eaten with boiled cassava, green bananas, and plantains.

PAULA COSTA

CALDEIRADA DE MARISCO

Portuguese Seafood Stew

Paula really, really loves cooking; and this love permeates her food, her blog, her cookbook collection, her generous portions, her personality. Her signature Portuguese dishes were part of some unforgettable Supper Clubs accompanied by live Afro-Brazilian *fado*, the painfully beautiful "blues" music of Lisbon and Coimbra. Food, like music, can be a medium of *saudade*, an aching nostalgia for times past.

Prep: 1 hr
Cook: 45 min

Makes: 4 to 6 generous servings

2 tbsp olive oil, plus more for drizzling

4 oz/115 g pancetta or bacon, cubed

1 heaping tbsp tomato paste

½ to 1 tsp dried crushed piri-piri peppers or red chili flakes

1 medium onion, sliced

2 small bay leaves, dried or fresh

1 medium red bell pepper, sliced

1 medium yellow bell pepper, sliced

4 cloves garlic, sliced

1 lb/450 g squid tubes, cleaned and cut into large rounds

Salt and freshly ground black pepper

3 to 4 medium potatoes, peeled and sliced

1 (28 fl oz/796 mL) can whole peeled tomatoes, undrained

¾ cup/175 mL Portuguese vinho verde or other dry white wine

1 lb/450 g mussels, rinsed and debearded

1 lb/450 g littleneck clams, rinsed

1 lb/ 450 g shell-on large shrimp (you can remove the shells if desired)

4 tbsp chopped fresh parsley

Crusty bread, for serving

In a large saucepan, combine the olive oil and pancetta and cook over medium heat until the pancetta is crispy, about 5 minutes. Remove the pancetta from the pan and set aside.

Stir the tomato paste into the flavoured oil and cook for 2 minutes. Add the crushed piri-piri peppers, onion, bay leaves, bell peppers, garlic, and squid. Season with a pinch each of salt and pepper. Cook, stirring occasionally, until the onion is soft, about 10 minutes.

Stir in the potatoes. Add the tomatoes, crushing them by hand as you do, along with the juices from the can. Add the wine and season with salt and pepper to taste. Bring the mixture to a simmer, then reduce the heat to medium-low, cover, and cook until the potatoes are just tender, 25 to 30 minutes.

Taste the tomato sauce and adjust the seasoning if needed. Stir in the mussels and clams, cover, and cook until the mussels and clams open, 5 to 7 minutes. Remove and discard any mussels and clams that have not opened.

Add the shrimp, cover, and cook until the shrimp are pink, about 1 minute. Remove the pan from the heat. Discard the bay leaves and stir in half of the parsley.

Ladle into bowls and garnish with the remaining parsley and reserved pancetta. Serve immediately with a drizzle of olive oil and lots of crusty bread to dip into the broth.

Growing up I did lots of dishes but didn't do any cooking. When I moved out on my own, I started feeling the urge to have that homestyle cooking. So I called my aunts. I called up my dad and asked, "How do you make this?" or "How do you make that?" For me cooking is definitely a love language, a way to be creative, and it gives me an outlet to just get lost in something. And if I have you over to dinner, it means I love you.

The scores of recipes on **Paula Costa's** blog, Dragon's Kitchen, chronicle her creative culinary adventures in food, from her Portuguese roots to more unexpected topics, like the seven deadly sins, or the final meal on the *Titanic*.
@dragonskitchen

ADOPT-A-RECIPE   John Leeson

I come from Tunisia. I've travelled a lot in my life and I lived in New York City in the '80s. Eight years. It was a great time. I worked at Petrossian, where I served so many stars, including Donald Trump, Elizabeth Taylor, Omar Sharif, Plácido Domingo. The plates were designed by Erté, a famous glass designer. In the back they had five seats, a banquette, only for the ladies. And every seat was covered in mink.

A veteran Toronto restaurateur, **Dali Chehimi's** storied career has seen him working at iconic restaurants such as Sassafraz, Sarkis, and Avec, as well as running Casbah, a catering company specializing in Tunisian fare. **@casbah707**

DALI CHEHIMI

TAGINE HOUT

Fish Chermoula Tagine

My love of North African food started with the couscous I first tried as a high school exchange student in France. I met Dali when he ran Casbah, a small street-food stall in a converted shipping container selling spicy merguez sausages and camel (!) burgers. Over the years, he would become a regular fixture in The Dep kitchen, always joking around with the friends he would enlist to give him a hand. Chermoula is an herbal green sauce used in North African countries as a marinade or to garnish fish and seafood, but it is also excellent on chicken or vegetables.

Prep: 15 min, plus a few hours to marinate

Cook: 30 min

Makes: 4 to 6 servings

Make the chermoula: In a food processor, combine the cilantro, garlic, ginger, spices, salt, olive oil, and lemon juice and pulse, adding a bit of water if needed to end up with a smooth, loose paste, about ¾ cup/325 mL.

Prepare the fish: In a nonreactive container, cover the fish in half of the chermoula and marinate in the fridge for at least a few hours or overnight. Refrigerate the rest of the chermoula until needed.

If using fresh tomatoes, bring a pot of water to a boil. Set up a bowl of ice water. Score an "X" on one end of each tomato and drop them into boiling water for about 30 seconds. Remove with a slotted spoon and transfer to the cold water to cool. Peel the tomatoes, chop, and set aside. (If using canned, chop roughly or crush with your hands.)

In a large skillet, heat the olive oil over medium-high heat. Add the garlic and onion and sauté, stirring, until they soften, about 2 minutes. Add the carrot and cook a few minutes more until the carrot softens a bit. Add the tomatoes and cook until the tomatoes start to break down, about 5 minutes more.

Add the marinated fish with its marinade, cover, and cook for 5 minutes or until fish is done to your liking.

To serve: Spoon over a bed of steamed couscous. Drizzle the plate with some of the reserved chermoula, garnish with lots of fresh cilantro, and lemon wedges.

Chermoula:

2 cups/80 g chopped fresh cilantro

4 cloves garlic, peeled

1 tsp grated fresh ginger

1 tbsp ground cumin

2 tsp paprika

¼ teaspoon saffron threads, crumbled

1 tsp salt

3 tbsp olive oil

2 tbsp fresh lemon juice

Fish:

2 lb 2 oz/1 kg firm-fleshed fish, such as cod, mahi mahi, or haddock

4 fresh tomatoes or about ½ (28 fl oz/ 796 mL) can peeled whole tomatoes, drained

2 to 3 tbsp olive oil

3 to 4 cloves garlic, finely chopped

1 onion, finely chopped

1 carrot, diced

For Serving:

Couscous

Fresh cilantro leaves

Lemon wedges

 Donna MacDonald

6½ cups/1.5 L
chicken or fish stock

A good pinch of
saffron threads

2 cloves garlic,
peeled but whole

3 tbsp roughly
chopped fresh
parsley, plus more
for garnish

Coarse salt

3 tbsp Spanish olive
oil, plus more as
needed

1 lb /450 g shrimp
(about 24 medium to
large shrimp)

1 medium onion,
finely chopped

1 red bell pepper,
finely chopped

1 teaspoon smoked
paprika

½ cup/125 mL
tomato purée
(tomato sauce will
work as well)

Juice of ½ lemon or
lime

3 cups/600 g bomba
rice (see Tips)

½ cup/80 g green
beans

½ cup/65 g frozen
peas

2 roasted red
peppers, cut into
strips

2 lemon or lime
wedges, for serving

JOSÉ ARATO
PAELLA DE CAMARÓN
Spanish Shrimp Paella

Paella is often thought of as the Spanish national dish, but it is really a speciality of the region of Valencia. Named after the *paellera*, the wide shallow pan it is cooked in, this classic dish is defined by a few key ingredients: short-grain rice (ideally Spanish bomba rice), saffron, pimentón (Spanish paprika), and olive oil.

José, a Venezuelan expat, fell deeply in love with Spanish food, and made paella one of his specialities. He could be found dishing it out from giant, metre-wide pans at farmers' markets or The Dep's Communal Table events. Cooked over an open flame, it would develop the elusive *socarrat*, the crispy, almost-but-not-quite burnt bottom layer of rice that is the hallmark of a perfect paella.

In a saucepan, bring the stock to a boil over medium heat. Remove ½ cup/125 mL of the hot stock to a small saucepan or bowl, add the saffron, cover, and set aside. Keep the remaining stock warm.

In a mortar and pestle or small food processor, mash the garlic, parsley, and some coarse salt to a paste.

In a paella pan or a very large skillet, heat the oil over medium heat. Add the shrimp and cook gently for a few minutes until just pink, remove from the pan, and set aside.

If the pan is dry, add more oil and return to the stove over medium heat. When the oil is hot, add the onion and bell pepper and cook until softened but not browned, about 5 minutes.

Add the smoked paprika, tomato purée, and the garlic/parsley mix, stirring to combine, about 1 minute. Add the saffron-infused stock and then top up with additional hot stock to cover by about ½ inch/1.3 cm and bring to a boil. Add the lemon juice and season with salt.

Add the rice and stir to mix with the stock and distribute evenly around the pan. Allow it to cook, uncovered, over high heat for 8 minutes.

Add the green beans and the peas and nestle the shrimp on top. *Do not stir!* Continue cooking over high heat until the rice is no longer soupy but some liquid remains to finish cooking the rice, another 2 to 3 minutes. If the rice is too dry, add a bit more warm stock. Reduce the heat to low. Arrange the strips of roasted red peppers on top of the paella.

Cover with foil and let the paella rest for 5 minutes. Garnish with the lemon wedges and parsley and serve directly from the paella pan.

TIPS:
Spanish bomba rice is ideal, but other short-grain rice, such as Arborio or Carnaroli, will work.

It's tricky to get even heat across the bottom of a large, thin-bottomed paella pan on a regular stove; using a barbecue or griddle instead is one cheat. Alternatively, if the paella pan does not fit properly on the stove burner, you can finish the cooking in an oven (preheated to 350°F/180°C) for another 10 minutes. This is less of an issue with a thick-bottomed pan, but you're less likely to get a tasty crust (socarrat) on the bottom. Remove from the oven when the rice still looks a bit wet.

"I find that when you emigrate there's a necessity to connect to your country, to your roots, and to your memories. There is a part of you that has been ripped from you and stays in your country. And you are always looking for that part. That is what makes you look for your food and to actually make it."

José Arato spent many years running Pimentón, a catering and gourmet food project specializing in Spanish and Mediterranean fine food, and his spectacular giant paellas were a beloved fixture of the Brickworks Farmers' Market. He now works for the Toronto District School Board.
@pimentonto

Mary Freij is a food entrepreneur and full-time chef. After hosting a popular brunch at The Dep and a food kiosk in downtown Toronto, Mary is now collaborating on a new Lebanese and Indonesian food stall in North York.
@Mazehcatering
@tetaskitchen.ca
tetaskitchen.com

MARY FREIJ

SAYADIEH

Lebanese Fish and Rice

Mary ran Mazeh, one of The Dep's most popular brunch residencies, before opening up her own Middle Eastern street-food kiosk next to what is now Toronto Metropolitan University. She returned often to The Dep to teach classes or make a dinner, like this Levantine speciality of fried fish with seasoned rice and creamy tahini sauce. Reflecting her Palestinian/Lebanese/Jordanian roots, this dish would be a familiar sight in countless fishing villages that dot the southwestern Mediterranean.

Prep: 45 min   **Cook:** 45 min   **Makes:** 4 servings

Prepare the fish and rice: In a large skillet, heat 3 tablespoons of oil over high heat, add the onions, and cook for 5 minutes. Reduce the heat to medium-low and cook until the onions are caramelized and golden, about 20 minutes. Set some aside for garnish.

In a bowl, stir together the lemon juice, garlic, remaining 4 tablespoons oil, and a sprinkle of salt. Set aside while you set up the rest of the dredge mixtures.

Set up a dredging station: On a flat plate that can fit the length of your fish, mix together the flour, cumin, and salt to taste. In a wide but deep bowl, whisk the egg. Add the reserved lemon/garlic/oil mix and stir to combine.

Dip the fish portions, one at a time, in the egg mix, then coat in the flour. For a crispier effect, repeat this step.

For frying, a deep-fryer will give the best effects, but pan-frying also works. Place enough neutral oil in the pan to cover the fish when frying, about 3 inches/8 cm. Heat the oil to 350° to 375°F/ 177° to 190°C. Fry the fish until crispy and lightly browned, 6 to 8 minutes. Remove from the fryer or pan and set aside. If desired, strain the frying oil and reserve for using when you cook the rice.

In a medium pot, combine the caramelized onions, water (or fish stock), 2 teaspoons salt, the coriander, cumin, turmeric, and 2 to 3 tablespoons oil (from the fish fry for flavour, if desired). Bring to a boil over medium heat and cook, covered, for 10 to 15 minutes to integrate the caramelized onion flavour.

Add the rice and continue to boil for 5 to 7 minutes. Cover the pot and let simmer until fully cooked, about 15 minutes.

Make the tahini sauce: In a bowl, mix together the tahini, vinegar, water, parsley, and salt to taste. If needed, add more water to achieve the desired consistency.

To serve: Once the rice is cooked, divide among plates and top with the fried fish and tahini sauce. Garnish with the chopped parsley. If desired, sprinkle with the pomegranate seeds and sliced almonds.

ADOPT-A-RECIPE   Gianni Chiappetta

Fish and Rice:

7 tbsp netural oil, plus more for frying

2 large white onions, thinly sliced

2 tbsp fresh lemon juice

3 cloves garlic, minced and mashed into a paste

Salt

1 cup/130 g all-purpose flour

½ tbsp ground cumin

1 large egg

14 oz/400 g haddock fillet (or any preferred white fish), cut into 4 portions

6½ cups/1.5 L water or fish stock

1½ tbsp ground coriander

1½ tbsp ground cumin

1 tbsp ground turmeric

3 cups/600 g basmati rice

Tahini Sauce:

½ cup/125 mL tahini

2 tbsp distilled white vinegar

¼ cup/60 mL water

2 tbsp finely chopped parsley

Salt

For Serving:

1 tbsp chopped fresh parsley

2 tbsp pomegranate seeds (optional)

4 tbsp sliced almonds (optional)

Prep: 30 min

Cook: 30 min

Makes: 4 servings

Sambal:

4 tbsp coarsely chopped fresh ginger

6 to 8 cloves garlic

1 small onion or 4 shallots

4 tbsp vegetable oil

1 tbsp shrimp paste (dry/block, not liquid sauce)

6 tbsp Rooster brand sambal oelek (or 10 fresh bird's eye chilies, puréed in a blender)

Crab:

2 Dungeness crab, cleaned (liquid, tomalley, and shell reserved; ask your fishmonger to do this; see Tips)

1 seafood bouillon cube (or ½ cube plus 1 tsp MSG)

½ cup/125 mL boiling water

4 tbsp tomato paste

1 tbsp brown sugar

2 tbsp soy sauce

To Finish:

2 large eggs, beaten

1 to 2 bird's eye chilies, sliced

4 to 6 sprigs cilantro

2 green onions, thinly sliced

2 limes, cut into wedges

NANTHA KUMAR

KETAM CILI SINGAPURA

Singapore-Style Chili Crab

Nantha and I go *way* back; we have a lot of friends in common and I think we even dated the same woman a million years ago. Nantha's mischievous personality and delicious Malaysian cooking are a few of my fond memories of my Montreal years. His scrappy little kitchen operating out of the back of a local dive bar might have been the first pop-up restaurant I ever encountered. It was a treat to have him host a few pop-ups at The Dep when he was in town, and to have him make one of his signature dishes for us at his Montreal pied-à-terre.

Make the sambal: In a blender, purée the ginger, garlic, and onion.

In a large pot, heat the oil over medium heat. Crumble the the shrimp paste and fry gently. (Be prepared: *it will stink!* You have never smelled anything so foul. Open windows, turn the exhaust fan to high, or, if you can, do it outdoors.) Try to break the shrimp paste into smaller pieces and blend into the oil. Cook, stirring constantly, until the shrimp paste is completely dissolved, 2 to 3 minutes.

Add the ginger/onion/garlic purée and sambal oelek (or puréed peppers) and stir (this also benefits from a well-ventilated space). After half the liquid has evaporated, reduce the heat to low, cover, and simmer for 10 minutes, stirring occasionally. Remove from the heat and set aside, covered. This is your sambal.

Prepare the crab: Cut each crab into 4 parts, reserving any juices, and set aside.

In a bowl, dissolve the seafood bouillon cube (and MSG, if using) in the boiling water. Add the crab juices, tomato paste, brown sugar, and soy sauce.

Reheat the sambal over high heat, pour in the bouillon mix, and bring to a boil. Stir, cover, and let cook for 3 to 4 minutes, adding a bit of water if it gets too dry. Place the crab shell directly into the sauce along with the rest of the crab, including any tomalley (the soft green fat from under the shell). Mix well, cover, and cook for 7 to 8 minutes. When the shells turn bright red, your dish is done.

Remove from the heat. Carefully remove the crab from the sauce, placing half-shells facing up on four plates, and divide the cooked crab around it.

To finish: In a small bowl, beat the eggs. Return the pot to the stove over high heat. At this point the sauce should have a gravy consistency. If too dry, you can add a bit more water. When the sauce starts to boil, reduce the heat to medium and pour in the beaten eggs in a slow steam, barely stirring until the eggs have set into loose clumps. Turn the heat off.

Divide the mixture among the upturned shells. Garnish with the bird's eye chilies, cilantro, and green onions. Serve with the lime wedges.

TIPS:

This is a very spicy dish in Malaysia and Singapore. You can reduce the heat level by reducing the amount of chili and adding some sugar (but I don't recommend it).

When cleaning the crab, the only thing you need to discard are the gills. If you are asking the fishmonger to clean it for you, make sure you tell them to keep the shell and any eggs, and to cut the body and the large claw into two pieces. Say you want to cook it "Chinese style."

The best crab to use for this recipe is Dungeness from BC. The recipe is normally made with mud crab from Asia. You can also use Alaskan king crab, snow crab, or lobster.

If you want to avoid frying the shrimp paste indoors, you can flatten it and bake for 10 minutes in the oven, double-wrapped in aluminum foil, then add to the sauce.

I ended up writing for the Montreal Gazette and was eventually doing restaurant reviews.

After I wrote a review of Elsa's [a bar in Montreal] I started hanging out there. Then Elsa basically gave me 300 bucks and said, "Go buy some food and come and cook next week." I said, "Why?" She said the chef I had written the review about had quit. It was a good review though. So that's how I started.

Nantha Kumar is a Montreal-based travelling chef. Former proprietor of Plateau restaurants Nantha's Kitchen and Cash & Curry, he now travels the world doing restaurant and bar pop-ups, cooking in people's homes, serving up street food, and giving classes on Malaysian and South Indian cuisine. @nanthas_kitchen

ADOPT-A-RECIPE Elissa McBride

After graduating from culinary school in Toronto, **Laura Guanti** continued to study and work in Italy. This amazing experience helped her better understand her own family traditions and roots, surrounded by beautiful Italian food.
@bellantievents

TIPS:

Potatoes absorb cooking water, so it is difficult to give exact quantities for flour and potato, but a ratio of 70 percent potato to 30 percent flour by weight is the key. Here is my formula for success:

After the potatoes are cooked and cooled, weigh them out. Then use the following formula to determine the weight of flour needed:

Cooked potato in grams divided by 0.7 = X
X times 0.3 = grams of "00" flour needed,
e.g. 1000 g cooked potatoes ÷ 0.7 = 1429
1429 x 0.3 = 429 g flour

Seppia (squid ink) can be found at most fishmongers, or some specialty stores or butcher shops. It is always found in the freezer section and needs to be kept in the freezer at all times. (It does not freeze solid, so can be used straight from the freezer.)
Note: It may stain hands and some cutting boards.

Tipo "00" flour is an extra-fine wheat flour used for pasta and pizza; all-purpose can be substituted in a pinch, but won't be quite as delicate.

In Italy, Parmesan is never added to seafood pasta.

LAURA GUANTI

GNOCCHI AL NERO DI SEPPIE CON CALAMARI, POMODORINI, E RUCOLA

Squid Ink Gnocchi with Calamari, Cherry Tomatoes, and Arugula

Prep: 3 hr
Cook: 30 min
Makes: 4 servings

Laura spent a lot of time studying and working in restaurants in Emilia-Romagna, home of some of Italy's best pasta, and brought that experience to her ever-popular gnocchi classes. Simple to make yet elusive to perfect, gnocchi, a humble little dumpling of potato, flour, and water, becomes a dazzling, elegant showstopper of a dish with the addition of *seppia* (black squid ink). Once you get the feel for the dough, gnocchi are an incredibly versatile base for any number of flavours or sauces.

Gnocchi:

1 lb 7 oz/650g russet (baking) potatoes

Salt

About 2¼ cups/ 290 g tipo "00" flour (see Tips)

1 tsp black squid ink (see Tips)

All-purpose flour, for dusting

Sauce:

4 tbsp extra-virgin olive oil

3 cloves garlic, minced

Pinch of crushed chili flakes

1 whole cleaned squid, with tentacles attached, sliced into rings

3 tbsp white wine

12 to 14 cherry tomatoes, halved lengthwise

Handful of arugula, roughly chopped

2 sprigs curly parsley, finely chopped

Make the gnocchi: Peel the potatoes and set them in a large pot. Cover with water, add a large pinch of salt, and bring to a boil over high heat. Reduce to a simmer and cook until the potatoes are tender, 20 to 30 minutes. Drain well.

Using a potato ricer, rice finely (or mash well using a potato masher or fork). Place the riced/mashed potatoes on a baking sheet or tray to cool completely.

Once the potatoes are cool, weigh them (see Tips), place them on a work surface, sprinkle the required weight of "00" flour over the potatoes, and lightly mix the two together. Make a slight well in the middle and add a generous pinch of salt and the squid ink to the centre of the well. With a fork, begin to whisk the centre of the well, gradually incorporating the flour/potato mix until it is all combined.

Dust the surface with flour and begin to knead the dough with the palm of your hands. The dough should eventually become a solid black colour with all ingredients mixed into one firm ball. (If it sticks to the table, add more dusting flour while kneading until it is less sticky.)

Cut the dough into 4 equal portions, dusting each one on the cut sides specifically with flour to prevent sticking. Keep one piece to roll out and cover the remaining dough with plastic wrap.

Starting from the centre outward, using the palms of your hands, very gently roll out the dough into a long rope about ½ inch/1.3 cm in diameter, dusting lightly with flour as needed. Once all the pieces are rolled out, cut them into segments 1 inch/2.5 cm long. If you'd like, you can texture the gnocchi by pressing them with your thumb against a gnocchi board, the back of a fork, or even a woven basket.

Line a tray with parchment paper and dust with flour. Toss all the gnocchi with extra flour to prevent sticking and place on the lined tray. Cover the tray of gnocchi with a towel or plastic wrap and place in the fridge or freezer (gnocchi cook perfectly directly from frozen).

When it's time to serve, bring a large pot of water to boil for the gnocchi. Add 2 tbsp salt when it begins to boil.

Meanwhile, make the sauce: In a deep saucepan, add the olive oil, garlic, and chili flakes and cook over low heat for 1 to 2 minutes (do not brown the garlic). Add the squid and cook for 3 to 4 minutes. When the squid begins to firm up, deglaze the pan with the white wine and cook to reduce the liquid by half.

Once the water for the gnocchi is boiling, gently drop the gnocchi into the pot (a bench scraper or the flat side of a knife works well to scoop them up). Leave for 30 seconds before stirring gently. Boil until they float to the top, 1 to 2 minutes, stirring occasionally. (If cooking from frozen, cook for an additional 1 to 2 minutes.)

Add a big ladle of the hot pasta cooking water to the sauce and stir. Using a spider or large slotted spoon, remove the cooked gnocchi from the water and add to the sauce.

Add another ladle of pasta water, the cherry tomatoes, and the arugula. Season and toss gently until the sauce emulsifies and coats the gnocchi, adding more pasta water if needed to keep it saucy.

Serve sprinkled with parsley.

JAMAICAN JERK CHICKEN

Jerk chicken, like the Jamaican patty, has become a fixture of Toronto's culinary landscape, perhaps unsurprising given that our Caribbean diaspora community is the second largest in the world. When I was a teenager in Toronto, it was one of the first dishes that got me excited about discovering new flavours. Every Jamaican cook worth their salt has their own secret recipe, so big of Avery for sharing his. This one works just fine in the oven, but really shines on a charcoal BBQ. It's traditionally served with Jamaican-style rice and peas and coleslaw.

4 chicken leg quarters (thigh plus drumstick)

1 tbsp kosher salt

1½ tbsp paprika

4 tbsp Jerk Paste (recipe follows)

Lemon or lime wedges, for serving

Jamaican Jerk Paste

Makes: 8 tbsp

4 tbsp roughly chopped white onion

3 tbsp roughly chopped garlic

3 Scotch bonnet peppers, seeded

2 tbsp chopped fresh ginger

½ cup/20 g fresh thyme leaves

2 tbsp ground allspice

2 heaping tsp freshly grated nutmeg

1 tbsp brown sugar

4 tbsp vegetable oil

Juice of ½ lemon

Prep: 20 to 30 min, plus 12 to 24 hr marinating

Cook: 45 min

Makes: 4 servings

Pat the chicken dry with a paper towel.

In a large bowl, mix the salt, paprika, and jerk paste. Rub this mix all over the chicken pieces, coating them thoroughly. Put in the fridge and allow to marinate for at least 12 to 24 hours and up to 2 days.

Preheat the oven to 375°F/190°C.

Spread the chicken out on a baking sheet and bake, basting with any drippings from time to time, until the chicken reaches an internal temperature of 165°F/74°C, 45 minutes to 1 hour.

Plate, drizzle with pan juices, and serve with a wedge of lemon or lime.

Jamaican Jerk Paste

In a food processor, combine the onion, garlic, Scotch bonnets, ginger, thyme, allspice, nutmeg, brown sugar, oil, and lemon juice and blend until you have a thick paste. Can be stored in a jar in the fridge for a long time.

TIP:
This jerk paste is also great on fish, cauliflower, and tofu!

I really love my Caribbean roots. My dad's from Grenada, and most of my dad's side of the family is from Trinidad. My mom's from Jamaica and they all have really unique cuisines and I really love learning about where I come from. The Caribbean was colonized by people from many different places so their cuisine isn't necessarily their cuisine per se—it has influences from other places, but they made it their own.

Avery Billy–aka Chef Billy Bass–is a young, ambitious professional cook with a passion for creating unique culinary experiences that reflect his Caribbean roots along with his love for international cuisines. **@gb_hospitality_ toronto**

Prep: 30 min

Cook: 1 hr

Makes: 4 servings

Roasted Chicken:

4 tbsp all-purpose flour

4 skin-on chicken legs (or 8 thighs)

2 tbsp olive oil

8 oz/225 g thickly sliced Bayonne ham or 8 thick-cut slices bacon, cut into ½-inch/1.3 cm strips

Piperade:

2 tbsp olive oil

2 medium white onions, sliced

8 bell peppers (green, red, and yellow), cut into medium-wide strips

8 medium tomatoes, diced

2 to 3 cloves garlic, chopped

1 or 2 sprigs fresh thyme or a pinch or two of dried

2 bay leaves, torn in half

½ tsp ground Espelette pepper (see Tips)

To Finish:

1 cup/250 mL dry white wine

Salt

Espelette pepper (optional)

POULET BASQUAISE

Basque Country Chicken

Over the course of several years Chantal took The Depanneur on a culinary tour of France, a gastronomic voyage across all eighteen regions of the country, exploring the seasonal specialities of each one. This dish, from Basque country in Southwest France, is traditionally garnished with Bayonne ham and seasoned with Espelette pepper, two unique ingredients from the area. You can substitute other hams or chilies and still get a tasty dish, but it will miss a little of that *je ne sais quoi*.

Roast the chicken: Preheat the oven to 350°F/180°C.

Place the flour on a plate. Roll the chicken in the flour to cover lightly.

Add the olive oil to a roasting pan and place the chicken pieces in it. Use a brush to oil the tops of the chicken. Roast until the chicken begins to brown, about 15 minutes.

Turn the chicken over and sprinkle the ham (or bacon) all around the chicken. Roast for another 15 minutes.

Meanwhile, make the piperade: In a skillet, heat the olive oil over medium-low heat. Add the onions and cook, stirring gently, until translucent, about 5 minutes. Add the bell peppers, tomatoes, garlic, thyme, and bay leaves and mix well. Cook, stirring occasionally, until the vegetables are softening but not falling apart. Add the Espelette pepper at the end.

To finish: Remove the roasting pan from the oven. Spoon the piperade over the chicken and add the wine. Return the pan to the oven and roast until the chicken is fully cooked, 20 to 30 minutes longer. Add salt to taste and more Espelette pepper as desired.

TIPS:

If you cannot find Espelette pepper, substitute Aleppo pepper, hot Spanish paprika, or a mix of paprika and cayenne pepper.

This dish will be even better the next day; just reheat and serve with rice.

Consider making extra piperade: it freezes well and is great with fish, pork, omelettes, etc.

Tempting croque-monsieurs at one of Chantal's French Mother Sauces workshops

In France we cook, we cook, and we eat! I'm sixty-six, and for a long time every woman in France cooked. Now, women work more, and they don't care for cooking every day, but before it was totally different. I saw my mother, my grandmothers, and my great-grandmother cooking. I never thought I would cook for a living because in France, if you're from a good family, you don't cook as a profession. Cooking is what a woman did at home. My mother cooked very well, but she didn't like it.

Chantal Véchambre is a classically trained French chef, pâtissier, and author of *French Taste in Atlantic Canada, 1604–1758*. After many years cooking, catering, and teaching in Toronto, Chantal has recently returned to the East Coast. @mycremecaramel

"When my mother was planning to cook at The Dep she thought, "Ok, maybe I shouldn't do African because maybe people will be too scared to eat it." You know, sometimes when you are growing up as a black person, as people of colour, it's easy to think, even if it's not true, that maybe you or your culture is inferior. So when people loved the food, it definitely made her happy. It made me happy as well."

—Terence Molombo

Chef Monique (Momo) Mulombo left her native Congo to study in Europe and has since embraced Spanish, French, and Italian cultures and cuisines along with her African heritage.
chefmomo.ca

MONIQUE MULOMBO
POULET À LA MOAMBE
Congolese Chicken in Peanut Sauce

Prep: 30 min
Cook: 45 min
Makes: 4 servings

Given the incredible size, history, and diversity of the African continent, its foods feel criminally underrepresented in Toronto's restaurant scene (thankfully this is finally starting to change). So, when Terence suggested that his mom, Monique, aka Chef Momo, could prepare some Congolese dishes for The Dep, I jumped at the chance.

In a large bowl, combine the lemon juice, ½ teaspoon of salt, and the black pepper. Add the chicken and allow to marinate for 10 minutes. Remove to a plate and pat dry with paper towels.

In a large deep skillet, heat 2 tablespoons of sunflower oil over medium-high heat. Add the chicken and brown all over, 2 to 3 minutes per side. Reduce the heat to medium-low and let the chicken cook for about 10 minutes (it will finish cooking in the sauce). Remove from the pan and set aside.

In the same skillet, heat the remaining 1 tablespoon oil if needed. Add the onion and bell pepper and cook until soft, about 5 minutes. Add the garlic and cook until fragrant, about 30 seconds. Set aside.

Meanwhile, in a medium saucepan, bring the 3 cups/710 mL water to a boil over high heat. Add the rice and turmeric, reduce the heat to low, cover, and cook until the liquid is absorbed, about 18 minutes.

In a medium saucepan, combine the peanut butter and the 1 cup/250 mL warm water. The mixture will appear chunky and poorly combined until it begins to heat. Add the palm oil, chili flakes (if using), paprika, bay leaf, and remaining ½ tsp salt. Heat over medium heat, stirring frequently, until the sauce is homogenous and rich, about 10 minutes. The sauce will thicken slightly but should still run smoothly and easily from the back of a spoon.

Return the chicken to the pan with the onion and pepper. Add the peanut sauce. Set over medium-low heat and simmer until the chicken is fully cooked, 15 to 20 minutes, diluting with a small quantity of water as needed to keep the sauce from becoming too thick. Add cayenne, if you like it spicier.

Serve the chicken and sauce over the rice. Garnish with the parsley and serve with hot sauce alongside.

TIPS:
Palm oil lends the dish a distinctive richness, red colour, and smoky flavour, but tomato paste can be used instead.

The rice can be prepared in a rice cooker; follow the manufacturer's directions.

Plantains makes a delicious accompaniment to this dish.

Juice of 1 lemon

1 tsp salt

½ tsp freshly ground black pepper

1 lb/450 g bone-in, skin-on chicken thighs (2 to 4 pieces)

1 lb/450 g boneless, skinless chicken breasts (2 pieces)

3 tbsp sunflower oil

1 medium onion, finely diced

1 red bell pepper, finely diced

2 cloves garlic, minced

3 cups/710 mL water

2 cups/400 g long-grain white rice (see Tips)

1 tsp ground turmeric

1 cup/250 g creamy peanut butter

1 cup/250 mL warm water

3 tbsp palm oil (see Tips)

1 tsp crushed chili flakes, or more to taste (optional)

½ tsp paprika

1 bay leaf

Cayenne pepper (optional)

1 tsp chopped fresh parsley, for garnish

Hot sauce, for serving

Nasir Zuberi ran a successful catering business in Karachi, Pakistan, during the '90s. After many years in international sales, he's now based in Toronto and running a new food business, Enze's Meals, featuring traditional home-style recipes using homemade spice blends, as well as a range of exquisite shortbread cookies.
@enzes_meals

NASIR ZUBERI
MURGH HARA MASALA
Pakistani Green Curry Chicken

Nasir first brought this unique "curry" to The Dep back in 2013; I had never seen or tried a dish like it in any South Asian restaurant: tender marinated chicken cooked in a luscious deep-green sauce of cilantro, mint, and spices. I fell in love with its fresh, complicated character and asked him to make it a few more times over the years. In addition to being very particular about his spices, selecting them carefully, roasting and grinding all his masala blends from scratch, Nasir is also a talented baker, making some of the finest shortbreads I have tried.

Prep: 45 min, plus 4 hr to overnight to marinate

Cook: 45 min
Makes: 4 to 6 servings

Marinated Chicken:

2 lbs/910 g bone-in, skinless chicken quarters (drumsticks, thighs, and whole breasts cut in half)

2 cups/80 g chopped fresh cilantro

½ to ¾ cup/10 to 15 g fresh mint leaves

2 to 3 medium green chilies (see Tips)

4 cloves garlic, peeled but whole

2 tbsp fresh lemon juice

1 tbsp cumin seeds

½ cup/145 g Greek yogurt

Salt

Sauce:

4 cups/120 g fresh cilantro

1 cup/20 g fresh mint leaves

5 to 6 green chilies (see Tips)

¾ cup/215 g Greek yogurt

Salt

To Finish:

5 tbsp canola oil, plus more for the baking sheet and chicken

4 cloves garlic, peeled but whole

2 inches /5 cm fresh ginger

1 large onion, finely chopped

1 tbsp plus 1 tsp cumin seeds

¼ tsp grated nutmeg

Marinate the chicken: Pat the chicken dry with a paper towel. Cut slits in each piece to allow the marinade to penetrate the meat and place in a large bowl.

In a food processor or blender, combine the cilantro, mint, chilies, garlic, lemon juice, cumin seeds, and yogurt. Season with salt and process until smooth.

Pour the marinade over the chicken and massage into each piece. Cover the bowl and refrigerate for at least 4 hours or ideally overnight.

Make the sauce: In a food processor, combine the cilantro, mint, chilies, and yogurt. Season with salt and process until smooth. Set the green sauce aside.

To finish: Preheat the oven to 350°F/180°C.

Grease a baking sheet with some oil. Reserving the marinade, remove the chicken and place on the baking sheet. Brush the chicken with more oil and bake for 30 minutes.

Meanwhile, in a blender or food processor, purée the garlic, ginger, and 1 to 2 tablespoons water to make a fine paste. Set the ginger/garlic paste aside.

In a nonstick medium pot, heat the 5 tablespoons oil over medium heat. Add the onion and sauté until translucent, 3 to 4 minutes. Add 1 tablespoon of the cumin seeds and sauté for 1 minute. Add the ginger/garlic paste and sauté for 2 minutes. Add 3 to 4 tablespoons of water to ensure the paste doesn't burn and stir well.

Add the green sauce along with the reserved marinade and stir well. Reduce the heat to medium-low, cover, and cook until somewhat reduced and the oil is separating, about 20 minutes.

Remove the chicken from the oven and add to the curry. Reduce the heat to low, cover, and cook until

the chicken is completely cooked through, about 10 minutes.

In a small dry skillet, toast the remaining 1 teaspoon cumin seeds over low heat until fragrant, then grind them in a spice grinder.

Add the toasted cumin and nutmeg to the chicken curry. Cover, remove from the heat, and let rest for 5 minutes before serving.

TIPS:
Increase or decrease the number of chilies to suit your spice preference.

Serve with basmati rice or naan bread.

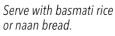

ELITA ROCKA

AYAM GULAI PADANG

Padang-Style Chicken Curry

Indonesia was the first non-Western country I ever visited, and in no time I had completely fallen in love with their food, in particular their complex, fragrant curries. Back in Toronto I was always on the lookout for an opportunity to eat them, but it was vanishingly rare. When Elita and her sister offered to bring it to The Dep, it was a little prayer finally answered.

Prep: 30 min

Cook: 1 hr

Makes: 4 servings

Spice Paste:

6 cloves garlic, peeled but whole

8 medium shallots (about 5 oz/150 g), peeled

8 red Thai chilies (about 2 oz/55 g; see Tips)

1 tsp cayenne pepper (see Tips)

1 inch/2.5 cm fresh ginger

1 inch/2.5 cm fresh turmeric or 1 tbsp ground turmeric

1 inch/2.5 cm fresh galangal root or 2 tsp galangal powder

4 candlenuts or Macadamia nuts

1 tsp coriander seeds or 2 tsp ground coriander

1 tsp cumin seeds or ½ tsp ground cumin

Neutral oil, if needed

Curry:

3 stalks lemongrass

3 tbsp cooking oil

6 makrut lime leaves (see Tips)

3 Indonesian bay leaves

2¼ lb/2 kg bone-in, skin-on chicken drumsticks, or drums and thighs

1⅓ cups/325 mL water

1½ tsp salt, plus more to taste

1 (1⅓ oz/35 g) block Indonesian coconut sugar (see Tips), plus more to taste

2 tsp tamarind paste

2½ cups/625 mL canned coconut milk

Steamed white rice, for serving

TIPS:

Ingredients can be found at most Asian supermarkets.

You can substitute 2 to 3 tbsp sambal oelek for the chilies and cayenne.

Indonesian coconut sugar can be replaced by panela, jaggery, or brown sugar.

The flavour of this curry improves with age; it tastes even better on the second or third day.

Make the spice paste: In a food processor or using a mortar and pestle, grind the garlic, shallots, chilies, cayenne, ginger, fresh turmeric, fresh galangal, candlenuts, coriander seeds, and cumin seeds into a smooth paste. Add a bit of oil if necessary to make grinding easier. If using turmeric powder or galangal powder and/or ground coriander or cumin, add them after grinding the fresh wet ingredients first. Set the spice paste aside.

Make the curry: Trim the ends from the lemongrass and remove the tough outer layers. Crush the stalks with the flat side of a heavy knife to "bruise" and release the aromatic oils. Cut into 1-inch/2.5 cm pieces.

Heat a large heavy-bottomed pot over medium heat. Heat 2 tablespoons of oil, then add the spice paste, lemongrass, lime leaves, and bay leaves. Stir until fragrant, about 5 minutes, scraping the bottom of the pot to prevent sticking.

Add the chicken to the pot and stir to coat with the spices. Cook until the chicken is no longer pink, 10 to 15 minutes.

Add the water, salt, coconut sugar, and tamarind paste and stir to combine. Increase the heat to medium-high and bring to a boil. Reduce the heat, cover, and simmer until the chicken is cooked through and tender, about 30 minutes.

Stir in the coconut milk and continue simmering for another 15 minutes.

Taste and adjust the seasoning. Serve with steamed white rice.

> *I signed my son into public school here and he really loved it. His skin is quite dark and there is a bias against that in Indonesia, so he felt more free and comfortable here. But after about a year I wanted to go back home. It was really hard for me, but because of my son I was trying. I rarely cooked in Indonesia, but I started to cook here because I missed my food from home.*

Elita Rocka comes from several generations of chefs. Moving to Toronto inspired her to start cooking authentic Indonesian food and, together with her sister, launched NaiNai Indonesian Food. **@nainai .indonesianfood**

My parents came from Tibet in the '60s, I was born in Nepal in the '70s, and I have a son who was born in 2005. You're a refugee in Nepal from generation to generation . . . you are not qualified to work, and you cannot have a piece of land in Nepal. These are the things that forced us to leave that beautiful country. So when I share this it makes me a little bit uncomfortable because I love Nepal; it's my birthplace.

As a Tibetan in exile in Nepal, **Tsewang Chodon** learned to cook from her father at a young age. She and **Lhundup** offer delicious Tibetan and Nepalese food at six markets in the city, as well as through their own storefront at TC Tibetan MoMo. @tctibetanmomos

TSEWANG AND LHUNDUP CHODON

KOTEY MOMOS

Tibetan Dumplings

Prep: 2½ hr

Cook: 15 min

Makes: 32 momos (4 servings)

I first encountered Tibetan-style momos in Northern India during the backpacking adventures of my twenties, and have loved them ever since. Simple, hearty, and soul-satisfying, they come to life with a spicy dipping sauce and tangy pickles. Tsewang and her husband, Lhundup, have developed a devoted following at several local farmers' markets, in part because they are just such warm, lovely people, but also because they insist on using local and organic ingredients grown by the other farmers.

Make the dough: In a medium bowl, mix together the flour, water, and turmeric (if using). Knead properly until the dough becomes soft and flexible, not sticky. Cover and let rest for at least 10 to 15 minutes.

Meanwhile, make the filling(s):

- For the chicken filling: In a bowl, combine the chicken, onion, and salt and mix well.

- For the tofu and spinach filling: Place the crumbled tofu and spinach in a bowl. In a small saucepan, heat the oil over medium heat and fry the garlic. Add to the bowl along with the salt and mix well.

To assemble the momos: Pinch off a small knob of dough (about 1½ tbsp/20 g). On a floured surface, roll it out into a round 4 inches/10 cm in diameter. Place 1 tablespoon filling in the middle.

Momos can be shaped in a variety of forms, such as crescent moon, ball, leaf, purse, etc. This recipe is made with the moon shape. To do that, holding the open momo in the palm of your hand, fold the dough over the filling to make a half-circle. Starting at the top, pinch a bit of the upper layer of dough together to make a small pleat, and then press it down into the lower layer to seal. Work your way down, making small pleats as you go until you reach the bottom and completely seal the momo. As you go, the momo will curl into a crescent moon shape, with a ridge of pleats along the top. (They can be frozen at this stage; just arrange them on a lightly floured baking sheet so they don't stick together. You can cook them from frozen; see Tips.)

A popular way to cook momos (called kotey) is to pan-fry them first before steaming (see Tips). In a nonstick skillet (that has a lid), heat 1 teaspoon oil over medium heat. Working quickly, carefully place as many momos as will fit, spaced at least 1 inch apart (they will increase in size when cooking), into the hot pan. Cook until the bottoms start to brown, 1 to 2 minutes. Add enough water to go one-quarter of the way up the momos. When adding the water, stand back as the hot oil can splash. Cover and steam for 10 to 12 minutes. The water should last until the end of cooking, but if it dries up too soon, add a few more spoonfuls. Uncover, swirl around to dislodge the momos and get rid of any residual water, and serve immediately.

Dough:

3 cups/390 g all-purpose flour, plus more for dusting

1 cup/250 mL water

¼ tsp ground turmeric (optional)

Neutral oil, for frying

Choice of Fillings: choose one or make half of each

Chicken Filling:

1 lb/450 g ground chicken

8 oz/225 g chopped onion

1¾ tsp salt

Tofu and Spinach Filling:

1 lb/450 g firm tofu, crumbled

5 oz/150 g spinach, chopped

1 tsp olive oil

2 cloves garlic, chopped

1 tsp salt

TIPS:

If momos are cooked from frozen, add 2 to 3 minutes to the cooking time.

To simply steam momos, cook them in a steamer basket for 15 minutes on high heat.

Momos are typically eaten with some condiments on the side: spicy kimchi, pickles, soy sauce, hot sauce, or chili oil. They are also wonderful in a bowl of broth.

ADOPT-A-RECIPE   Richard Joy

HÓNG SHĀO RÒU

Crispy Skin Red-Braised Pork Belly

Alex Chen has lived and worked across Canada, and the great mosaic of cultures he has encountered along that journey has influenced his identity as a Canadian and the food he cooks. This dish is a fusion of cooking techniques built around his Taiwanese heritage, braising pork belly in a combination of spices, while leaving the skin exposed to achieve maximum crispness.

Prep: 20 to 30 min
Cook: 3 to 4 hr
Makes: 4 servings

1 lb 5 oz/600 g pork belly (skin on)

1 tsp vegetable oil

1 cup/250 mL dark soy sauce

1 cup/250 mL brewed coffee

½ cup/125 mL maple syrup

2 medium shallots, finely chopped

6 cloves garlic, smashed

5 to 6 thin slices peeled fresh ginger

1 to 2 star anise (see Tips)

1 to 2 Thai bird's eye chilies (see Tips), chopped

6 tbsp whisky (plus any extra for the cook)

6½ to 8½ cups/ 1.5 to 2 L stock (vegetable, chicken, or beef) or water

Salt (optional)

2 green onions, finely chopped, for garnish

Position racks in the centre and upper third of the oven and preheat the oven to 300°F/150°C.

Using a sharp knife, score a diamond pattern in the pork belly skin, being careful not to cut into the meat. (Alternatively, ask your butcher to do this.)

In a large cast-iron skillet or roasting pan coated with the oil, sear the pork belly, skin-side down, until the skin starts to brown and turn crispy, 1 to 2 minutes.

Meanwhile, in a large bowl, combine the soy sauce, coffee, maple syrup, shallots, garlic, ginger, star anise, chilies, and whisky. Stir to combine. Add the stock. The braising liquid should taste sweet and savoury. Add salt if necessary; if it is too salty, dilute with additional stock or water.

Transfer the pork belly, skin-side up, to a lightly oiled roasting pan (if you seared the pork belly in a roasting pan, simply turn it over). Add enough braising liquid to submerge most of the pork belly, leaving the skin exposed. Reserve any excess braising liquid.

Transfer the pan to the centre rack of oven and oven-braise until the meat is fork-tender, 3 to 4 hours. You may need to top up the braising liquid to keep the meat (but not the skin) covered.

Once the braise is done, pour the braising liquid through a fine-mesh sieve and set aside. Let it settle a bit and then scoop as much excess fat from the braising liquid as possible.

Set the oven to broil. Move the pan to the upper rack in the oven and broil until crisp, 3 to 5 minutes. Watch it very carefully as it can burn fast.

Remove the pork belly and let it rest for 5 to 10 minutes.

Slice thinly and garnish with the green onions. Serve with the reserved braising liquid.

TIPS:

A range is given for the star anise and chilies, depending on your preferences.

Serve the pork belly with steamed bok choy and rice. It is also delicious in tacos, or as a sandwich on French bread.

Eight or nine years ago, I was living on the Sunshine Coast of British Columbia for a co-op job.... I ended up staying at a Buddhist temple for four months. You'd meet a lot of people there because they'd come and pray every weekend. It was an important experience for me because it really taught me how food is community-building. All the great things about humanity can be seen at the table; we show kindness, we show compassion. I guess that's what I learned there—not the Buddhist stuff.

Alex Chen grew up in Coquitlam, British Columbia. A data scientist by day, he enjoys collecting knives and cooking for lots of people. @alexaca79

NIKY SENATER

VARZĂ CĂLITĂ

Romanian Braised Pork Hocks with Sauerkraut

I definitely got my love of food and my adventurous palate from my dad. Whether he was taking us for dim sum, turning Romanian *mittiei* on the BBQ, or garnishing a platter of something extravagant for a dinner party, the kitchen was an extension of his aesthetic curiosity. There are a handful of my favourite comfort food recipes that come straight from his repertoire, like this dish of slow-cooked smoked pork hocks, cabbage, and sauerkraut. He's always been a fan of more challenging textures—knuckles, joints, and tendons—made luscious and unctuous by long, slow cooking, and as I get older, I am inheriting this too.

You know, before I started cooking, it seemed sort of mysterious and magical, how the food would end up on the plate. But once I started cooking myself, the enigma kind of evaporated. There was a transition from thinking, "Oh, this is mysterious and amazing, how is it being done?" to you knowing how to do it yourself and then off you go and do it.

Niky Senater is a retired award-winning jewellery designer, artist, and sculptor. He is also my dad. @nikycarves

Prep: 30 min
Cook: 1½ to 2 hr
Makes: 6 to 8 servings

2 tbsp vegetable oil

1 medium onion, finely chopped

2 lb/900 g green cabbage, shredded or chopped (about 8 cups/2 L shredded)

18 oz/510 g sauerkraut, fresh or canned, drained

1 tsp salt, or to taste

½ tsp freshly ground black pepper, or to taste

2 lb/900 g smoked pork hock (see Tips), cut into 2-inch/5 cm cubes (ask the butcher to do this)

½ tsp caraway seeds

2 bay leaves

1 (28 fl oz/796 mL) can diced tomatoes

1 tbsp Worcestershire sauce

3 to 4 drops liquid smoke (optional)

In a large heavy-bottomed pot or Dutch oven pot, heat the oil over medium heat. Add the onion and sauté until soft and translucent, 3 to 5 minutes.

Add one-third of the cabbage on top. Add the sauerkraut, salt, pepper, and half of the cubed pork hock, then another one-third of the cabbage. Sprinkle with the caraway seeds and bay leaves. Add the diced tomatoes, remaining pork hock, and remaining cabbage. Add the Worcestershire sauce and liquid smoke (if using).

Mix well in the pot, making sure it doesn't stick to the bottom. Stir constantly until the fresh cabbage softens and releases liquid, 5 to 10 minutes.

Reduce the heat to low, cover, and cook for 1½ to 2 hours, depending on how soft you want the cabbage to be. Stir occasionally to make sure it doesn't burn on the bottom. When ready, the meat should be very tender and the cabbage soft. Taste and adjust the seasoning.

TIPS:

Use a food processor or mandoline to quickly shred the cabbage.

Smoked pork hocks can be found at most European butchers. You can also use fresh pork hock; just start by browning the meat in oil and don't omit the liquid smoke.

I often substitute smoked turkey legs or thighs for pork hock for a lighter version of this dish.

This dish can be cooked in a pressure cooker or electric pressure cooker in about half the time.

Enjoy over soft corn polenta–known as mamaliga in Romanian–with sour cream on the side.

ADOPT-A-RECIPE   Ingo Holzinger

My mother was brought up in Winnipeg, on a very bread and potatoes and canned mushrooms kind of diet. Although I did always think that my mother's cooking was great and she introduced me to ginger and all these other flavours, it was always a little bit restrained. So when I first tasted Sichuan pepper in my early twenties it was like seeing a new colour.

Leo Moncel is a freelance writer on food and the restaurant industry. He wrote and presented local food tours for a few years, and now works as a butcher at Sanagan's Meat Locker in Kensington Market in Toronto.
@leomoncel

LEO MONCEL
DANDAN MIAN
Dan Dan Noodles

Dan dan noodles—fresh wheat noodles tossed in a rich, spicy sesame sauce, topped with a mild ground pork topping—have all the comfort-food qualities of spaghetti and meat sauce, with the added punch of the potent spices and aromas of Sichuan cooking. The name comes from the traditional street vendors whose bamboo shoulder poles make the onomatopoeic *dan-dan* clacking sound.

Prep: 45 min
Cook: 8 min

Makes: 4 generous servings

Sauce:

2 tbsp Sichuan peppercorns (see Tips)

8 tbsp Chinese sesame paste (zhī ma jiàng; see Tips)

8 tbsp homemade unsalted stock (pork, chicken, or vegetable; see Tips) or water

2 tbsp dark soy sauce

1½ tbsp Chinkiang vinegar

1 tbsp peanut or vegetable oil

1 tbsp chili oil (with sediment), or more if you like it spicy

2 tsp sesame oil

4 tbsp finely chopped pickled mustard greens

2 tbsp Shaoxing cooking wine

4 tbsp Sichuan chili bean paste (doubanjiang or Pixian)

1 tbsp soy sauce

1½ lb/675 g ground pork

16 stems yu choi or other sturdy Chinese greens

1 lb 5 oz/600 g fresh Shanghai-style wheat noodles (see Tips)

4 tbsp sesame seeds, toasted, for garnish

Assembly:

4 green onions

Peanut or vegetable oil, for cooking

8 cloves garlic, finely chopped

Make the sauce: In a small dry skillet, toast the Sichuan peppercorns over medium-low heat until fragrant, about 3 minutes. Cool and grind to a powder in a spice grinder or mortar. Measure out a pinch for the sauce and set the rest aside for garnishing.

In a large bowl, slowly whisk the sesame paste and stock together. Whisking constantly, slowly drizzle in the soy sauce, vinegar, peanut oil, chili oil, and sesame oil. Stir in the reserved pinch of the ground Sichuan pepper. Set the bowl of sauce near the stove at the ready.

To assemble: Cut the whites from the tops of the green onions and slice them into rounds that are as long as they are wide. Slice the green onion tops into very fine rings. Keep separate.

Heat a large wok or very large skillet over medium heat. Add 1 to 2 tablespoons oil, enough to coat the pan. When the oil is hot and flowing smoothly, add the whites of the green onions, then the garlic. Add the pickled mustard greens. When the garlic and onions are three-quarters cooked, about 1 minute, increase the heat to medium-high and add the cooking wine. Cook off some of the alcohol, about 1 minute.

Add the chili bean paste and soy sauce to the middle of the pan. Give a vigorous stir and quickly add the ground pork. Let the heat build back up and stir the meat, breaking the ground meat apart as it cooks. Turn off the heat when the pork is fully cooked (lightly browned, no more pink, and easily separated into small pieces).

Bring a large pot of water to a boil. Do not salt.

Lightly blanch the yu choi, 1½ to 2½ minutes depending on the size. You should see some whiteness in the middle of the stem, indicating it is still crunchy.

Remove the choi from the water and put it into a colander to drain. When cool enough to handle, cut into thirds.

Add the noodles to the boiling water and cook according to the package directions. Using tongs, transfer the hot noodles to the bowl of sauce, carrying over some of their cooking liquid. Stir and toss thoroughly.

Divide the noodles among four bowls. Top each bowl evenly with the cooked meat mixture. Garnish with a pinch of Sichuan pepper, a generous smattering of sesame seeds for crunch, and finally a sprinkling of green onion tops. Plate the blanched yu choi alongside.

Stir well and keep stirring as you eat, mixing the unseasoned greens with the stronger flavoured noodles and topping.

TIPS:

All of these products can be sourced at a Chinese specialty supermarket.

Chinese sesame paste (zhī ma jiàng) is essential to the taste of the finished dish. Do not substitute tahini. Chinese sesame pastes are roasted before processing; look for a darker one.

If you do not have unsalted stock on hand, use water; do not substitute canned stock or the dish will be too salty.

When buying Sichuan pepper (huājiāo), always buy the whole peppercorns, which are actually the dried rind of a tiny citrus fruit. Look for a dusky red colour. After it has been toasted and ground, it will start to lose its aromatic potency.

Shanghai noodles can come in a variety of thicknesses. I like a medium thickness, a little wider than spaghetti, smaller than udon.

Depending on your tastes, you can substantially increase the amount of both chili oil and Sichuan pepper in this dish.

If cooking for guests, prepare them for the lip-tingling effect of Sichuan pepper—the unprepared may mistake the pins and needles effect for an allergic reaction!

BBQ PULLED PORK

Jason and I have some things in common. We both had perfectly serviceable, well-paying careers that we abandoned to pursue a passion for food, trading in a steady paycheque for something more difficult yet rewarding.

Jason became enamoured of BBQ around twenty years ago, founded a popular BBQ blog, and competed on the international competitive BBQ circuit under the banner of Pork Ninja. In the early days of The Dep, his competition leftovers were the basis of a weekly pulled pork night, so this dish has a lot of memories for me. He also earned a place in Dep history with Porknography, his nine-course Supper Club that featured pork in every dish—including dessert!

Prep: 30 min, plus up to 24 hr curing time

Cook: 7 to 12 hr

Makes: 10 to 12 servings (see Tips)

Pork:

1 whole pork butt/ shoulder (see Tips), 7 lb/3.2 kg bone-in (recommended) or 5 lb/2.3 kg boneless

1 tbsp kosher or noniodized salt

Rub:

3 tbsp brown sugar

3 tbsp granulated sugar

3 tbsp paprika

1 tbsp garlic powder

½ tbsp freshly ground black pepper

½ tbsp ground ginger

½ tbsp onion powder

½ tbsp ground rosemary

4 tbsp ballpark mustard

For the pork: Coat all sides of the pork butt with the salt and set on a wire rack set in a sheet pan. Refrigerate, uncovered, to cure for at least 30 minutes or up to 24 hours.

Meanwhile, make the rub: In a small bowl or food processor, combine the brown sugar, granulated sugar, paprika, garlic powder, black pepper, ginger, onion powder, and rosemary and mix well with a whisk or pulse in your food processor.

Coat the outside of the pork with the ballpark mustard to create a "glue" to hold the rub. (Please use ballpark mustard and not a fancy mustard.) Coat all sides of the pork with the rub. Save any extra rub mix.

To grill/smoke: Prepare a barbecue (see Tips) or smoker to 250°F/120°C.

Place the pork over indirect heat and cook to an internal temperature of 200°F/93°C, about 8 hours. (Cooking time depends on the size of the pork butt.)

In the oven (see Tips): If you don't have a barbecue or smoker, it is possible to cook the pork in the oven (but it just isn't the same). Place the coated pork on a rack with a drip pan underneath. Add a cup of water to the drip pan to prevent smoking/burning. Cook at 250°F/120°C to an internal temperature of 140°F/60°C, about 4 hours.

Wrap the pork in foil and increase the oven temperature to 350°F/180°C. (Adding 1 to 2 tablespoons brown sugar, apple cider, or wine when you wrap the pork will layer more flavour.) Roast until the internal temperature reaches 200°F/93°C, about 3 more hours.

Remove from the heat and let rest for 30 minutes before pulling. Add more of the reserved rub (to taste) to the meat as you pull it.

TIPS:

For number of servings, figure on 5 to 8 oz/ 140 to 225 g raw pork per person

Although a smaller piece will cook faster, the best pulled pork is made with an entire pork butt or shoulder, cooked slowly over low heat.

Pork butt and pork shoulder are interchangeable for the purposes of this recipe.

If you are using a gas barbecue, light one side of the grill and place the pork on the "cold" side of the grill. Create smoke packs with wood chips in foil and place them on the hot side of the grill.

If you smoke the pork on the barbecue overnight, in the morning wrap it in foil and place it in an insulated cooler until ready to pull and serve; it will stay hot for several hours.

If you cook the pork in the oven, you can add a splash of liquid smoke either before wrapping it in foil or before pulling the cooked meat.

A set of cotton gloves with a pair of medical gloves overtop them (known in the BBQ world as "hot gloves"), make it easy to handle large, hot roasts of meat on the grill, and along with some forks, can help when pulling the pork.

If you make extra rub, you can store it in an airtight container in a cool, dry place for up to 6 months.

Make sure you have a good-quality meat thermometer.

You can freeze leftovers in zip-seal plastic storage bags for up to 6 months. Pulled pork freezes well and is an excellent leftover, great for tacos, quesadillas, or with eggs for brunch.

Serving suggestions: Pile high on large buns, add your favourite BBQ sauce, and top with coleslaw.

About twenty years ago I happened to be near a barbecue contest and they were short on judges so I got sworn in as a judge! Around fifteen years ago I decided to take it more seriously and I became a certified judge for the Kansas City Barbecue society. In 2010 I competed on a barbecue team that got the best pork score for the Canadian team at the World Championship. I was on a barbecue team that literally made the best pulled pork in the world. Yet it's not my best seller at the restaurant.

Jason Rees is an award-winning BBQ pitmaster and runs Earlscourt BBQ in Toronto.
@porkninjas

CHENG FENG

LAOYOUFEN

Old Friend Noodles

It is said that the Chinese culinary repertoire exceeds eighty thousand dishes, perhaps unsurprising given the vast geography and deep history of the world's most populous nation. This dish, a typical street food in the city of Nanning, in Guangxi province, is interesting for its use of tomatoes, something relatively uncommon in Chinese food. The combination of *dou-chi* (fermented black beans) and a distinctive Guilin-style chili paste creates the complex sour/salty/spicy flavour profile of this region.

Prep: 30 min

Cook: 10 min, plus 8 hr for broth

Makes: 4 servings

Make the broth: Rinse the pork hocks and bones and set aside.

In a large stockpot, heat the vegetable oil over high heat. Add the garlic, ginger, and green onion whites and sauté until lightly browned, about 4 minutes.

Add the wine and cook until most of the alcohol has burnt off, about 1 minute. Add the pork hocks and bones, the daikon radish, lotus roots, and water. Bring to a boil, then reduce the heat to low and simmer for at least 8 hours, skimming every 45 minutes to remove any scum that rises to the top. It will reduce by about half, to around 3 to 3.5 L, a little more than you'll need. Taste and adjust the seasoning with salt. Keep warm if serving right away, or cool, cover, and refrigerate, reheating when you're ready to make the noodles.

Make the noodle mixture: Slice the pork loin into thin, finger-length strips and season with salt and pepper. Set aside.

In a large pot, heat the vegetable oil over medium-high heat. Add the tomatoes and cook until juices start to release, about 4 minutes. Quickly add the ginger, garlic, bamboo shoots, fermented black beans, and chili paste and cook until fragrant, about 1 minute. Add the pork strips, soy sauce, and oyster sauce and cook to about half done, around 2 minutes.

Ladle in 8 cups/2 L of the warm broth. (Store any leftover strained broth in the refrigerator for a week, or in the freezer for several months.) Increase the heat to high and bring to a boil. Reduce the heat to medium and add the bean sprouts, lettuce, and rice noodles. Cook until the noodles are just warmed through, about 2 minutes or less, stirring gently. Taste and adjust the seasoning.

Meanwhile, make the topping: Crush the pork rinds into small pieces, then season with the garlic powder and salt to taste.

To serve, divide the broth and noodle mixture evenly among four bowls and garnish with the reserved green onion tops and the crumbled pork rinds.

TIPS:
Salted fermented black beans (dou-chi), Guilin-style chili paste (Guìlín làjiāo jiàng) and other specialty items can be found in local Asian grocery stores or online.

Ho-fen noodles are already cooked, so they just need to be warmed through; adding them at the same time as the lettuce and bean sprouts will keep them from overcooking.

Broth:

4 lb/1.8 kg pork hock, about 4 pieces

1 lb/450 g pork bones

3 tbsp vegetable oil

2 tbsp minced garlic

2 inches/5 cm fresh ginger, sliced

1 bunch green onions (about 6), white part only, thinly sliced (reserve greens for garnish)

2 tbsp Shaoxing cooking wine

1 lb/450 g daikon radish, peeled and sliced into thick slices

1 lb/450 g lotus roots, peeled and thickly sliced

6 qt /6 L cold water

Salt

Noodle Mixture:

1 lb/450 g lean pork loin

Salt and freshly ground black pepper

3 tbsp vegetable oil

4 Roma tomatoes, cut into 1-inch/ 2.5 cm cubes

1 tbsp slivered fresh ginger

1 tbsp minced garlic

1 tbsp slivered pickled bamboo shoots

1½ tsp salted fermented black beans (dou-chi), lightly crushed

1 to 2 tsp Guilin-style chili paste (Guìlín làjiāo jiàng) or sambal oelek

1 tbsp soy sauce

1 tbsp oyster sauce

½ cup/56 g bean sprouts

½ cup/30 g roughly chopped romaine lettuce

1½ lb/675 g Chinese fresh wide rice noodles (ho-fen)

Topping:

1 cup/15 g store-bought crispy pork rinds

1 tbsp garlic powder

Salt

Prep: 1½ hr
Cook: 2 to 2½ hr
Makes: 4 servings

Pork Carnitas:

2½ lb/1.13 kg boneless pork butt, cut into 3-inch/ 7.5 cm pieces

1 tbsp kosher salt

½ tbsp garlic salt

1 tsp ground cumin

4 tbsp lard or vegetable oil

2 bay leaves

½ white onion

Grated zest and juice of 2 oranges

2 cups/480 mL water

Pickled Onions:

1 red onion, thinly sliced

½ cup/125 mL boiling water

Juice of 4 limes

Pinch of salt

Tomato Sauce:

1 (28-oz/796-mL) can stewed tomatoes

½ cup/125 mL water

½ white onion

3 cloves garlic, peeled but whole

½ teaspoon ground cumin

1 teaspoon salt

6 whole cloves, crushed

¼ teaspoon black peppercorns, crushed

1 tsp dried oregano (Mexican, if you can find it)

Chili Sauce:

1 cup/250 mL water

20 dried árbol chilies

¼ white onion

2 cloves garlic, crushed

¼ cup/60 mL distilled white vinegar

1 teaspoon salt

¼ teaspoon black peppercorns, crushed

½ teaspoon ground cumin

Assembly:

1 tablespoon vegetable oil

1 (16-oz/454-g) can refried beans

4 sourdough rolls or 1 baguette cut into 4 lengths

1 avocado, sliced

4 radishes, sliced

4 tbsp chopped fresh cilantro

2 limes, cut into wedges

KATIE KRELOVE

TORTA AHOGADA

Mexican "Drowned" Sandwich

I have always found it odd that given the insatiable popularity of tacos in Toronto, that the joys of a good torta (sandwich) remained largely unsung. This one is particularly spectacular, from the city of Guadalajara, where Katie once lived and worked. Made with luscious pork carnitas, refried beans, pickled onions, and *ahogada* (literally "drowned") in two sauces—one savoury and one spicy—it is impossibly messy and utterly craveworthy.

Make the pork carnitas: Preheat the oven to 325°F/160°C.

In a Dutch oven or other heavy ovenproof pan, rub the pork pieces with the kosher salt, garlic salt, cumin, and lard/oil. Add the bay leaves, onion, orange zest, orange juice, and water. Cover with a lid or aluminum foil, slide into the oven, and bake for 2 hours.

Spoon out half of the cooking liquid and return to the oven to cook, uncovered, until tender but with some golden crispy bits, about another hour. You can moisten with reserved braise as needed.

Make the pickled onions: Place the red onion slices in a glass jar or bowl. Cover with boiling water for 20 seconds, then drain off the water. Add the lime juice and salt. Cover and let sit for at least 30 minutes.

Make the tomato sauce: In a food processor or blender, combine the stewed tomatoes, water, onion, garlic, cumin, salt, and crushed cloves and peppercorns and process until very smooth. Alternatively you can add whole cloves and peppercorns after blending, but they'll need to be strained out before serving.

Transfer the sauce to a small saucepan and add the oregano. Bring to a boil over medium heat. Reduce to a simmer, cover, and heat for 20 minutes, or until ready to use. Add water as needed to keep it thin (like tomato juice). Adjust the seasoning to taste.

Make the chili sauce: In a small saucepan, combine the water, chilies, onion, and garlic and bring to a boil. Once boiling, remove from the heat and let cool. Transfer the mix to a food processor with the vinegar, salt, crushed peppercorns, and cumin. Blend until smooth. This is a very hot sauce!

When ready to assemble: In a saucepan, heat the vegetable oil over medium heat, add the refried beans, and heat until warm, 3 to 4 minutes, stirring to blend.

To assemble the tortas: Cut the pork carnitas into bite-size chunks. Slice the sourdough rolls in half (but not all the way through). Spread some refried beans on one half and add a good amount of pork carnitas and avocado slices.

To serve, pour a ladle of the tomato sauce on each plate or wide shallow bowl. Place the tortas on the plates and "drown" them in more tomato sauce (about 2 ladles per sandwich). Top with a tablespoon of chili sauce (or serve the chili sauce separately to be added to taste–remember, it is hot!). Garnish with the pickled onions, radish slices, and cilantro. Serve the lime wedges for squeezing.

Don't forget the napkins!

I have anxiety, and cooking helps to alleviate that anxiety; it helps me relax like no other thing does. Possibly it's because I have to think about it, but I don't have to think about it too much. And I don't have much stress around it because it doesn't have to be perfect. I also find cooking is great for social anxiety. If I'm having a party and I'm sitting on the couch and talking to people, I'll be socially anxious. But if I'm in the kitchen and I'm cooking, I'll be able to talk and interact much better.

TIPS:

This sandwich demands a sturdy roll, ideally sourdough, that won't disintegrate.

Don't be stingy with the tomato sauce–this sandwich is meant to be drenched!

You can freeze any leftover carnitas and sauces for later use.

Katie Krelove is a food-lover, gardener, outdoor eco-educator, environmental activist, and keen urban forager. @katiekrelove

SONYA GAMMAL

TOURTIÈRE

Québécois Pork and Beef Pie

A classic Québécois recipe, this hearty meat pie is traditionally served at *réveillons*, festive dinners held on the nights before Christmas or New Year's. Sonya, a French-trained chef who taught many of our sourdough bread and knife skills workshops, made this dish one of her specialities, sometimes cooking more than a hundred of them over the holidays.

> *My father was born in Cairo, Egypt, and my mom is from Atlanta, Georgia, with some Irish sprinkled in. So I'm a little bit of a mixed bag. They nurtured a multicultural aspect in our lives that continues today. When it comes to food, I like the authenticity of a particular dish that has a story. But the country next door, or across the continent may have something similar. I find that very interesting with food, the etiology of it.*

Sonya Gammal is a trained chef and culinary educator. Since 2020, she has been running Slow Green Cuisine, a zero-waste food delivery business. Most recently, Sonya became the Chef Instructor for the Cooking for Life Program at Covenant House Toronto. @slowgreencuisine

Prep: 1 to 1½ hr
Cook: 2 hr

Makes: one 9-inch/23 cm pie (8 servings)

Filling:

Salt

1 small potato, peeled and diced

7 oz/200 g ground pork

7 oz/200 g lean ground beef

1 tbsp olive oil

½ medium onion, diced

⅓ cup/45 g finely diced peeled carrot

⅓ cup/35 g finely chopped celery

1 clove garlic, minced

1 bay leaf

2 to 4 tsp mix of fresh or dried parsley, sage, savoury, thyme (see Tips)

1 to 2 tsp mix of allspice, cinnamon, nutmeg, cloves (see Tips)

2 tbsp fine dried bread crumbs

2 tsp apple cider vinegar

1½ tsp Dijon mustard

1 tbsp Worcestershire sauce

1 tbsp ketchup

⅓ cup/75 mL beef stock

½ tsp freshly ground black pepper

Pastry Dough:

3 cups/330 g pastry flour, plus more for dusting

16 tbsp (8 oz/225 g) very cold butter, cubed

½ cup/110 g cold water

1½ tsp/8 g salt

1 egg yolk

Egg wash: 1 large egg whisked with 1 tbsp water

Make the filling: In small pot of boiling salted water, cook the potato until tender. Drain and set aside.

In a sauté pan or skillet, cook the pork and beef over medium heat until no longer pink. Transfer to a plate and set aside.

In the same sauté pan, heat the olive oil over medium heat and sauté the onion, carrot, and celery until tender, about 10 minutes. Add the garlic and sauté another minute. Mix in the meat, bay leaf, herb mix, and spice mix until well combined. Add the bread crumbs, vinegar, mustard, Worcestershire sauce, ketchup, beef stock, ½ teaspoon/3 g salt, and the pepper. Bring to a simmer and cook until most of the liquid is absorbed, about 15 minutes. Remove from the heat, stir in the potato, and let cool to room temperature. (This can be prepared a day in advance.)

Preheat the oven to 375°F/190°C.

Make the pastry dough: Put the flour in a medium bowl. Add the butter and use a pastry blender or two knives to incorporate into the flour until pea-size pieces remain. Add the cold water to a measuring cup and mix in the 1½ teaspoon salt and egg yolk with a fork. Pour the liquid into the flour/butter mixture. Mix until it just comes together. Add a drop or two more water if needed to make the dough cohere. Divide the pastry into 2 equal portions and shape into balls or discs. Cover in plastic wrap and chill in the fridge (or freezer) for a minimum of 15 minutes or until the butter solidifies.

When ready to shape the dough, pull one ball out of the fridge, set it on a well-floured work surface, and sprinkle with more flour. Roll out to a round about 12 inches/30 cm in diameter and ⅛ to ¼ inch/ 3 to 6 mm thick.

ADOPT-A-RECIPE   Christine Manning

Transfer to a 9-inch/23 cm pie plate and gently shape the pastry to line the bottom of the pan (do not press hard). Use scissors to trim away excess dough, leaving 1 inch/2.5 cm hanging over the edge of the pie plate. Use a fork to prick the pie crust all over the bottom and sides. Place a square of parchment over the dough and fill with pie weights or dried beans, at least halfway up.

Bake the bottom crust until it just begins to turn golden at the edges, 12 to 15 minutes. Remove the parchment and pie weights from the pie crust and return to the oven for 2 to 3 more minutes. Remove from the oven, but leave the oven on.

Let the parbaked bottom crust cool for 3 to 5 minutes, then use scissors to trim any excess crust so it meets flush with the edge of the pie plate. Let cool completely before continuing.

When the crust has cooled, add the filling. Pull the second half of the dough from the fridge and roll out the top crust on a lightly floured surface to about ¼ inch/6 mm thick. Unfurl the dough on top of the pie. Use scissors again to trim the excess dough from the sides, leaving about ½ inch/1.3 cm all around the edge. Tuck the excess dough from the top crust under the parbaked bottom crust using a small offset spatula or knife to help, if needed. Seal the bottom and top crusts together by crimping with a fork.

Brush the top crust with the egg wash. Cut a couple of vents in the crust. Return to the oven and bake until the filling is heated through and the top crust is golden brown, 40 minutes to 1 hour.

Remove from the oven and let rest for 5 to 10 minutes, then cut your first slice and serve!

TIPS:

You can use some or all of the herbs and spices listed, and the exact ratio is up to you.

The tourtière *can be made up to 2 days in advance and reheated in a 300°F/150°C oven.*

You can do this without parbaking the bottom crust if you make some adjustments: Make the bottom crust thinner, like ⅛ inch/ 3 mm. To bake the filled tourtière, *preheat a pizza stone or sheet pan before placing the pie in the oven on the stone or pan (this will help brown the bottom crust).*

Alternatively, opt out of the bottom crust altogether; I prefer a thick top crust on my meat pies, so I often make it with no bottom crust at all.

ROBERT YEE

XĪNJIĀNG KǍO CHUÀN

Xinjiang Spicy Lamb Skewers

When Robert, a computer programmer with an abiding passion for food, offered to make some of these spicy kebabs, you know I was on board. A speciality of northwestern China, they feature lamb, potently seasoned with cumin, fennel, chili powder, and salt, grilled over hot coals. One of the most iconic of Xinjiang dishes, they are found in street stalls and markets throughout the region.

Prep: 15 min
Cook: 10 min
Makes: 10 skewers

1 kg boneless lamb shoulder

4 tbsp plus 1 tsp cumin seeds

1 tbsp fennel seeds

5½ tsp ground chili powder (see Tips)

2½ tsp sea salt

3 to 4 tbsp vegetable oil

Cut the lamb shoulder into 1-inch/2.5 cm cubes.

In a spice grinder, combine 3 tablespoons plus 1 teaspoon of cumin seeds with the fennel seeds and grind. Place in a small bowl and mix in the remaining 1 tablespoon cumin seeds, the chili powder, and the salt.

In a large bowl, mix the cubed lamb with the vegetable oil until well coated. Add the spice mixture and toss well.

Prepare a charcoal barbecue for direct high-temperature grilling.

Skewer the cubes of lamb onto thin metal skewers.

Grill the skewers over direct heat until fully cooked and crisp on the outside, 5 to 10 minutes. Enjoy immediately.

TIPS:

This recipe calls for pure ground chili pepper, not the "chili powder" that is a seasoning blend for making chili. Use as much or as little chili powder as you want, depending on how hot you like it.

Len's note: I've cheated and made these under a hot broiler. It's not as good or as authentic as over charcoal, but it worked in a pinch.

Robert Yee works as a software developer by day and pursues culinary arts training at night. An avid traveller who "eats the world," he brings global inspirations and techniques back to his kitchen. **@superbgourmand**

ADOPT-A-RECIPE   Greg Clow

I started cooking when I decided to become a vegan. At the same time I went on a trip around Africa for about three years, to different places in West and East Africa, like Ghana, Nigeria, Eritrea, Egypt—a kind of a food tour. As a nutritionist, I realized that I wasn't preparing healthy food and realized that I was healing faster when I went back to the traditional village food. Because while tofu is great, it's not the best thing for me.

Selam Teclu was born in Eritrea and immigrated to Canada at an early age. She currently lives in Toronto where she works as an urban farmer, Registered Holistic Nutritionist (RHN), holistic chef, culinary instructor, and writer.

SELAM TECLU

DUBA BAMIA

Eritrean Pumpkin, Okra, and Beef Stew

Selam made an indelible impression on me in the early days of The Dep. She hosted an Earth Day Supper Club featuring unique dishes typical of rural Eritrean villages. She invited musician Moyo Rainos Mutamba to play the *mbira* and engage the guests in traditional African storytelling. While Moyo shared stories, Selam roasted green coffee beans with incense in preparation of the traditional coffee ceremony. The whole experience was deeply moving, offering connections on so many levels: sounds, tastes, smells, stories, gestures, and rituals, revealing the depth and the power of a meal to reach from one culture deep into the heart of another.

Prep: 30min
Cook: 45 min to 1 hr
Makes: 4 servings

2 tbsp sunflower oil or butter

1 medium red onion, finely chopped (about 1 cup/180 g)

2 cloves garlic, finely chopped

1 tsp ground coriander

2 tbsp berbere spice blend

4 tbsp tomato paste

10½ oz/300 g stewing beef, cut into 1-inch/2.5 cm cubes (about 2 cups)

6 to 7 oz/170 to 200 g pumpkin, cut into 1-inch/2.5 cm cubes (about 1½ cups)

2 cups/475 mL water (or more if you like more sauce)

1 tsp sea salt

5 oz/150 g okra, chopped or whole

In a heavy-bottomed pot or Dutch oven, heat the oil/butter over medium heat. Add the onion and garlic and cook until soft and translucent, about 5 minutes.

Add the coriander and berbere, mix well, and, when fragrant, add the tomato paste. Reduce the heat to a simmer and cook, stirring constantly to prevent burning at the bottom, until it turns into a brown paste, about 15 minutes. If it sticks to the bottom or is too dry, add a teaspoon or two of water.

Add the beef, pumpkin, water, and salt and let it cook down for 15 more minutes.

Add the okra, cover, and cook, stirring occasionally, until the oil is floating to the top and the pumpkin is soft but not mushy, 15 to 25 minutes.

Serve over injera bread or rice.

TIP:
Recipe can be made vegetarian simply by omitting the beef and using some extra pumpkin.

ADOPT-A-RECIPE   Mary Hulbert

SARME

Bosnian Cabbage Rolls

My family is Romanian, and they take their cabbage rolls pretty seriously. But these ones, using leaves from whole cabbages that Ksenija's family ferments for half a year, and luscious lamb fat that they smoke themselves, elevates these to the best *sarme* I have ever tasted.

I was always in the kitchen with my grandma, I'd choose that over playing out with the other kids. Fishing with my father, seeing him catch the fish, put herbs in it, then make a fire and fry it in a pan by the river, that was one of my first experiences of cooking.

Photo: Katy MacLachlan

Ksenija Hotic
is a freelance photographer and food stylist, based in Toronto. This is her fourth cookbook, and she is also working on her own book about Bosnian food and her journey to Canada.
@khzen

Prep: 1 hr to 1 hr 15 min

Cook: 3 to 3½ hr

Makes: about 30 (depending on size of cabbage leaves)

1 head pickled cabbage (see Tips)

Filling:

2 lb/900 g ground meat (see Tips)

Up to 8 oz/225 g Balkan dry-smoked meat (suho meso), finely chopped (optional, see Tips)

2 cups/400 g white rice, rinsed

2 medium onions, finely chopped (about 2 cups/320 g)

½ cup/35 g chopped fresh parsley

2 tbsp smoked paprika

2 tsp dried thyme

2 tsp salt

2 tsp freshly ground black pepper

½ tsp cayenne pepper or to taste (optional)

2 tsp Vegeta (optional; see Tips)

Braise:

1 tbsp oil

8 oz/225 g Balkan dry-smoked meat coarsley chopped, including fat and bones

4 cups/1 L beef or vegetable stock

1 (28 fl oz/796 mL) can tomato sauce or crushed tomatoes

Roux:

4 tbsp vegetable oil or 60 g butter

4 tbsp all-purpose flour

1 tsp paprika

1 tsp salt

½ tsp freshly ground black pepper

For Serving:

Chopped fresh parsley, for garnish

Crusty bread

Sour cream

Separate the leaves of the pickled cabbage head and lay them out on a large round plate, placing the core end towards you. Very large leaves can be cut in half along the stem if necessary. If the centre core is very thick, pare it down a bit to make it malleable and easier to roll. Keep any trimmings to add to the pot.

Make the filling: In a large bowl, combine the ground meat with the rinsed rice, onions, parsley, smoked paprika, thyme, salt, and black pepper, adding optional ingredients (smoked meat, cayenne, Vegeta) if desired, and thoroughly mix together with your hands.

Make the rolls: Place a large meatball-size amount of filling at the bottom edge of a cabbage leaf (adjust the amount of meat filling as needed to work with the size of the cabbage leaf), leaving a 1-inch/ 2.5 cm border on each side. Roll the leaf away from you, folding in the side edges as you go. You want a tight, tucked and sealed roll that won't fall apart while cooking.

Coat the bottom of a large soup pot with the oil. Place any chunks of cabbage core in the pot and carefully place a layer of rolls over the top. Poke each cabbage roll twice with a toothpick.

Sprinkle with some of the remaining chopped smoked meat. Make another layer of rolls. Add the stock and tomato sauce to cover the cabbage rolls.

Cover and bring to a boil over high heat. Reduce the heat to medium and cook for 3 to 3½ hours, depending on how soft you like them, reducing the heat to low for the last hour of cooking. Check regularly and add water as needed so the liquid does not reduce below the top level of rolls.

Make the roux: In a medium skillet, heat the oil over medium heat. Add the flour, whisking constantly, until it becomes smooth and the colour turns light gold, 3 to 5 minutes. Reduce the heat to low and add the paprika, followed by the salt and pepper. When combined and aromatic, pour the roux over the simmering cabbage rolls and let simmer on low for another 5 minutes. Remove from the heat and let them sit covered until you are ready to serve.

Garnish with some chopped parsley and serve with crusty bread and a dollop of sour cream.

ADOPT-A-RECIPE   Stephen Bulger

TIPS:

Pickled cabbage (kiseli kupus), Balkan smoked meats (suho meso), and Vegeta, a seasoning mixture, are available in most Eastern European grocery stores. Vacuum-sealed whole heads of cabbage are preferred.

For the ground meat in the filling, I prefer beef and lamb in a ratio of 3 parts beef to 1 part lamb, but you can use any combination of ground meat you like.

For the smoked meat, use lamb and/or beef, some with bones if possible. If you like a more intense smoky flavour, you can also add some extra smoked meat or sausage to the meat stuffing mixture. Keep the best finely chopped meat for the filling, and any leftover bones, fat, or bits can be added to the pot.

Sarme freeze well, so don't be afraid to make a big batch and save some for later. When reheating, for 2 cabbage rolls add about ½ cup/125 mL of water (or a bit of tomato sauce) in a pan and simmer the cabbage rolls on low, turning them so they get heated thoroughly, 10 to 15 minutes.

Photo: Rick O'Brien

> *I was born in Bosnia in 1981. In 1992, the civil war began and went on for three years. . . . There were concentration camps. We would see men loaded onto buses and taken away and you don't see them again.*
>
> *We had to sleep in the storage lockers downstairs, as many of us as could fit. You never really could sleep by the window; you slept in hidden areas. Basic survival. Honestly, no access to food. There was no electricity and things were bombed out. We were trapped there for seven, eight months.*
>
> *When we did flee it was for many months, and then when we got out of Bosnia the bus was attacked by the Serbian army, by planes—literally bombarded. You think you're out, you're not really out. It didn't really end until we were in Croatia. Life was pretty normal there. We were driving out and I remember seeing bananas on the side of a road and I remember grabbing my brother's hand and waking him up on the bus and being like, "Look, bananas! They have bananas!!!"*

KSENIJA HOTIC

Ksenija Hotic grew up very close to nature in Kljuc, Bosnia, cooking in her grandmother's kitchen, foraging in the mountains, and fishing in the rivers. At age eleven, she and her family were forced to flee the genocidal civil war. They barely escaped, relocating nearly a dozen times through Croatia, Slovenia, and Austria, before finally ending up in Berlin, displaced and homeless—an experience that would define much of the trajectory of her life.

They were finally able to resettle in Canada in 1995, where she worked in a German delicatessen while pursuing degrees in sociology (with a focus on global migration) and German studies, as well as studying photography. In time she found work in mental healthcare at CAMH (Centre for Addiction and Mental Health), but after more than a decade in a high-pressure institutional career, Ksenija, like me, found herself burnt out and disconnected from herself.

Also like me, something about food called to her as a path back to herself. I met her at TUM (Toronto Underground Market), a popular food festival, where she was one of the event coordinators, and eventually a vendor as well, serving up hundreds of Bosnian *sarme* (cabbage rolls). We immediately clicked over our shared enthusiasm for food and its ability to connect people. Soon enough Ksenija was in The Dep kitchen with her parents preparing traditional Bosnian food under the banner of *Cookin' Like a Boz*.

Photo: Rick O'Brien

It was a meeting that would tilt both our lives, giving momentum and encouragement to her move towards a new career in food and photography—you are now holding her fourth published cookbook. In 2015, I invited Ksenija to do a Table Talk, to share a bit of her history, culture, and personal journey. **The talk helped crystallize the connection between her culture and identity, her history and trauma, and the place of food in healing.** The years to follow, and more than thirty events at The Dep, would culminate in an intense, year-long collaboration on the beautiful photography for this book.

Ksenija is now returning to her own project, a deeply personal cookbook of traditional Bosnian food interwoven with her experiences as a refugee and immigrant. For both of us, food has offered a pathway to meaning, self-discovery, and healing.

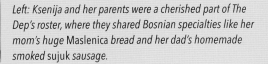

Above: Ksenija worked on this book for over a year, styling and shooting thousands of photographs.

Left: Ksenija and her parents were a cherished part of The Dep's roster, where they shared Bosnian specialties like her mom's huge Maslenica bread and her dad's homemade smoked sujuk sausage.

The Depanneur Cookbook   **191**

Back in India I had everything: I had a career in banking, I had family, I had a romantic relationship, friends, and everything broke at once. . . . I wanted to leave town and start again. I had no friends or family here and I was in a very vulnerable state of mind; I think I lost myself. . . . I'd never cooked outside my own home but I did one night, and then another and through this process I found myself again. I found my calling, and my joy. I healed myself with cooking.

Ridhima Kalra is a banker by profession and baker by passion. Her journey in the kitchen started at a very early age and remains an integral part of her life. **@raag.to**

RIDHIMA KALRA

GOSHT DO PYAZA

Goat Curry

Prep: 15 min

Cook: 1 hr

Makes: 4 servings

Ridhima is an *amateur* cook in the true sense of that word in that she does it for the love of it. This is different than just skill or technique, something a little rarer and more precious, something that The Dep sought to give a home to by inviting cooks like her into its kitchen. The care and attention they pour into their meals, the joy they get from diners' enjoyment of their food, are worth more, at least to me, than any Michelin star.

Do pyaza, meaning "double onions," is a rich meat stew with variations found in Persia, Afghanistan, and Northern India; it gets its name from the generous amount of onion used in different ways at two stages in the preparation of the dish.

4 tbsp/60 g ghee or butter

1 tbsp cumin seeds

1 bay leaf

4 whole cloves

4 black peppercorns

1 tbsp ginger-garlic paste (see Tips)

1 cup/250 mL onion paste (see Tips)

1 tbsp MDH gosht masala (see Tips)

2 lb/900 g goat meat, cut into bite-size pieces

1 cup/250 mL water

½ cup/125 mL plain Greek-style yogurt

1 tbsp ground coriander

1 tbsp ground red lal mirch chili powder

1½ tsp ground turmeric

Salt

2 fresh green chilies, seeded and diced

1 tbsp dried fenugreek leaves, crumbled (or powder)

2 cups/230 g sliced onions

2 tbsp cilantro leaves, or more to taste, for garnish

Warm naan or cooked basmati rice, for serving

In a heavy-bottomed saucepan, melt the ghee or butter over medium-high heat. Add the cumin seeds, bay leaf, cloves, and peppercorns. When the seeds begin to splutter, add the ginger-garlic paste, onion paste, and gosht masala. Sauté until the onion paste starts to brown.

Add the goat, stir, and continue to fry until the pieces no longer look raw, 4 to 6 minutes. Reduce the heat to low, add the water, cover, and cook until tender, 45 minutes to 1 hour.

Stir in the yogurt, taking care it does not curdle. Keep cooking until the fat begins to separate and float to the top. Add the coriander and chili powder, turmeric, and salt to taste. Increase the heat to medium-high, add the green chilies, fenugreek leaves, and onions and stir to fully incorporate. Continue cooking over medium heat for a few minutes until the fat separates again but the onions remain a bit crunchy.

Serve hot, garnished with the chopped cilantro, with warm naan or basmati rice.

TIPS:

Ginger-garlic paste is a convenient jarred product commonly used in Indian cooking; you can substitute equal parts finely minced fresh ginger and garlic that have been mashed together with a little salt.

Onion paste, too, can be purchased in Indian markets. You can substitute 2 chopped onions that have been microwaved for 5 minutes, then blended to a smooth paste with a bit of water and salt.

MDH is a brand of Indian spice blends readily available in most South Asian shops; Shan is another popular brand. Gosht masala is a blend specifically for goat or lamb, but you can substitute garam masala in a pinch.

ADOPT-A-RECIPE Monika Rau

Prep: 40 min plus soaking time

Cook: 40 to 50 min

Makes: 4 servings

Meatballs:

1 lb/450 g ground meat (a mix of lamb and veal works best)

½ medium onion, grated

4 cloves garlic, grated

1 tsp ground coriander

½ tsp salt

1 tsp freshly ground black pepper

½ cup/125 mL dried sour plums, soaked in water (see Tip), pits removed

Sauce:

1 cup/250 mL dried sour plums, soaked in water (see Tip), pits removed

5 tbsp vegetable oil

1 cup/160 g chopped onion

5 cloves garlic

½ tsp ground turmeric (optional)

1½ cups/270 g chopped tomatoes

½ tsp ground cumin

¼ tsp salt

½ tsp freshly ground black pepper

2 cups/475 mL water

1 tbsp chopped fresh cilantro, for garnish

FRISHTA GHAFOORI

KOFTE ALOO BOKHARA

Lamb Meatballs with Sour Plum Sauce

For millennia, Afghanistan was a place where important trade routes between India, China, the Middle East, and Europe converged. Marco Polo crossed the country en route to China; Arab travellers and the British passed through on their way to India. A rich culture took hold at this crossroads, and with it a varied Afghan cuisine influenced by Persia, India, and Mongolia, but with a style all its own.

Make the meatballs: In a medium bowl, combine the ground meat, onion, garlic, coriander, salt, and pepper and mix thoroughly with your hands to allow the meat to absorb the flavours. Add the pulp of the soaked dried plums and mix in well.

Shape into 2-inch/5 cm balls and set them aside to rest while preparing the sauce.

Make the sauce: In a food processor, purée the soaked plums.

In a large skillet, heat the oil over medium heat. Add the onion and garlic and fry until golden, 5 to 10 minutes. Stir in the turmeric (if using). Add the tomatoes and continue cooking, stirring constantly, until the tomatoes are broken down and the oil starts separating, 5 to 10 minutes.

Season the sauce with the cumin, salt, and pepper and mix well. Add the plum purée and water and stir to incorporate. Add the meatballs to the sauce, one by one, in a single layer. Reduce the heat, cover the pan, and cook at a low simmer until the meatballs are cooked through, 25 to 30 minutes. If the sauce seems thin, uncover and let simmer for 5 more minutes until the sauce thickens.

Garnish with the fresh cilantro before serving.

TIP:

Soak the dried plums in water for at least 1 hour and as long as overnight. You can use hot water to speed the softening process.

ADOPT-A-RECIPE Colette Snyder

Tuba Tunç was a marketing professional in Istanbul for ten years, but her true passion has always been cooking. She has worked in various restaurants including managing Anatolia, one of the oldest Turkish restaurants in Toronto. Tuba recently founded Lokum Eats, where she showcases Turkish and Ottoman cuisine, as well as her take on international cuisines.
@lokumeats

TUBA TUNÇ
HÜNKAR BEĞENDI

Sultan's Delight (Turkish Eggplant Purée with Braised Beef)

The sprawling Ottoman Empire transformed the cuisines of a huge swath of the Western world, from the Balkans to the Middle East to North Africa. Its legacy lives on in the vast repertoire of Turkish dishes—supposedly over a hundred for eggplant alone—of which this is one of the most famous. This dish is traditionally served with the meat atop a bed of eggplant béchamel, but using the eggplant shells makes for an attractive presentation.

Prep: 1 to 1½ hr
Cook: 2 to 3 hr

Makes: 4 or 5 servings

5 to 7 eggplants

Braised Beef:

2 lb/900 g beef (boneless blade roast, rib eye roast, or stewing meat) or boneless lamb leg

Olive oil

Salt and freshly ground black pepper

2 medium onions, chopped

2 to 3 cloves garlic, grated

3 tbsp Turkish tomato paste (*salca*) or tomato paste

3 tbsp Turkish sweet pepper paste (*tatlı biber salçası*; see Tips)

3 tbsp Turkish hot pepper paste (*acı biber salçası*; see Tips)

2⅓ cups/560 mL tomato sauce or grated fresh tomato

Sprig of fresh thyme or rosemary (optional)

Béchamel:

8 tbsp/120 g butter

½ cup/65 g all-purpose flour

1¼ cups/300 mL milk, plus more as needed

½ whole nutmeg, grated

7 oz/100 g *kashar* cheese (see Tips), grated

Salt and freshly ground black pepper

Fresh parsley leaves, thyme, or rosemary, for garnish

Preheat the oven to 450°F/230°C. Line a baking sheet with parchment paper.

Rinse and dry the eggplants, then pierce them several times with a skewer or fork. Place them on the lined baking sheet and roast, turning occasionally, until the flesh is soft enough to scoop out, about 45 minutes.

Meanwhile, prepare the braised beef: Remove the silver skin and excess fat and cut the meat into 1-inch/2.5 cm cubes.

In a medium pot, heat 1 to 2 tablespoons olive oil over high heat. When the oil is hot, add the meat, and season with salt and pepper. Reduce the heat to medium and turn the pieces of meat to brown evenly, 4 to 6 minutes. Add the onions and sauté until translucent, about 5 minutes. Stir in the grated garlic. At this stage the meat may release juices, so cook it until evaporated.

Add the tomato paste, sweet pepper paste, and hot pepper paste and cook for a few minutes, incorporating more olive oil if too dry. Add the tomato sauce (or grated tomato), reduce the heat to low, and simmer for 1 hour, stirring occasionally to avoid sticking. If it's getting dry, add a bit of water, ¼ cup/60 mL at a time. When close to done, add the herb sprig (if using).

Carefully cut the eggplants lengthwise and scoop out the insides; try to avoid tearing the skin. If you want to use the "shells" for presentation, set the tidiest ones aside (1 or 2 per serving depending on the size of the eggplants). Keep warm or reheat gently when ready to use.

Chop the roasted eggplant flesh roughly and place in a mesh sieve to drain off the juices.

Make the béchamel: In a heavy-bottomed pan, melt the butter over medium heat. Add the flour and whisk constantly, allowing the mixture to cook until golden in colour, about 5 minutes.

Add the drained eggplant, mixing well with a whisk to avoid lumps. Cook for 5 minutes, then add the milk and nutmeg, continuing to stir. Once the whole mixture is well combined, add the cheese and keep stirring until the mixture becomes creamy. (Add more milk if needed for a creamy texture.) Remove from the heat, check the seasoning, adding salt and pepper as needed. If the meat is not ready yet, cover the eggplant béchamel directly with plastic wrap to avoid forming a skin on top.

Ladle some eggplant béchamel into the eggplant "shells" and top with the braised meat and more sauce. (Alternatively, serve the traditional way by placing the eggplant béchamel on a serving plate, topping with the meat, and drizzling with the braising juices.) Garnish with fresh parsley, thyme, or rosemary.

TIPS:

Turkish tomato paste, sweet pepper paste, hot pepper paste, and kashar *cheese are all available at Middle Eastern shops.*

To substitute for the sweet pepper paste (tatlı biber salçası), use more tomato paste (50 g).

To substitute for hot pepper paste (acı biber salçası), use ½ tbsp chili flakes.

To substitute for kashar *cheese, use any melty, mild cheese, such as mozzarella.*

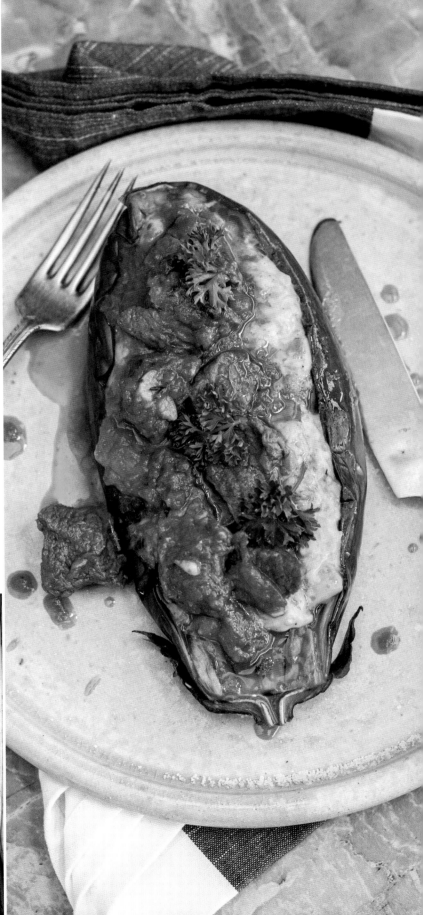

Prep: about 2 hr

Cook: 40 to 45 min, depending on the size of the manti

Makes: 50 to 60 pieces, depending on the size of the manti (8 to 10 servings)

Dough:

1 cup/250 mL water, plus more as needed

4 cups/520 g all-purpose flour

1 large egg

1 tsp salt

Filling:

1¾ lb/800 g lamb stewing meat

7 oz/200 g lamb fat (see Tips)

1 large onion

14 oz/400 g butternut squash

1 tsp freshly ground black pepper

2 tsp salt

1 tsp ground coriander

1 tsp ground cumin

Assembly:

½ cup/125 mL or more vegetable oil, for brushing the steamer

Melted butter, for serving

Sour Cream Sauce:

½ cup/125 mL sour cream

½ cup/125 mL yogurt

1 clove garlic, crushed and finely chopped

Salt

Tomato Sauce:

1 cup/250 mL tomato sauce or canned crushed tomatoes with their juice

1 red bell pepper, seeded and cut up

1 clove garlic, peeled but whole

Salt

ZHANAR KHAMITOVA

MANTI

Kazakh Lamb and Squash Dumplings

Toronto must have one of the most diverse food scenes in the world, but there were still cuisines that even a dedicated, curious foodie like myself never seemed to encounter. When Fatima Khamitova approached The Dep suggesting that her mom, Zhanar, could make a meal of traditional Kazakh dishes, you know she did not have to ask twice.

Making dumplings from scratch is typically not something one does just for oneself; it is something done with others and for others, usually for a gathering or celebration. There is something about the patient process that is itself a little ritual of connection, an excuse to spend some time together, a quiet pleasure in the anticipation as comforting as any plate of steaming dumplings.

Every time we travelled we would go to a supermarket abroad, get groceries, and smuggle them back into the country because my mom would be like, "I need this vanilla powder." Even after the Soviet Union collapsed there were a lot of groceries that weren't imported, so we used to bring back everything from everywhere and she would incorporate them into her cooking.

— Zhanar's daughter, Fatima

Make the dough: In a stand mixer fitted with the dough hook, combine the water, flour, egg, and salt and mix to form a stiff dough, about 5 minutes. (You could also knead the dough by hand.) Let it rest, covered, for 20 to 30 minutes.

Make the filling: Cut the lamb, lamb fat, onion, and squash into ¼-inch/6 mm dice. Place in a large bowl and add the pepper, salt, coriander, and cumin and mix thoroughly.

Divide the dough into 4 equal portions. Using a rolling pin or a pasta machine, roll the dough out until very thin (#4 setting, a scant ¹⁄₁₆ inch/1 mm). Lay each sheet of dough on a floured surface and cut into 4-inch/10 cm squares or 4- to 5-inch/10 to 12 cm rounds. You should end up with 50 to 60 pieces.

Assemble the manti: Place about 1 tablespoon of filling in the centre of each square/circle. Pick up the four corners/edges to form a small pouch and pinch together at the top. Work your way down any open seams, pinching to seal completely, gently

squeezing out any extra air as you go. Place the shaped mantis on a floured surface or parchment-lined baking sheets.

Fill a large pot two-thirds with water and bring to a boil.

Brush steamer baskets (see Tips) with vegetable oil. Evenly arrange the manti in the steamer baskets, leaving some space between them to avoid sticking to each other. Place the steamer baskets over the pot of boiling water, cover, and steam for 40 to 45 minutes.

Meanwhile, make the sour cream sauce: In a small bowl, stir together the sour cream, yogurt, garlic, and salt to taste.

Make the tomato sauce: In a food processor, combine the tomato sauce, bell pepper, garlic, and salt to taste and process until smooth.

When the manti are cooked, toss with a little melted butter and serve with the sauces.

TIPS:
You can substitute beef for the lamb (and keep the lamb fat) or you can omit the lamb fat and use beef and lamb meat.

Add ½ cup/125 mL water to the filling if you like them juicier.

You can substitute potato or cabbage for the butternut squash, or make the filling with just meat and onions.

Uncooked manti freeze well, and can be steamed directly from frozen (add 10 to 15 minutes).

If possible, use a multi-tier steamer to be able to steam several layers of manti at once. Otherwise, steam them in batches.

Zhanar Khamitova has been cooking all her life, feeding family, friends, and friends-of-friends. Originally from Astana, the capital city of Kazakhstan, she studied baking in the UAE, before relocating to Toronto to be with her daughter, Fatima. **@zhanarbakes**

ADOPT-A-RECIPE Tom Yim

FATIMA KHLIFI AND ZEYNEB BEN REJEB

KOSKSI

Tunisian Couscous

In Tunisia, a large platter of couscous topped with meat, seafood, or vegetables is the quintessential Sunday dinner for many families. Cousins Zeyneb and Fatima brought that cozy family vibe to their meals, cooking lots of delicious food with laughter and music, re-creating a familiar feeling far from home, warmed with a dollop of their spicy homemade harissa.

Couscous is prepared in a variety of ways across North Africa, but the most traditional is in a *couscoussier*, a split-level pot that cooks the couscous in the fragrant steam from the stew cooking below; fortunately, it can still easily be made without one. In the Tunisian style, the couscous is thoroughly moistened and coloured by mixing in some of the flavourful broth from the stew before serving.

Having roots is very, very important to us, to say, "Okay, that's where I come from." Cooking the food of our home is like travelling. Couscous takes a lot of steps, and a lot of touching. You mix the couscous with your hands. And you have the smell of the olive oil and the salt. And so even if it takes twenty minutes, for twenty minutes you're back in your childhood.

Zeyneb Ben Rejeb and Fatima Khlifi are cousins, but grew up in two different countries; Zeyneb in Tunisia and Fatima in France. Zeyneb joined Fatima in Toronto with her family to do her PhD at the University of Toronto. Despite living far apart, they were connected by their Tunisian roots and memories of spending summer holidays together in Tunisia.
@Zeynouba_ben_rejeb
@FatiCookInMix

Prep: 20 min, plus overnight soaking (optional)

Cook: 1 hr 15 min
Makes: 4 to 6 servings

Couscous:

1½ cups/250 g fine or medium couscous

1 tsp salt, or to taste

½ tsp freshly ground black pepper, or to taste

1 tbsp olive oil

2 tbsp warm to hot water

Stew:

4 tbsp olive oil/vegetable oil mix

1 medium onion, finely chopped

10 to 12 oz/300 to 350 g stewing beef, cut into medium pieces

1½ tbsp tomato paste

1 tsp harissa paste, hot paprika, or chili powder, or to taste

½ tbsp ground coriander

½ tsp ground turmeric

1 tsp salt

½ cup/100 g dried chickpeas, soaked overnight and drained, or 1 (15 oz/425 g) can chickpeas

2 medium carrots, halved lengthwise and cut crosswise into 1½- to 2-inch/3 to 5 cm lengths

2 medium potatoes, peeled and each cut into 8 wedges

1 zucchini, peeled in strips for a striped effect, cut crosswise into 1½- to 2-inch/3 to 5 cm lengths

Prepare the couscous: Place the couscous in a large bowl and sprinkle with the salt and black pepper. Drizzle on the olive oil and water and mix everything with your hands.

If using a couscoussier, place the couscous mix in the upper pot and set the pot aside. (You'll place it on the top of the cooking pot once the stew is underway.) If not using a couscoussier, cover the bowl and set aside until the stew is finished.

Make the stew: In the lower pot of a couscoussier or in a heavy-bottomed pot or Dutch oven, heat the oil over medium heat. Add the onion and sauté until soft and translucent, 2 to 5 minutes. Add the beef and sauté for a few minutes until it begins to brown. Add the tomato paste, harissa, coriander, turmeric, and salt and mix well for 2 more minutes.

Add the soaked and drained chickpeas (if using canned, do not add at this stage) and carrots. Pour in enough hot water to cover the meat. Cover and cook until tender, about 30 minutes. Add water as needed to keep the meat covered.

Add the potatoes. If using a couscoussier, set the upper pot with the couscous over the stew (if not using a couscoussier, you will cook the couscous later). Cook the potatoes for 10 minutes, then add the zucchini and cook until softened, about 20 minutes. If using canned chickpeas, add them towards the very end of the cooking. Taste and adjust the seasoning. At the same time, let the couscous steam over the stew for 20 to 25 minutes.

Once the stew is ready, use a slotted spoon or spider to scoop the meat and veggies into a separate pot or bowl.

At this point, if you did not use a couscoussier, add about 2 cups/475 mL of the sauce from the pot, while it is still very hot, to the bowl of dry couscous. Do not mix. Cover tightly with a lid or plastic wrap, leave it for 10 minutes, and then toss with a fork, breaking up clumps. If you did use a couscoussier, transfer the steamed couscous to a large bowl or deep serving plate.

In both cases, finish the couscous by adding 2 more ladles of sauce, mix to combine, cover, and let rest a few minutes until the couscous is moist and soft. Repeat with another ladle of sauce if necessary.

To serve, mound the couscous on a serving plate or platter. Arrange the meat, veggies, and chickpeas on top and drizzle generously with some of the remaining sauce. Ideally, have a bit of harissa on hand for those who like to turn up the heat.

TIPS:

You can use fine or medium couscous, as you prefer.

It is important to cook the stew with the lid on so that the liquid doesn't evaporate too much. You will need enough sauce—at least 3 to 4 cups/700 to 950 mL—at the end to finish the couscous. Top up with a bit of hot water if needed. If desired, garnish with hot or sweet peppers fried in a generous amount of oil until soft.

TAYLOR PARKER
VENISON IN THE WOODS

I met Taylor, a talented hired gun of a professional chef, when he came in to assist on an event. At some point our conversation turned to his Mohawk roots and the dire underrepresentation of First Nations food in Toronto's restaurant scene. Since then, Taylor has played an instrumental part in what I feel is some of The Dep's most important work: an annual Canada Day Supper Club built around Taylor's take on Indigenous ingredients, culture, and culinary philosophy.

Chef's Note: This dish uses a mix of hunted and foraged ingredients, combined with canned goods. Most Indigenous communities struggle to keep to their roots of hunting, fishing, and foraging, adding store-bought items for the sake of making things quick and easy.

Prep: 10 min, plus as much time as you wish to spend outside

Cook: 2½ hr

Makes: 4 servings

Venison:

1 cup/150 g blueberries

2 cups/500 mL red wine (or 2 cups/500 mL water and ¼ cup/60 mL cider vinegar)

2¼ lb/1 kg venison, roughly cut into 1-inch/2.5 cm cubes

Salt and freshly ground black pepper

2 tbsp neutral oil

5 sprigs thyme

Foraged ingredients (see Tips): such as white cedar, white fir needles, juniper berries, bergamot leaves, staghorn sumac, rosehips, elderberries, or elderflowers

Beans:

2 (15 oz/425 g) cans beans of your choice, rinsed and drained (if you can make them from scratch, it's better)

1 cup/150 g chopped fresh herbs (half parsley and half chives is lovely), plus more for garnish

2 lemons, 1 zested and 2 juiced

Salt and freshly ground black pepper

Prepare the venison: In a bowl, stir together the blueberries and red wine (or water plus vinegar).

Season the venison with salt and pepper.

Heat a large Dutch oven until very hot and add the oil. Working in 2 to 3 batches, add the venison and sear, turning only when the meat releases easily and is nicely browned. When all the meat is done, throw it all back into the pot with the fresh thyme. Add any foraged herbs.

Add the wine and the blueberries, stirring to incorporate all the browned bits. Cover and cook over low heat on the stovetop for 2½ hours or bake in a 350°F/180°C oven for the same amount of time. You may need to occasionally top up with enough water just to cover the meat.

Meanwhile, make the beans: In a large bowl, combine the beans, chopped fresh herbs, lemon zest, and lemon juice. Season to taste with salt and pepper. Set aside.

After the venison has been cooking for 2½ hours, or when it's tender, uncover and place over medium-high heat and cook until the liquid thickens to a sauce consistency.

Plate by piling beans first, then add the venison with some of the thickened sauce.

Garnish with some of the fresh herbs. If you found a few edible flowers while you were out on your forage hunt, top with those.

TIPS:
You can substitute almost every component of this dish; use your imagination and get creative. Seared wild mushrooms, for example, would be great to add, even more so if they were in season.

Use what you have but always do your research. Best part is your recipe will be ever-changing. Use what fits in your five fingers (not in your palm).

I grew up on Six Nations reserve in the centre of Hamilton. My parents are the foremost experts on plants native to North America, so I got a horticulture degree basically slammed into my brain before I was eighteen. And I just took all the knowledge they taught me about basic plants and condensed it down into food knowledge.

Taylor Parker is from Six Nations of the Grand River Reserve, where he inherited an extensive knowledge of native plants and foraged foodstuffs from his parents. Taylor has spent much of his professional life working in a diverse range of professional kitchens and as a freelance chef, and recently launched FOR4GED Candle Company in Brantford, Ontario. **@turok_parker @for4gedcandleco.ca**

ADOPT-A-RECIPE   Sean Moore

TAYLOR PARKER

In 2017, when the Canadian government came up with the laughably tone-deaf motto, "Canada 150," its glib erasure of thousands of years of pre-colonial history made me itchy as hell. I was already frustrated by the underrepresentation of Indigenous food in Toronto's food scene in general, and at The Depanneur in particular. I reached out to Taylor

Parker, an accomplished freelance kitchen pro who had come in as a hired gun on a few other private events. Taylor came from the Six Nations of the Grand River near Brantford, and in addition to his professional cooking chops, he had also inherited a lot of indigenous plant knowledge from his family, who had run a nursery and farm on the reserve.

Our conversations turned to the creative possibilities of Native American cuisine. A Canadian concept of terroir—the flavour of a place—would need to start by embracing and celebrating indigenous culinary heritage. **What did the place where I live actually taste like? I realized I had basically no idea.** To begin to understand what the idea of Canadian food means, our food and our food systems desperately needed to reconnect to the land where we live. Over the past few years, the locavore movement and farmers' markets have begun to emphasize the environmental and economic importance of eating locally grown produce, but how many of those ingredients were themselves actually endemic to Ontario?

I invited Taylor to offer a culinary response to the shortsighted Canada 150 idea, and together with Chef Matthew Knight-Barton, they put on Canada 1500 —A First Nations Dinner. The meal showcased a range of wild ingredients harvested by Taylor on the Six Nations reserve: wild garlic chives, berries, mustard greens, and herbs. Taylor smoked and maple-glazed wild-caught Ontario salmon—I hadn't even known we had salmon in Ontario. The Three Sisters (corn, beans, and squash) were given their place of honour in a stunning wild rice pilaf. Young tart apples picked in downtown Toronto became fritters for dessert. What

"I use a lot of wild foraged ingredients that people don't use or see on most menus. In our cuisine there's not the idea of authentic. I guess I could say corn soup is authentic, but I could have corn soup with venison, or bear, or buffalo. Or maybe if I didn't have corn, maybe it's just a soup. It was always about using what you have; some days that's the shank, some days it's the leg. Some days it could just be the marrow. Authentic to me is just using what you have."

had been billed as Ontario venison turned out to be moose, hunted by a cousin, gifted to the chef, and technically forbidden to sell to the public. Good thing this was a free meal included with one's membership to the Rusholme Park Supper Club!

Everything was prepared and plated with the skill of a veteran of fine-dining restaurant kitchens, but the story of the meal ran much deeper. It spoke to the history of the place where we all lived, of what grew and thrived there, of relationships formed over centuries by the people who shared that land. It made me realize my own profound ignorance—abetted by an utter lack of education—of the people and foodways that defined this place long before any settlers set foot upon it.

Over the next few years Taylor would return to The Dep to do a variety of events, and always as a chef of honour on Canada Day. I don't know if it was my own late awakening that made me more aware, or if it was part of a larger, long-overdue societal evolution, but those years also saw a growing recognition of aboriginal voices across the cultural landscape. From political and environmental activism, to arts and culture, to policy and history, the call to decolonize our systems was growing louder. Land acknowledgements became de rigueur; though inadequate, and often glib, their very presence reflected a tectonic shift in Canadians' understanding of our relationship to our place in the world. These dinners became a special offering, the most expensive dinners I hosted, and I made a point of reserving seats to gift to members of First Nations communities, to ensure they had a place at the table, both literally and figuratively.

The more I learned about food history and sustainable food systems, the more things pointed to Indigenous knowledge, values, and wisdom. True to form, Taylor taught me without telling me the answers, but rather by leading me to the truth. Getting menus for his dinners was always a bit of a battle; I'd pester him for weeks and often get only what seemed like a vague list of ingredients. Having spent years trying to craft evocative descriptions for Dep events, I was very attached to the idea of setting clear expectations, and thought it was essential for sales and marketing.

The big lesson came in 2019 when Taylor teamed up with Chef Mark Cutrara, who had largely introduced Toronto to the idea of nose-to-tail dining at his influential restaurant Cowbell. The idea was a "Hunt & Gather" dinner: A group of chef friends would go on an ice-fishing and hunting trip together and make a dinner of what they brought back. As usual I pressed Taylor for a menu that would let me start promoting the event, insisting that people needed to know what was going to be served. As usual, he was hesitant, but ultimately I extracted enough that I could create a write-up. In the end, the chefs' fishing trip was a bust, as they simply sometimes are, and they hadn't caught anywhere near enough to feed twenty-four guests.

Strings were pulled and fish procured from other Indigenous fishers who had stock. A beautiful meal graced the table, but the lesson had finally sunk in: **the very idea of the restaurant, with its set menu and expectations that anything can be eaten on demand, its implication that nature can, or should, be bent to the whim of the chef or the diner, itself was deeply colonial.**

Perhaps to actually embrace an Indigenous cuisine was to forego the notions that any ingredient can be had at any time, that there should be a set menu of dishes with specific names, that can be reproduced year after year, regardless of the season or the fertility of the land. Perhaps the definition of a chef also needed to change: not as someone who can faithfully execute (!) a recipe, but as someone who could bring to life whatever Mother Nature had decided to share. Perhaps every meal is a unique improvisation of availability, and a chef's skill is marked not by the perfection of a fixed dish, but by their ability to make something delicious and nourishing under any circumstances. Perhaps that gift is made more valuable when it serves the whole community and not just a marketplace. Perhaps it embodies a reciprocity with the land that sustains it, with all the people and species that share it, who all must eat from this dish with one spoon.

It is definitely not for me to say what any indigenous cuisine should or should not be—it can be and is many things all at once—but I am grateful to Taylor for quietly reframing my understanding of where I live, what I eat, what I do, and why.

SWEETS

Pies and Tarts

MARDI MICHELS
TARTE FINE AUX POMMES ET À LA CRÈME D'AMANDE
Apple Tart with Almond Cream

SHINJI YAMAGUCHI
MOM'S YOGURT CAKE

LESLIE LINDSAY
BLUEBERRY RHUBARB PIE

PETER MINAKI
EKMEK KADAYIFI
Shredded Phyllo with Custard

SHIELA LABAO
HAUPIA PIE
Chocolate Coconut Pie

Cakes and Bakes

MOMO YOSHIDA
OCHA-IRI SUKŌN TO OCHA JERĪ
Matcha Scones with Tea Jelly

AMIRA ESKENAZI
MONTREAL-STYLE CHEESE "BAGELEH"

FRANÇOISE BRIET
BANANA RUM CAKE WITH BEER-CARAMEL SAUCE

RALUCA COJOCARIU
PRAJITURA CU SUC DE ROSII
Romanian Tomato Juice Cake

TONIA DI RISIO
KUGELHOPF
Austrian Yeast Cake

DORIS FIN
MEDOVIK
Russian Honey Cream Cake

DANIEL HOLLOWAY
PURPLE YAM SCONES WITH PASSION FRUIT CREAM

Sweets and Treats

ROBIN "SQUIGGY" DUTT
PURPLE FRENCH TOAST

LAURA REPO
SEEDY GRANOLA

MIRELLE BLASSNIG
RICO PAVÊ
Brazilian Chocolate-Caramel No-Bake Cake

KEISHA LUKE
KEY LIME KUPS

ABEL CARTAYA-CARRAL
CASCOS DE TORONJA
Cuban Candied Grapefruit Shells

SHEM BARKER
CROP OVER CONKIES
Barbadian Dessert Tamales

MARIA ROZYNSKA
KUTIA
Barley and Poppy Seed Pudding

CHRISTINE MANNING
SEVILLE ORANGE MARMALADE

MARDI MICHELS

TARTE FINE AUX POMMES ET À LA CRÈME D'AMANDE

Apple Tart with Almond Cream

I'm not much of a baker, but this recipe is fantastic: fast, easy, virtually foolproof, beautiful to behold, and somehow even more delicious than it looks. The only hard part is not eating it all.

Prep: 30 min

Cook: 30 min

Makes: 4 to 6 servings

Almond Cream:

2 tbsp/30 g unsalted butter, at room temperature

2 tbsp granulated sugar

1 large egg yolk, at room temperature

½ tsp pure vanilla extract

4 tbsp almond meal

¼ tsp fine sea salt

Galette:

1 sheet (about 8 oz/250 g) puff pastry

2 to 3 small unpeeled apples (about 9 oz/250 g), very thinly sliced

1 tbsp/15 g unsalted butter, melted

½ tbsp brown sugar

1 large egg, lightly beaten

1 tbsp apricot jam

1 tbsp warm water

Make the almond cream: In a bowl with a handheld mixer, beat the butter and granulated sugar on high until smooth and creamy, about 2 minutes. Add the egg yolk and vanilla and beat until well combined. Your mixture may look a little curdled, but that's okay. Using a rubber spatula, gently fold in the almond meal and salt until paste-like. Cover the mixture with plastic wrap and set aside until ready to use.

Prepare the galette: Preheat the oven to 400°F/200°C. Line a baking sheet with parchment paper.

On a lightly floured surface, roll out the puff pastry into a rectangle about 10 × 12 inches/25 × 30 cm. Place on the lined baking sheet and spread the almond cream evenly over the top, leaving a border of around ¾ inch/2 cm on all sides. Smooth the almond cream with an offset spatula.

Layer the apple slices on top of the almond cream in a single layer, overlapping slightly. Brush with the melted butter and sprinkle with the brown sugar.

Using the tines of a fork, mark the border around the edge and brush the beaten egg around these edges.

Bake until the pastry is golden brown around the edges, the almond cream is slightly puffy, and the apples are baked, 25 to 30 minutes.

Meanwhile, in a small bowl, combine the jam and warm water.

When the galette comes out of the oven, brush the apples gently with the jam mixture. Serve warm or at room temperature.

TIP:

Other flavours of jam can be used instead of apricot, if desired, but be aware that any jam that is not clear/colourless will add a slight colour to the top of the apples.

> *I'm a full-time teacher and I teach French to seven- to twelve-year-old boys. I also teach them cooking. It's not something that you'd expect, but they're really into cooking and they love making pastry. I've learned a lot from teaching kids because they have no fear, and that is the way that you have to go into something like pastry. You just have to think, "We're doing it, it's going to work, or it might not work but we'll learn something from it."*

Mardi Michels is a full-time French teacher and the author of *In the French Kitchen with Kids*, as well as *eat.live.travel .write*—a blog focusing on culinary adventures near and far. @eatlivtravwrite

ADOPT A RECIPE   Peter Hanson

The yogurt cake I made for the cookbook is no fancy recipe or technique— it's what my mother cooked for me. I really missed this cake when I moved out from my parents' house, so I learned from my mom how to make it. When I moved to Canada, I started making it for friends, and they were asking for the recipe. So this is for my mother, Yumoko. I really want to show her that her cake has been shared with so many people.

Shinji Yamaguchi is the chef and owner behind Gushi Foods, specializing in creating authentic Japanese street food experiences. His *karrage* (Japanese-style fried chicken), and *kushi-katsu* (panko-coated skewers of meat or veggies) have been recognized as some of the best street food in Toronto. @gushitoronto

SHINJI YAMAGUCHI
MOM'S YOGURT CAKE

Shinji's friendly and generous personality evokes *omotenashi*, the Japanese spirit of thoughtful hospitality. It is informed by Zen philosophy, which suggests that any activity, if done carefully and mindfully enough, can be a spiritual path. Shinji so clearly loves sharing his culture and cuisine, and his delight so genuine when people enjoy his food, that I think he is well on his way. While not a "cake" exactly—more of a panna cotta—this light, refreshing dessert has a special place in Shinji's heart.

Prep: 30 min
Cook: 20 min, plus 3 hr chilling time
Makes: 6 to 10 servings

¾ cup/175 mL whole milk

½ cup/100 g sugar

1 tbsp unflavored gelatin powder (10 g, from 1½ envelopes)

¼ cup/60 mL boiling water

1 cup/250 mL whipping cream (35%)

1 cup/250 mL plain yogurt

Topping:

4 kiwis

4 tbsp sugar

Juice of ½ lemon

4 tbsp blueberry jam

In a medium saucepan, combine the milk and sugar and heat over low heat until the sugar melts, about 5 minutes. Remove from the heat.

In a small bowl, combine the gelatin and boiling water and let stand until the liquid is absorbed, about 3 minutes. Add the warm milk/sugar mixture and stir to dissolve the gelatin. Let cool to room temperature.

In a medium bowl, using a whisk or hand mixer, whip the cream until stiff peaks form.

Stir the yogurt into the cooled milk/gelatin mix and then gently fold in the whipped cream.

Pour the mixture into a 9-inch/23 cm springform pan and cover with plastic wrap. Refrigerate for 3 hours to set.

Prepare the topping: Peel 2 of the kiwis and finely dice. In a small skillet, combine the diced kiwis, sugar, and lemon juice and cook over low heat, stirring gently, until the sugar melts and the excess liquid evaporates, 5 to 10 minutes. Set aside to cool.

When the cake is set, run a knife around the edge to loosen it. Unlatch the sides of the springform pan and gently lift away the ring.

Top with the cooked kiwi mixture and blueberry jam. Slice the remaining 2 kiwis and arrange on top.

TIPS:
Make sure to hydrate the gelatin well in order to achieve the correct texture.

The cake can be topped with any fruit, depending on your personal preference. You can use a combination of fresh or canned fruits, compote, or jam.

Note that if you use fresh kiwis or pineapple, garnish just before serving so the ezymes in the fruit don't melt the gelatin.

 ADOPT-A-RECIPE Momoyo Yoshida

Things like communal eating make you feel part of a community; it makes you feel seen. You can do everything online, but what does that leave you? Humans hunger for touch and connection. You know, saying hi to the guy behind the cash register as you buy your coffee. You're connected: these invisible threads are tying you to your neighbourhood and your community. These things are really, really important.

You'll find **Leslie Lindsay** at the intersection of food and culture. She is an enthusiastic, frugal foodie who embraces local terroir and its potential for unique flavour as an expression of place.

LESLIE LINDSAY

BLUEBERRY RHUBARB PIE

Prep: 40 min

Cook: 45 min

Makes: one 9-inch/23 cm pie (6 servings)

Leslie worked at the nearby Dufferin Grove Park, helping coordinate their farmers' market, community dinners, and baking in their wood-fired bread ovens. Somewhere along the way I thought to ask her to bring over one of her amazing pies as a dessert for my weekly Drop-In Dinners. Seasonal and often still warm, served à la mode with vanilla ice cream, they became the iconic finish to many of the meals I cooked at The Dep.

Crust:

1½ cups/195 g unbleached all-purpose flour

Pinch of sea salt

8 tbsp/120 g chilled unsalted butter

½ cup/125 mL ice-cold water

Filling:

3 cups/445 g blueberries

1 cup/100 g chopped rhubarb

1 cup/200 g granulated sugar

1 tbsp fresh lemon juice

¼ tsp grated nutmeg

All-purpose flour

Make the crust: Place the flour in a large bowl. Add the salt and stir with a fork to combine. Add the butter and use a knife to chop it into pea-size pieces, allowing the pieces to be coated with flour as you go. Next, using clean hands, begin incorporating the butter into the flour, gently breaking the pieces up until you have a shaggy mixture of flour combined with small lumps of butter. Go gently and try not to overwork the dough.

Dribble a bit of the ice water into the bowl, turning the dough with your hands as you go. The goal is to incorporate enough water to make a cohesive dough that holds together without making the mixture too wet. When the dough begins to hold together, lightly press it into a ball. Transfer the ball of dough into a clean kitchen towel, wrap it, and put it into the fridge to chill whilst preparing the filling.

Make the filling: In the same bowl that you mixed the dough, combine the blueberries, rhubarb, sugar, lemon juice, and nutmeg. Mix thoroughly. The remnants of the flour from the crust will combine with the fruit and help to thicken the filling. Sprinkle another 1 to 2 tablespoons flour over the filling mixture.

Position a rack in the centre of the oven and preheat the oven to 425°F/220°C.

Take the pie dough out of the fridge. Lightly flour a counter space and rolling pin. Place the ball of dough in the centre of the lightly floured space. Begin to roll into a round from the centre outwards until you have a round 13 to 14 inches/33 to 36 cm across. Fold the dough in half and then in half again. Pick it up and place it into a 9-inch/23 cm pie plate (preferably glass) so that the point is in the middle, then unfold and drape the dough evenly across the pie plate.

Spoon the fruit filling into the centre of the pie crust and even it out. Fold the edges of the dough up and over the filling, making a rustic edge. Try to drape the dough so that it looks pleasing to the eye and evenly distributed around the pie plate.

Transfer the pie to the oven and bake for 5 minutes. Reduce the oven temperature to 375°F/190°C and continue to bake until the crust is evenly browned, the filling is juicy and bubbling, and the pie is "singing" in the oven as a heavenly smell of pie fills the kitchen, about 40 more minutes. If the crust begins to burn before the filling has cooked sufficiently, cover the darkening edges with strips of aluminum foil to prevent over-browning and return it to the oven until the fruit is done.

Take the pie out of the oven and let it cool before slicing. This will give the filling time to set and thicken before serving.

TIPS:

This basic pastry dough recipe can be used for many fruit pies. You can swap in fresh apples for instance, a mix of other fresh berries, pears with a grating of fresh ginger, and so on.

I like to serve pies with softly whipped cream that has been lightly sweetened with a little maple syrup.

EKMEK KADAYIFI
Shredded Phyllo with Custard

Prep: 1 hr, plus 1 hr thawing and 4 hr chilling

Cook: 45 min

Makes: 9 to 12 servings

Peter is big, brash, loud, and friendly—he reminds me of a few of my old Greek friends in Montreal. He is also a very knowledgeable and capable chef, and one of the only people I know who makes his own phyllo pastry from scratch. This luscious dessert actually comes together pretty easily, with delicate shredded *kataifi* pastry now available in many supermarket freezers. It features a hint of the unique flavour of *mastiha*, aka mastic, a piney resin from the island of Chios; it's more authentic with it, but still totally delicious without.

Pastry:

½ lb/225 g frozen kataifi pastry (see Tip)

1¾ cups/425 mL water

2 cups/400 g granulated sugar

3 strips of lemon zest

1 small cinnamon stick

4 tbsp/60 g unsalted butter, melted

Custard:

4 cups/950 mL whole milk

½ tsp ground mastiha (see Tip)

3 large eggs

6 tbsp fine semolina

1½ tbsp corn starch

½ cup/100 g granulated sugar

Assembly:

1½ cups/350 mL whipping cream

1½ tsp vanilla extract

4 tbsp icing sugar

1½ tbsp powdered milk

¾ cup/75 g finely chopped pistachios or almonds

Prepare the pastry: Set the frozen kataifi pastry on the counter and let it thaw for 1 hour. You may refreeze the remainder in the package for future use.

In a medium pot, combine the water, granulated sugar, lemon zest, and cinnamon stick and bring to a boil. Reduce the heat to medium and simmer for 8 minutes. Remove from the heat and allow the syrup to cool. Discard the lemon zest and cinnamon stick.

Position a rack in the centre of the oven and preheat the oven to 350°F/180°C.

Place the thawed kataifi in an 11 × 13-inch/28 × 33 cm baking pan and untangle it with your hands. Pour the melted butter over the kataifi and toss with your hands to ensure the butter has coated all of the pastry. Spread the kataifi evenly over the surface of the pan. Place in the oven and bake until golden, about 30 minutes.

Remove from the oven and while still hot, ladle the syrup over the pastry. Allow to cool.

Make the custard: In a medium pot, combine the milk and ground mastiha and bring to just scalding over medium heat.

In a large bowl, whisk the eggs, semolina, corn starch, and granulated sugar until smooth.

Whisking with one hand, slowly add 2 to 3 ladles of the scalded milk to warm the eggs (this is called tempering). Now pour the tempered custard mixture into the remaining milk in the pot, set over medium heat, and stir until the mixture has thickened to a custard consistency, about 10 minutes. Remove from the heat, place plastic wrap directly on the surface of the custard so a skin doesn't form, and let cool for at least 30 minutes.

Once the custard has cooled (your kataifi base will also have cooled by now), pour the custard over the kataifi base and spread it out evenly. Allow to cool to room temperature and then refrigerate for at least 4 hours.

For assembly: In a bowl with a whisk or hand mixer, beat together the cream and vanilla. As you beat, gradually the add icing sugar until soft peaks form. Sprinkle in the powdered milk and continue to mix until stiff peaks form.

Place the whipped cream in a piping bag fitted with a star tip and pipe out rosettes on top of the custard. Sprinkle the chopped nuts over the whipped cream. Serve immediately or place in the fridge until ready to serve. Cut into 9 to 12 slices.

TIP:
Kataifi *pastry and ground* mastiha *(mastic) can be found at Greek or Middle Eastern specialty shops.*

ADOPT-A-RECIPE   Ann Ball

There's a lot of good and bad history between Turkey and Greece, and this recipe came to mainland Greece, as we know it today, with Asia Minor Greeks. There were a lot of Turks living in what is now Greece, and there were Greeks living in what is now Turkey. When the Ottoman Empire fell, the powers that be said, "We're kicking everybody out," so there were massive population exchanges. They brought many dishes with them, such as this.

Peter Minaki puts his passion for authentic Greek cuisine front and centre. His blog and cookbooks are reliable sources for delicious Mediterranean recipes. **@kalofagas**

SHIELA LABAO

HAUPIA PIE

Chocolate Coconut Pie

Seriously, who doesn't love pie? But I don't know a lot of people who love it quite as much as Shiela, who used The Dep as a springboard to turn a ten-plus-year hobby/obsession into a new career as a pie maker and instructor. This pie is inspired by Hawaiian haupia pie, a coconut and chocolate cream pie; Shiela adds *macapuno*, a kind of soft, sweetened coconut preserve common in Southeast Asian desserts, and a connection to her Filipino roots.

I'm originally from the Philippines but I spent a considerable amount of time in the Middle East and later, moved to North America to a very tiny town called Kalamazoo in Michigan. My parents are Baptist and know that joining a church is a good way to find community. Of course, in the Midwest, everyone bakes, so there was a group of church ladies who would just take kids away and say, "Let's bake." It was there that I learned how to bake an apple pie. And I was obsessed.

Shiela Labao is a self-taught baker of over ten years who recently opened a new pie company, called, appropriately enough, New Pie Co. @newpieco

Prep: 30 min, plus overnight chilling
Cook: 35 min

Makes: one 10-inch/25 cm pie (8 to 10 servings)

Crust:

1 cup/130 g all-purpose flour

4 tbsp sweetened shredded coconut

½ tsp salt

8 tbsp/120 g cold unsalted butter

⅓ cup/75 mL cold water

1 large egg, beaten

Filling:

6 tbsp corn starch

½ cup/125 mL water

1 (13.5 oz/400 mL) can coconut milk

1½ cups/350 mL whole milk

½ cup/100 g granulated sugar

1 tsp vanilla extract

1 tsp coconut extract

3 oz/85 g dark baking chocolate, roughly chopped

3 tbsp macapuno preserves or shredded coconut

Assembly:

1½ cups/350 mL heavy cream (at least 35%)

1 tsp vanilla extract

5 tbsp toasted coconut flakes, for garnish

Make the crust: In a bowl, combine the flour, shredded coconut, and salt. Cube the butter and add to the dry ingredients. Break the butter chunks into smaller pieces by flattening them out in between your fingers, tossing the smaller pieces into the flour as you go–you are aiming for large but flat chunks of butter.

Once you have flattened all the pieces, add the cold water in three stages, gently squeezing to incorporate as you go. When the dough is able to come together in one large piece, turn it out onto a clean work surface.

To create a flaky crust, you want to create long, thin layers of butter in the dough. Start by slightly flattening the dough and then smearing it forward using your palms. Scrape up the dough, fold in half, and repeat this step three times. The result should be cohesive but not fully uniform. Wrap the dough in plastic wrap and refrigerate for at least 10 minutes until the butter solidifies.

Roll out the dough to a thickness of ⅛ inch/3 mm. Transfer the dough to a 10-inch/25 cm pie plate and press the dough into the bottom and sides of the pie plate, ensuring that there is no space between the dough and the plate. Trim the excess dough using scissors, leaving about 1½ inches/4 cm of dough over the rim of the plate to create your favourite crimp style. (Beginners: fold over the extra dough and press in place with equally spaced thumb prints or a fork.) Place the pie crust back in the fridge to help re-solidify the butter.

Preheat the oven to 400°F/200°C.

Place the crust on a baking sheet and brush the beaten egg over the top of the crimps. Line the bottom of the crust with parchment paper and fill with pie weights or dried beans. Bake the crust until golden brown, 25 to 30 minutes.

Remove the weights and parchment paper and bake until the bottom of the crust is no longer translucent, another 3 minutes. Set the crust aside to cool.

Make the filling: In a small bowl, combine the corn starch and water and mix well until completely smooth. Set aside.

In a medium pot, combine the coconut milk, whole milk, sugar, and vanilla and coconut extracts. Heat the mixture until steamy but not boiling and whisk in the corn starch mixture. Bring to a boil while constantly whisking and scraping the bottom and sides of the pot. In about 5 minutes it will thicken and you will start to see big bubbles rising from the bottom. Remove from the heat.

Divide the mixture in half in separate bowls. Mix the dark chocolate into one of the bowls, turning it into a chocolate pudding. Mix the macapuno preserves into the other bowl. Cover the puddings with plastic wrap to prevent a skin from forming and let them cool slightly.

Assemble the pie: Pour the chocolate pudding into the crust. Level the surface with a spoon. Pour the coconut pudding on top and level the surface again. Let the pie cool; cover the pie loosely with plastic wrap and set in the fridge overnight.

When ready to serve, combine the heavy cream and vanilla in a bowl and whip until soft peaks form (see Tips). Top the pie with the whipped cream and garnish with the toasted coconut flakes. Store leftovers in the fridge.

TIPS:
If possible, use pure extracts to get the best flavour.

If you'd like to stabilize the whipped cream to last longer, combine 4 tsp unflavored gelatin powder and ¼ cup/ 60 mL cold water and mix well. Heat up in the microwave (or a double boiler) for 10 to 15 minutes until liquid, then add to a mixer bowl with the whipping cream and vanilla extract. Whisk on high speed until medium to stiff peaks form.

Zen philosophy is a big part of the tea ceremony, and from Zen we learn the expression: "Ichi-go ichi-e," or "Once in a lifetime." Every single moment, even right now with you and me chatting, this is only once in a lifetime. We're never going to have the exact same conversation again. So, that means you have to enjoy every single moment. If you think that way, especially if you have the tea in front of you, that moment is just so valuable and so special. That's the essence of the tea ceremony.

Momo Yoshida is a Certified Tea Sommelier and the founder and owner of Momo Tea. @momoteatoronto

OCHA-IRI SUKŌN TO OCHA JERĪ

Matcha Scones with Tea Jelly

Prep: 30 min, plus steeping and cooling
Cook: 20 to 30 min
Makes: 16 scones

Momo is a serious tea lover. A Certified Tea Sommelier, a member of Tea Guild of Canada, as well as the Urasenke school of *chanoyu* (Japanese tea ceremony), her tea workshops at The Dep were a friendly, approachable introduction to the history, philosophy, and rituals of traditional Japanese tea. Presented by her wearing one of her beautiful kimonos, the experience illuminated the complex relationships between food, drink, culture, and identity. At the same time, Momo also loves the simplicity of a fresh cup of tea with a tasty scone, and so developed this recipe that connects Japanese matcha with the joys of an afternoon tea.

Tea Jelly:

1½ cups/350 mL strong steeped tea (green, or your favourite kind)

1 cup/200 g granulated sugar

1 g kanten (agar) powder

Scones:

2 cups/350 g all-purpose flour

⅓ cup/80 g sugar

1 tbsp/15 g baking powder

½ tsp/2 g baking soda

¾ tsp/3 g salt

8 tbsp/120 g cold unsalted butter

1 large egg

¼ cup/90 g plain yogurt

1 tsp/5 g matcha powder

2 tsp/10 g genmaicha tea (see Tips), ground to a powder in spice grinder

Make the tea jelly: Start by using 1½ cups/350 mL water to steep your favourite tea, but twice as strong as you would normally make it. Steep for 30 minutes, then strain the tea into a small pot.

Add the sugar to the pot and stir to dissolve. Add the kanten powder and bring to a boil over medium heat. Remove from the heat and let it start to gel as it cools down. Once it is completely cool, transfer to a small jar or bowl and refrigerate.

Make the scones: Position a rack in the upper third of the oven and preheat the oven to 375°F/190°C.

In a large bowl, mix the flour, sugar, baking powder, baking soda, and salt. Cut the cold butter into cubes and use your hands to incorporate into the flour. Work fast, making sure the butter doesn't melt.

In a small bowl or measuring cup, combine the egg and yogurt. Add to the flour and mix until the dough just comes together. Divide the dough in half.

Incorporate the matcha powder into half of the dough and the genmaicha into the other half and mix roughly—it should not be fully incorporated, but rather offer some visual texture. (If only using one flavour, you can add the tea powder to the dry flour mixture to start out with.) Flatten each type of dough into a disc 1 inch/2.5 cm thick. If the butter melted while mixing the dough, chill the discs for 30 minutes to firm up the dough.

Cut out the scones using a 2-inch/5 cm scone/biscuit cutter. Transfer the scones to a baking sheet and bake until lightly golden on top, 20 to 30 minutes.

Remove from the oven and transfer to a wire rack to cool slightly.

Serve the tea jelly with the warm scones and tea.

TIPS:

As an alternative to the genmaicha (brown rice tea) powder, you can use 1½ tsp/5 g hojicha (roasted green tea) powder.

The tea jelly and the dough for the scones can be made the day before and refrigerated.

AMIRA ESKENAZI

MONTREAL-STYLE CHEESE "BAGELEH"

As a fellow Jewish ex-Montrealer, Amira and I connected right out of the gate. When I invited another one—author David Sax (*Save the Deli*)—to host a Table Talk about the history of Montreal, Jews, and delis, I instantly thought of this old-school dessert, and tapped Amira to make it for the event. Needless to say, she absolutely nailed it.

Despite the name, these are not "bagels" per se; rather they are similar to a lightly sweet cheese Danish, made with a flaky flat dough instead of puff pastry, and are found almost exclusively in a handful of Montreal Jewish bakeries.

The recipe I've included is very very symbolic of my childhood. . . . I made it because I didn't see it anywhere and I've worked in maybe fifteen countries. There's just nothing quite like it. It's super comforting and delicious, not too sweet, and the dough is perfectly flaky, but not too puffy. It's perfect with a cup of coffee or tea. It's just the best.

Amira Eskenazi is a veteran international chef having worked on a number of continents over the past two decades. She was Head Chef on tour with Cirque du Soleil for five years and then she spent seven years as a chef on private yachts in the US, the Caribbean, and Europe. She recently relocated to Los Angeles to work as a private chef on Harry Styles's world tour.
@sister_chef

Prep: 1 hr (including dough resting time)
Cook: 40 min
Makes: 8

Dough:

2 cups/260 g all-purpose flour

2 tsp baking powder

1 tbsp sugar

¼ tsp salt

8 tbsp/120 g unsalted butter, cut into cubes

½ cup/125 mL full-fat sour cream

1 large egg

Filling:

1 lb/450 g dry full-fat cottage cheese or farmer cheese

1 large egg

½ cup/100 g sugar

¼ tsp salt

2 tbsp orange zest

1 tbsp flour

To Finish:

Egg wash:
1 egg + 1 tbsp water

1 cup/200 g sugar

Make the dough: In a large bowl (or food processor), combine the flour, baking powder, sugar, and salt. Blend by hand (or pulse the processor a few times). Add the butter and rub between your fingers until it's incorporated (or pulse until the mixture resembles chunky sand). Add the sour cream and egg and mix (or pulse) until the dough comes together. It should be soft. Flatten the dough into a square and wrap with plastic wrap. Refrigerate for 30 minutes.

Meanwhile, make the filling: In a medium bowl, stir together the cottage cheese, egg, sugar, salt, orange zest, and flour. Refrigerate until ready to use.

To finish: Preheat the oven to 350°F/180°C. Line a standard sheet pan with parchment paper.

Divide the dough in half and let rest on the counter for 15 minutes to soften slightly. With your hands, gently shape each half into a 3 × 7-inch/7.5 × 18 cm rectangle. On a lightly floured surface, roll out the dough into a 12 × 16-inch/30 × 40 cm rectangle, about ⅛ inch/3 mm thick.

Cut the rolled-out dough lengthwise into two 6 × 16-inch/15 × 20 cm rectangles. Don't move them. Repeat with the other half of the dough for a total of 4 long rectangles.

Brush one long edge of each rectangle with the egg wash. On the opposite side of the dough (no egg wash), place one-quarter of the filling, by the spoonful, along the edge, leaving a ¼-inch/6 mm border. Slowly lift the edge closest to the filling and roll the dough over the filling. Continue rolling until the filling is enclosed and the seam is underneath the roll.

Repeat with the remaining dough and filling.

Using half the sugar, sprinkle 1 tablespoon in each of 8 spots on the prepared baking sheet.

Take each roll and cut it in half (for a total of 8 pieces). Form each half into a horseshoe, pinching the ends to seal. Gently place it on top of the sugar on the baking sheet. Brush with the egg wash and sprinkle each horseshoe with 1 tablespoon sugar.

Bake until the bagels are golden brown and starting to crack on top, about 40 minutes. Remove to a rack and let cool.

Serve at room temperature or warm with sour cream and berries if you wish, or just on their own.

FRANÇOISE BRIET

BANANA RUM CAKE WITH BEER-CARAMEL SAUCE

Françoise packs a lot into a little package: scientist, chef, nutritionist, and beer aficionado. Her fascination with incorporating the diverse flavour profiles of local craft beers into dishes has led to some pretty tasty places, like the beer caramel sauce that elevates this luscious cake. And seriously, who isn't looking for something amazing to use up those dying bananas?

Cake:

5 ripe bananas

1½ cups/250 g all-purpose flour

2 tsp/10 g baking powder

Salt

½ cup/150 g butter, at room temperature

¾ cup/175 g light brown cane sugar

4 large eggs, separated, at room temperature

3 tbsp/45 ml gold or dark rum

Sauce:

½ cup/125 mL local craft beer (choose your favourite pale, Scottish, or amber ale)

½ cup/100 g dark brown/demerara sugar

1 tbsp/15 g butter

1 tsp/5 mL vanilla extract

½ cup/125 mL whipping cream (35%)

Preheat the oven to 410°F/210°C. Grease a 9-inch/23 cm square cake pan.

Make the cake: In a bowl, mash the bananas with a potato masher or a fork. Set aside.

In a separate bowl, whisk together the flour, baking powder, and ½ teaspoon salt. Set aside.

In a stand mixer fitted with the paddle (or in a bowl with a handheld mixer), beat the butter on high speed until smooth and creamy, about 1 minute. Add the brown sugar and beat on high speed for 2 minutes until creamed together. Scrape down the sides and bottom of the bowl with a rubber spatula as needed. Add the egg yolks to the butter/sugar mixture one at a time, beating after each. Beat in the mashed bananas and rum, scraping down the sides of the bowl as needed.

Add the flour mixture and mix until just incorporated. Do not overmix. The batter will be slightly thick, with a few lumps.

In a separate bowl, whip the egg whites with a pinch of salt until they hold stiff peaks. Gently fold the beaten egg whites into the batter. Spread the batter into the prepared pan.

Bake for 10 minutes. Reduce the oven temperature to 320°F/160°C and bake until a toothpick inserted in the centre of the cake comes out clean, another 50 minutes.

Remove the cake from the oven and cool completely in the pan on a wire rack.

Make the sauce: In a small saucepan, bring the beer to a gentle boil over medium heat. Reduce the heat to medium-low and simmer, stirring occasionally, until the beer is reduced to about ¼ cup/60 mL (about 10 minutes). Remove from the heat and allow to cool for a few minutes.

In a medium saucepan, combine the brown sugar, butter, and 3 tablespoons beer reduction over high heat, and boil for 2 minutes. Remove from the heat. Stir in the vanilla and heavy cream, return to the heat and bring to a boil again. Boil for 1 minute. Remove from the heat and allow to cool. (The caramel will thicken as it cools.)

Serve slices of cake with a drizzle of beer-caramel sauce.

TIPS:

I like to serve this cake with Icelandic yogurt, or a mix of whipped cream and mascarpone infused with freshly ground pepper and a pinch of sugar.

For a gourmet presentation, I sprinkle the top with caramelized coconut chips or beer-caramelized pecans to add some crunchiness.

For a lighter, healthier version, replace 5 tablespoons of sugar in the cake batter with ground hemp seeds, which bring a nice nutty flavour to the cake.

If the beer-caramel sauce gets too thick, add a bit of the leftover beer reduction.

 Brent McLaughlin

Françoise Briet is the former chef of the General Consulate of France in Toronto, and the owner of Malty and Hoppy Delicacy, a company that uses Ontario craft beer in small-batch artisan jellies, jams, and other delicacies. Before that, Françoise was a clinical research scientist in the area of metabolic nutrition.
@maltyand hoppydelicacy

This is a cake that my mom used to make a lot when I was growing up in Romania. Now, looking back, I can see how it was difficult for my parents, because there was an economic crisis. It was a little hard to find ingredients such as butter and whipping cream. But my mom did a good job, and always cooked good meals on the healthy side. When you grow up with good home-cooked food, you can't really stray too far from that.

Raluca Cojocariu is a chef and food entrepreneur. She travels to eat and learn new recipes. She loves farmers' markets, food stories, and new ingredients. **@ralucasfoodnotes**

RALUCA COJOCARIU

PRAJITURA CU SUC DE ROSII

Romanian Tomato Juice Cake

Prep: 2 hr
Cook: 1 hr
Makes: 16 servings

Raluca connected with The Dep in many ways, as a customer and as a cook, and then when the cookbook came into being, as a project manager and recipe tester. Raluca and I both have Romanian backgrounds, so I tapped her for a family recipe. This attractive, not-too-sweet cake features an unexpected ingredient—tomato juice—to leaven and colour the cake, which is layered with a lemony cream of wheat custard and a stripe of tart plum marmalade. (And no, it doesn't taste like tomato!)

In a medium bowl, whisk together ¾ cup/90 g of the icing sugar, the tomato purée, and oil. Add the ammonium carbonate and mix well. Add all the flour and incorporate into the mix with a rubber spatula.

Place the dough on a floured surface and knead for a few minutes until the dough is uniform. Divide the dough in 4 equal portions, wrap in plastic, and refrigerate for 15 minutes.

Meanwhile, in a medium saucepan, combine the milk and remaining 1½ cups/180 g icing sugar and bring to boil over medium heat, stirring constantly. When the milk starts to boil, reduce the heat and slowly whisk in the cream of wheat, whisking constantly to prevent lumps. Cook until it thickens to a custardy consistency, 6 to 10 minutes.

Remove from the heat and add the lemon zest, lemon juice, and butter and mix well. Cover and set aside to cool down and firm up.

Preheat the oven to 350°F/180°C. Coat an 8 × 12-inch/20 × 30 cm sheet pan with oil.

Remove one ball of dough from the fridge and using a rolling pin or glass bottle, roll out directly into the pan, making sure that the entire surface is covered and evenly distributed.

Bake until golden brown, 10 to 12 minutes. Keep an eye on it as it can easily burn! Remove from the oven, gently slide a cake spatula under to help detach from the pan, and slide the biscuit layer onto a rack to cool. Be careful as it is very fragile when hot and can easily break, but you only need 1 out of 4 layers to be intact.

Repeat with the rest of the dough balls, making sure the pan is cleaned and oiled every time.

When the biscuit layers have cooled, they will firm up and you can start assembling the cake. Save the best-looking biscuit layer for the top.

Place a sheet of parchment paper at the bottom of the same sheet pan and add one biscuit layer. Top with half of the custard and spread evenly. Place a second biscuit layer on top and cover evenly with the plum marmalade. Follow with a third biscuit layer and the rest of the custard. Finish with the best-looking biscuit layer.

Cover with parchment paper and wrap the whole thing in plastic wrap. Place a cutting board or another tray topped with a plate on top to slightly compress the cake. The biscuit layers will soften as they absorb some of the moisture from the custard and the marmalade. Refrigerate overnight.

Cut into diamonds, triangles, or squares.

2¼ cups/270 g icing sugar

14 tbsp/200 mL plain strained tomato purée (passata), or a mix of tomato paste and tomato juice

¾ cup/175 mL vegetable oil, plus more for the baking pan

1 tsp ammonium carbonate (baker's ammonia) or baking soda

4 cups/520 g all-purpose flour, plus more as needed

2 cups/500 mL milk

6 tbsp cream of wheat (fine semolina)

Grated zest and juice of 1 lemon

10 tbsp/150 g unsalted butter, cut into 1-inch/2.5 cm cubes

1 cup/250 mL tart plum marmalade (see Tip)

TIP:
Romanian plum marmalade is a thick jam that is usually cooked without added sugar. You can substitute with any jam as long as it is tart, smooth enough to spread evenly, and adds a bit of colour. If the jam is too sweet, add some lemon juice or pomegranate molasses to balance it out.

Prep: At least 2 hr (this includes two rises of the dough)

Cook: 30 min

Makes: 1 cake (10 to 12 servings)

5 cups/650 g bread flour or all-purpose flour

½ cup/100 g granulated sugar

1 tsp salt

1 (¼ oz/7 g) envelope quick-rise (instant) yeast

16 tbsp/240 g unsalted butter (see Tips)

1¾ cups/425 mL milk (1%, 2%, buttermilk all okay)

2 large eggs, beaten

6 heaping tbsp light brown sugar

2 tbsp ground cinnamon

Baking spray (with flour)

1 cup/100 g walnuts, chopped (optional; see Tips)

1 tbsp sifted icing sugar, for dusting

TONIA DI RISIO
KUGELHOPF
Austrian Yeast Cake

Tonia is a visual artist whose projects often involve food. She came to The Dep with her collaborator Claire to give a Table Talk about Alchemy, their artists' retreat that explores the relationships between artistic practice and the growing, cooking, and sharing of food in a community setting. For dessert that night, Tonia baked this kugelhopf, a brioche-like Austrian cake, in the ceramic mould her grandmother brought with her to Canada in the '50s. It gives the cake its tall, distinctive shape—which explains its nickname, "Hat Cake"—but a regular Bundt pan will also work fine.

In a large bowl, combine the flour, granulated sugar, and salt. Stir in the yeast. Make a well in the centre of the mixture.

In a small saucepan, melt the butter over medium heat. Add the milk and heat until it is just warm or hot to the touch.

Pour the warm butter/milk mixture into the well in the flour mixture. Add the beaten eggs and mix together with a wooden spoon until you have a smooth dough.

Cover the bowl with plastic wrap or beeswax cloth. Leave it to rise in a warm place until it doubles in size, at least 45 minutes to 1 hour. If you have a cool space, cover the bowl with a towel (sometimes I use a big old wool scarf).

In a small bowl, mix the brown sugar and cinnamon and set aside.

Thoroughly coat the inside of a 10-cup/2.5 L kugelhopf pan (see Tips) or Bundt pan with baking spray.

When the dough has risen, beat the dough with a wooden spoon to knock it back. With well-floured hands, divide the dough into 4 equal portions. In the prepared pan, take 1 portion of the dough and stretch it around the base until it is covered. Sprinkle with one-quarter of the cinnamon/sugar mixture and one-quarter of the nuts (if using). Take a second portion of dough and stretch it over the first one. Sprinkle with another one-quarter of the cinnamon sugar and one-quarter of the nuts. Repeat twice more. Leave to rise for at least 15 minutes (you can leave it longer).

Meanwhile, position a rack in the centre of the oven and preheat the oven to 425°F/220°C.

Bake the cake for 20 minutes. Reduce the oven temperature to 375°F/190°C and bake until the cake has risen, another 5 to 10 minutes. The internal temperature of the cake should be 200° to 205°F/93° to 96°C; or do the toothpick test to make sure it is baked through. If the exposed cake starts to turn dark brown during baking, cover it lightly with a sheet of foil.

Let the cake cool in the pan on a wire rack for 10 to 15 minutes. Then turn it out onto the rack to cool overnight.

Before serving, dust the cake with icing sugar and serve in slices.

TIPS:

You can use anywhere from 12 to 20 tablespoons/ 170 to 285 g of butter; the more butter the richer the cake!

You can substitute any nut for the walnuts or omit entirely.

A traditional kugelhopf pan can be purchased at any local bakeware store. If you do not have one, a Bundt pan works well.

This cake freezes nicely. Cut into serving slices and place in a zip-seal plastic freezer bag. Take out pieces 20 minutes before serving.

Dry, stale cake can be sliced and toasted or used for French toast.

ADOPT-A-RECIPE Loretta Chang

In recent years I have been working on an artist residency project called Alchemy. We bring artists interested in food and community and art together, typically for two weeks at a time. In 2021 we layered in art installations at farms and vineyards in Prince Edward County where we've been feeding the seasonal agricultural workers.

Tonia Di Risio is an artist, who together with Claire M. Tallarico runs Alchemy, an international artist residency held in Prince Edward County that explores the synergy between artistic and culinary practices in a community setting. **@alchemy_artist_ residency**

DORIS FIN

MEDOVIK

Russian Honey Cream Cake

Doris just radiates positive energy, a walking bundle of good vibes. Even though her speciality is healthy foods, when she made this decadent cake for a Russian dinner, I completely fell in love with it, and had to ask her very nicely to share such an indulgent recipe. It's a bit challenging, but a real showstopper with a unique flavour and texture. It can be made ahead and freezes well, so make it when you have some spare time, and then crack it out for a special occasion.

Chef's Note: I strongly encourage you to use organic ingredients wherever possible. Also note that this cake needs to be refrigerated for 24 to 48 hours to allow the cake layers to soften and the flavours to meld, so plan to make it at least one day ahead of when you need it.

My family's from Russia. They encouraged me to help in the kitchen since I was seven years old. I thought they were alchemists when I saw how they would take a raw chicken, put it in the oven, and then it would come out beautiful and crispy and delicious. My mother taught me how to use the stove, my father taught me to use the oven. I would take out cookbooks from the library every weekend and just read them for inspiration.

Chef Doris Fin
teaches interactive culinary classes and caters retreats. When she isn't foraging in the wild, she is making and selling plant-based organic ice cream cakes and bars.
@chefdorisfin

Prep: 1½ hr

Cook: 45 to 90 min (depending on the size of your oven)

Rest time: 24 to 48 hr

Makes: 1 cake (12 to 16 servings)

1¼ cups/380 g dulce de leche (see Tips)

1½ cups/505 g honey

4 cups/1 L whipping cream (35%)

1 tsp salt

1 tsp ground cinnamon

2 tsp baking soda

16 tbsp/240 g unsalted butter

½ cup/100 g cane sugar

5 large eggs, at room temperature

3½ cups/455 g unbleached all-purpose flour, sifted

Fresh berries, for serving (optional)

Trace 9-inch/23 cm circles on 4 pieces of parchment paper, using a cake pan as a guide. (If using transparent silicone baking mats, only 1 traced circle will be needed.)

In a small bowl, stir together the dulce de leche, ½ cup/168 g of honey, ¾ cup/175 mL of cream, and ½ teaspoon of salt. Refrigerate until needed.

Place a stand mixer bowl (or regular bowl if using a hand mixer) in the freezer.

In a small bowl, combine the remaining ½ tsp salt, the cinnamon, and baking soda. Set aside.

In a medium pot, bring 2 inches/5 cm of water to a boil. Reduce the heat to a simmer and place a large heatproof bowl on top, ensuring the bowl doesn't touch the water. In the bowl, combine the butter, cane sugar, and remaining 1 cup/335 g honey. Stir occasionally until the butter completely melts, then whisk well to combine. The temperature should remain warm, not hot.

While the honey/butter mixture is warm (and still sitting over the simmering water), whisk in one egg at a time, then whisk in the cinnamon mixture until it begins to foam, about 30 seconds. Remove the bowl from the heat and whisk in the sifted flour in two to three additions, fully incorporating the flour after each addition. Whisk until completely smooth. Place the bowl on top of the preheating oven to keep warm (this helps the batter spread more easily).

Position a rack in the centre of the oven and preheat to 350°F/180°C.

Depending on the size of your oven and baking sheets, you'll bake 1 or 2 cake rounds at a time, and while they bake, you'll prepare the next cake round(s). Turn the ink side on the parchment paper upside down (or set the circle underneath the transparent silicone mat) and use a ⅓-cup/75 mL measure to measure the batter and a spoon/spatula to help pour into the centre of the circle(s). Use an offset spatula or a spoon to evenly spread the batter to the edges of the circle(s). If needed, add a touch more batter in sparse areas. Gently lift and transfer the parchment paper (or mat) to a baking sheet.

Bake until the cake(s) turns a deep caramel colour and springs back when gently touched, 6 to 7 minutes. Do not overbake. Allow the layer(s) to cool a few minutes

ADOPT-A-RECIPE Sandy Nicholson

on the pan before transferring from the parchment/mat to a wire rack to cool completely. Scrape off any remaining crumbs from the parchment/mat using a bench scraper or metal spatula and set them aside.

Repeat with the remaining batter. You should end up with 11 to 12 layers. Place the cooled layers on top of each other on a plate. After the last layers are baked, leave the oven on but reduce the temperature to 250°F/120°C.

Place the least attractive layer (and any crumbs collected) on a baking sheet and bake for 15 minutes or until dry and deep reddish brown. Let cool completely, then grind into fine crumbs in a food processor. Set aside.

Remove the stand mixer bowl (or other bowl) from the freezer and pour in the remaining 3¼ cups/775 mL cream. On the stand mixer fitted with the whisk (or using a handheld mixer), whip the cream at medium speed to soft peaks. While mixing slowly, pour in the chilled dulce de leche mixture and whip to medium-stiff peaks. If your bowl is smaller than 5 quarts/5 L, you may need to whip in two batches.

To assemble, on a 10-inch/25 cm cake board round or flat serving plate, top one cake layer with ¾ cup/175 mL of whipped cream. Spread the cream evenly with an offset spatula or a spoon. Continue alternating layers of cake and whipped cream, ending the last layer with cream. Smooth the sides of the cake with any remaining whipped cream. Any revealing edges will be covered up by the crumbs.

Place the assembled cake on a sheet pan and use your hands to gently press the crumbs into the sides. Cover the top with crumbs, if desired.

Cover the cake with a large pot, bowl, or box and refrigerate for at least 24 hours before serving. Leftover cake can be refrigerated for up to 3 days or frozen in an airtight container for up to 3 months.

Serve as is, or with fresh berries.

TIPS:

Depending on your preference, you could use a strongly flavoured wildflower honey or a milder floral-noted honey such as clover. Both will produce excellent results.

Baked cake layers can be separated with parchment paper and frozen in an airtight container for up to 1 year. You can choose to use up all of the cake layers or freeze a few for a smaller cake later.

Daniel Holloway is a professional chef who, together with partner, Marie Fitrion, founded Urban Acorn in 2012 to pursue innovative plant-forward connections between food and community.
@urbanacornca
@chefholloway
@voodoohaggis

DANIEL HOLLOWAY

PURPLE YAM SCONES WITH PASSION FRUIT CREAM

Shortly after they moved to Toronto, Dan and his partner, Marie, approached me with the idea of a Scottish-Haitian fusion dinner—Voodoo Haggis—that reflected their respective backgrounds. I absolutely loved the idea, which became the first of many collaborations, and one of my go-to examples of the kind of creative culinary play that The Dep encouraged. They went on to establish their own culinary studio, Urban Acorn, which, like The Dep, sought to blur the lines between restaurant, cooking school, event venue, and community hub. This dish was on that original menu, and can be served up simply as tasty scones with yummy toppings, or cheffy-chef style, artfully layered and elegantly plated.

Prep: 30 min
Rest time: 20 min
Cook: 2 hr

Makes: 8 scones
Vegan

Scones:

½ cup/125 mL baked purple yam purée

2 tsp vanilla or rum extract

Grated zest of 1 lime

2 cups/260 g all-purpose flour, plus more for dusting

6 tbsp granulated sugar

4 tbsp brown sugar

2 tsp baking powder

½ tsp ground allspice

½ tsp salt

8 tbsp/113 g vegan butter, chilled or frozen

Passion Fruit Cream:

4 to 6 tablespoons passion fruit juice (about 3 passion fruits) or purée

½ cup/120 g icing sugar, or to taste

2 tbsp arrowroot or corn starch

½ cup/125 mL coconut milk

Pinch of salt

Tablet Kokoye:

2 cups/170 g coarsely grated fresh coconut or coconut shavings (see Tips)

1 tbsp grated fresh ginger

½ cup/125 mL coconut milk

1½ cups /300 g brown sugar

¼ tsp baking powder

2 cups/500 mL water

2 cinnamon sticks

2 bay leaves

2 tsp vanilla extract

Make the scones: In a small bowl, whisk together the purple yam purée, vanilla, and lime zest .

In a large bowl, mix together the flour, 4 table-spoons of the granulated sugar, the brown sugar, baking powder, allspice, and salt.

Grate the vegan butter using a box grater and add to the flour mixture. Combine using two forks, or the tips of your fingers until the mixture comes together in pea-size crumbs.

Add the yam purée mix to the flour/butter mixture and mix together until everything appears to form a loose ball; don't overknead. Refrigerate for at least 30 minutes and up to 1 hour.

Preheat the oven to 400°F/200°C. Line a baking sheet with parchment paper.

Dust a work surface with a bit of flour and place the dough onto the surface. Work the dough using a rolling pin or your hands and as best you can form into a disc about 1½ inches/4 cm thick. If it's too sticky, add a little more flour. If it seems too dry, add 1 to 2 more tablespoons water.

With a sharp knife or bench scraper, cut the dough into 8 wedges. Place 3 inches/7.5 cm apart on the lined baking sheet. Sprinkle with the remaining 2 tablespoons granulated sugar.

While the oven is preheating, place the scones on the baking sheet (if your fridge has space!) and refrigerate for at least 20 minutes.

Bake until golden brown around the edges and lightly browned on top, 18 to 26 minutes.

Remove from the oven and cool for a few minutes before serving.

Make the passion fruit cream: In a small bowl, whisk the passion fruit juice and icing sugar together.

In a small pot, combine the arrowroot or corn starch and coconut milk. Whisk over medium heat until it thickens. Remove from the heat and slowly incorporate the passion fruit mixture, whisking until all lumps are dissolved. Whisk in the salt.

Store airtight in the fridge (it will keep for up to 2 days) until ready to serve with the scones.

Make the *tablet kokoye*: In a pot, combine the grated coconut, ginger, coconut milk, brown sugar, baking powder, and water. Bring to a boil over high heat. Stir in the cinnamon sticks and bay leaves. Reduce the heat to medium-high and cook, stirring occasionally, for 1 hour. As the consistency begins to thicken, remove the bay leaves and cinnamon sticks. Add the vanilla. Cook for another 30 minutes, stirring constantly as it becomes stickier, until the consistency is very thick and sticky. The tablet is ready when it reaches caramel consistency (if using a thermometer, it should reach 270° to 290°F/ 132° to 143°C).

Remove from the heat. Using a large spoon, transfer dollops of your preferred size onto a baking sheet. Let it cool down for 30 minutes before serving. The tablet will keep 1 week in an airtight container at room temperature.

To plate, top the scones with passion fruit cream and shards of crumbled tablet kokoye, or just set it all out and let people DIY.

TIPS:

Scones will keep well in an airtight container at room temperature for 2 days or in the refrigerator for 5 days.

Use unsweetened grated fresh coconut or coconut shavings, not dried shredded coconut.

ROBIN "SQUIGGY" DUTT

PURPLE FRENCH TOAST

Robin's background was in theatre, and he brought that creativity and theatricality to the series of Squiggfeasts he hosted at The Dep, each one a different culinary and technical challenge. His insatiable curiosity has taken him through many great kitchens, but it has also made him keenly aware of the many problematic issues in our food system, something he insightfully explores through social media.

Prep: 15 min
Cook: 15 min
Makes: 4 servings

Blueberry-Infused Maple Syrup:

½ cup/125 mL maple syrup

¾ cup/110 g blueberries

French Toast:

4 large eggs

¾ cup/175 mL whipping cream (35%)

1 cup/150 g blueberries

½ cup/100 g granulated sugar

2 tsp vanilla extract

2 tsp ground cinnamon

Pinch of salt

8 slices white bread (day-old works best)

Butter, for cooking French toast

To Serve:

Lemon curd

Blueberries, strawberries, and mint, for garnish

Icing sugar, for dusting

Make the blueberry-infused maple syrup: In a small saucepan, combine the maple syrup and blueberries and bring to a simmer over medium heat. Turn off the heat and leave to infuse. (You can serve as is or blend to make a smooth sauce.)

Make the French toast: In a blender or with a hand mixer, blitz together the eggs, cream, blueberries, sugar, vanilla, cinnamon, and salt into a smooth batter and pour into a small baking pan or dish that can fit the bread to be coated.

Preheat the oven to 200°F/90°C with a baking sheet set in it.

Place the bread in the batter, flip over, and let soak for a couple minutes.

Heat a large nonstick skillet over medium heat. Add a knob of butter, and once the butter has foamed, working in batches, place the soaked bread into the pan. Brown on one side before flipping. Once browned on both sides, transfer the toasts to the baking sheet in the oven to keep warm while cooking the rest.

To serve: Swipe some lemon curd on a plate; place 2 pieces of French toast on top; drizzle with some blueberry-infused maple syrup; garnish with fresh blueberries, strawberries, and mint; and dust with icing sugar.

Prior to being a chef, I was a backstage theatre technician. Once I was flown to Switzerland for a weekend gig to do lighting design for a breakdancer crew. After, I went to one of the breakdancers' houses and they served macaroni salad. And it was amazing. People need to recognize that to cook for people, you don't have to cook Michelin three stars. As long as you cook with care and love, that's all that matters.

After many years in theatre production, **Robin "Squiggy" Dutt** moved from the stage to the *stage*, working his way through many professional kitchens in Montreal and Toronto. These days he works full time as a chef in Prince Edward County and is a vocal advocate of social justice issues. **@the_brown_ squiggy**

ADOPT A RECIPE Peter Voore

Laura Repo is an accomplished and award-winning songwriter, singer, and guitarist, as well as Registered Massage Therapist, and the founder of Go Slow Mama, which offers creative and supportive workshops for new mothers.
@laurarepomusic

LAURA REPO

SEEDY GRANOLA

I'd known Laura, a talented local musician, for many years. Then by happy coincidence we ended up living around the corner from each other. She would often pop by The Dep and used my kitchen on a handful of occasions to make big batches of her fabulous granola. She'd tithe a bit to me in return, and it was always a treat, especially served Laura's favourite way, with yogurt and peaches.

Prep: 15 min
Cook: 45 min
Makes: 10 to 12 servings
Vegan

4 cups/360 g large flake oats

1 cup/140 g sunflower seeds

1 cup/130 g pumpkin seeds

1 cup/120 g coarsely chopped walnuts

1 cup/100 g pecans (half chopped and half left whole)

1 cup/145 g almonds, coarsely chopped (optional)

½ cup/65 g sesame seeds

¾ cup/175 mL maple syrup, or to taste

½ cup/125 mL vegetable oil

Pinch of ground cinnamon

1 tsp vanilla extract

Pinch of salt

1 cup/80 g coconut flakes

1 cup/160 g dried cranberries, chopped

Preheat the oven to 400°F/200°C. Line two baking sheets with parchment paper or grease with some oil.

In a large bowl, combine and thoroughly mix the oats, sunflower seeds, pumpkin seeds, walnuts, pecans, almonds (if using), and sesame seeds.

In a small saucepan, combine the maple syrup, oil, cinnamon, vanilla, and salt and gently warm over medium heat. Do not boil! Reserve a tablespoon of this mixture.

Add the maple syrup mix to the bowl of oat mixture and mix until the dry ingredients are soaked in the wet mixture. Let sit for a few minutes.

Divide the ingredients between the prepared baking sheets and even out to a layer about 1 inch/2.5 cm thick.

Place the baking sheets in the oven and reduce the temperature to 350°F/170°C. Bake until the granola is a rich golden brown, about 45 minutes. Check every 15 minutes to make sure the edges aren't burning and stir if necessary.

Test the granola. If it isn't sweet enough, add the reserved tablespoon of maple syrup/oil mixture to the pan and stir. Divide the coconut flakes between the baking sheets and stir. Return to the oven for 2 more minutes.

Remove from the oven, add the cranberries, and allow to cool.

TIPS:

You can customize the ingredients to your liking—more or less of any ingredient. This applies to the amount of sweetener/maple syrup and oil as well. You can also replace the cranberries with other chopped dried fruit, but raisins are not allowed with this recipe!

The key to the crunch is a dark golden roast. If it's only golden blonde, leave it in longer, but stay close to the oven so you can keep an eye on it.

Serve with yogurt or milk, along with berries and/or fresh or canned sliced peaches.

ADOPT-A-RECIPE Jillian Brant

MIRELLE BLASSNIG

RICO PAVÊ

Brazilian Chocolate-Caramel No-Bake Cake

Cookies, caramel, chocolate, and cream are a pretty foolproof combo for a tasty dessert. *Pavê* is a silky and luxurious Brazilian spin on the no-bake refrigerator cake that's as *rico* as it is *suave*.

Prep: 30 to 45 min, plus overnight refrigeration

Cook: 20 to 30 min

Makes: 8 servings

2 (300 mL) cans sweetened condensed milk

2 cups/500 mL 2% milk

2 tbsp corn starch

4 egg yolks

2⅓ cups/560 mL chocolate milk, divided

2 tbsp cocoa powder

1 (7 oz/200 g) package Maria cookies, or other rich tea biscuits

2 cups/500 mL whipping cream (35%)

In a heavy-bottomed medium saucepan, combine 1 can of condensed milk, the 2% milk, 1 tablespoon of corn starch, and 2 of the egg yolks. Cook over medium heat, stirring constantly, until the mixture thickens to a custard consistency, 4 to 5 minutes. Pour into a medium bowl and cover with plastic wrap. Refrigerate until chilled, 2 to 3 hours.

In a clean heavy-bottomed medium saucepan, combine the remaining can of condensed milk, 2 cups/475 mL of the chocolate milk, the cocoa powder, remaining 1 tablespoon corn starch, and remaining 2 egg yolks. Cook over medium heat, stirring constantly, until the mixture thickens to a custard consistency, 4 to 5 minutes. Pour into a medium bowl and cover with plastic wrap. Refrigerate until chilled, 2 to 3 hours.

To assemble the pavê, spread a thin layer (about ½ cup/125 mL) of the chilled milk cream at the bottom of a 9-inch/23 cm square glass baking dish.

Pour the remaining ⅓ cup/75 mL of chocolate milk into a shallow bowl. Dip the cookies into the chocolate milk and soak until they absorb liquid and soften up.

Arrange a layer of milk-soaked cookies on top of the milk cream. Top with a thin layer (about ½ cup/125 mL) of chocolate cream. Repeat the layers. Cover and refrigerate overnight.

When ready to serve, in a large bowl, using a whisk or hand mixer, whip the cream until stiff peaks form. Top the pavê with whipped cream.

I am much more of a food person than I am a dessert person, but when I tried this recipe, it was amazing. It's actually a Brazilian dessert—my husband is originally from Brazil. And the interesting thing about Brazil, for me, is that it's in Latin America, but they speak Portuguese—their culture is completely different. My mom was from Guatemala, so I have a Latin background, so we always have this conversation: "Are Brazilians Latinos?"

Mirelle Blassnig is an avid home cook, who loves entertaining and dabbles in catering. She rode her love of Latin American food all the way to the shortlist for *MasterChef Canada*–twice! **@Cocina.de.Alvarez**

ADOPT-A-RECIPE   Matthew J. Clark

KEISHA LUKE

KEY LIME KUPS

Keisha is a tiny powerhouse with a giant personality. Her Healing the Gut workshops were perennially popular, especially in January as people sought to start off a new year on the right foot and maybe repent for a bit of holiday overindulgence. These delicious vegan, gluten-free, and dairy-free treats make a great guilt-free dessert or snack.

Prep: 30 min, plus 2 to 3 hr to freeze

Makes: 6

Vegan

1 cup/140 g cashews (see Tips)

½ cup/80 g pitted dates

2 cups /254 g fine almond flour

2 tbsp coconut oil

1 tsp grated lime zest

Juice of 5 to 7 Key limes or 3 regular limes (see Tips)

1 cup/250 mL full-fat coconut milk

2 tbsp maple syrup

1 tsp vanilla extract

In a bowl, cover the cashews with room temperature water and soak overnight if possible, but for at least 15 minutes. Drain well.

In a small bowl, cover the dates with water and soak for 20 minutes. Drain well.

In a food processor or blender, combine the almond flour, dates, and coconut oil and pulse to a crumbly texture.

Line 6 holes of a muffin tin with cupcake liners. You can also use small canning jars or ramekins, lightly greased with coconut oil.

Fill each cupcake liner (or jar/ramekin) about halfway with the date and almond crumble and push down in the centre with a spoon to create the crust.

In a food processor or blender, combine the soaked cashews, lime zest, lime juice, coconut milk, maple syrup, and vanilla and process until smooth.

Pour the Key lime filling into a piping bag (or a medium zip-seal plastic bag; seal and snip a corner off) and fill each crust with the filling.

Place in the freezer for 2 to 3 hours to set. Let soften slightly for 10 minutes before serving.

TIPS:

Make sure to use raw unsalted cashews.

In a pinch, you can use bottled lime juice.

Any additional crust mixture can be rolled into protein balls.

Prep: 30 min, plus
soaking time

Cook: about 2 hr

Makes: 12 servings

Vegan

3 large grapefruit

3 cups/600 g sugar

3 cups/750 mL water

1 cinnamon stick

1 star anise

Zest strips of 1 small
lime (optional)

CASCOS DE TORONJA

Cuban Candied Grapefruit Shells

Abel is one of my oldest and dearest friends, and my own personal ambassador and guide to Cuban culture. We have travelled together to Cuba many times, for birthdays or New Year's Eve, Carnival, or the epically insane Las Parrandas de Remedios. I invited him to do a Cuban dinner at The Dep, largely as a ruse to get him to make me this unforgettable dessert that I first tried at his family's house in Havana.

Cascos de toronja is a traditional Cuban dessert of grapefruit peels poached in an infused simple syrup until translucent. It is a great example of resourcefulness amidst adversity, the transformation of waste—via patience, skill, and ingenuity—into something exquisite.

Use a vegetable peeler to carefully remove the thin outermost coloured layer (the zest) of the grapefruits in strips, leaving as much of the white pith as possible. (Save the strips of zest for other recipes like baking or marmalade.)

Quarter the grapefruits and carefully remove the fruit segments, keeping the pith shells intact. (The fruit segments, too, can be saved for another use.) Set the pith shells in a bowl of cold water and soak for at least a few hours, preferably overnight. Drain.

In a medium saucepan, combine the shells with cold water to cover. Bring to a boil over high heat. When it reaches the boiling point, drain, add more cold water and repeat this two more times to remove bitterness. Transfer them to a bowl of cold water to cool down.

Drain the shells in a sieve and press them gently to remove as much water as possible, then place on paper towels. At this point they should be sponge-like and ready to absorb the syrup.

In a medium saucepan, combine the sugar and 3 cups/750 mL water and stir over medium heat until dissolved.

Add the cinnamon stick, star anise, lime zest (if using), and grapefruit shells. Bring to a boil, reduce the heat, and simmer until the shells are soft and translucent (see Tips) and the syrup is thickened, 1 to 1½ hours. The shells will take on the colour of the syrup.

Remove from the heat. Allow the shells to cool to room temperature in the syrup. Discard the cinnamon stick and star anise. Transfer the shells and syrup to a large bowl and refrigerate until ready to serve.

Serve the shells drizzled in syrup.

In Cuba it is often served with small wedges of nutty, creamy, salty cheese, like Edam, Gouda, or Havarti.

TIPS:

Don't overcook the shells; you want to leave a hint of the bitterness.

These will keep indefinitely in the fridge, and the fragrant syrup is lovely on ice cream, fruit salad, or in cocktails.

This also works well with Seville oranges or pomelos, both of which have generous amounts of pith.

ADOPT-A-RECIPE   Vivien Cy Wong

Abel Cartaya-Carral teaches elementary school in Toronto. Originally from Havana, he has been in Canada since 1992. He is one of my favourite people in the world. @abelcartaya

"I came to Canada from Barbados on the refugee program because of my lifestyle. I'm gay. I'm a gay, homosexual person and there is a lot of discrimination back home. So for my safety, I came here. I'm actually happy, but I'm one of those ones who have recently got turned down with their case. Okay, so it's a depressing moment for me right now, but I am going to appeal."

A graduate of the Barbados Hospitality Institute, **Shem Barker** immigrated to Toronto in 2018. He is the owner of Shem's Kitchen, which features Shem's unique style, a cuisine inspired by the food, festivals, and culture of the Caribbean. **@shembarker**

SHEM BARKER

CROP OVER CONKIES

Barbadian Dessert Tamales

Prep: 1 hr 15 min
Cook: about 2½ hr
Makes: 32 conkies

Shem's serious, dedicated professionalism hides a wild, flamboyant personality. Both are deeply informed by his Caribbean roots, a source of great pride but also deep personal conflict. Shem's food embraces and celebrates a love for a culture that still struggles to accept him as he is. Conkies are a kind of sweet tamale, traditionally made in November after the corn, sweet potatoes, and pumpkins have been harvested—crop over—and a beloved part of Barbados's Independence Day celebration.

1 package frozen banana leaves (see Tips)

1 lb/450 g pumpkin, peeled and grated

½ lb/225 g sweet potatoes, peeled and grated

1½ cups/125 g fresh or frozen shredded coconut

1½ cups/198 g cornmeal

1½ cups/300 g granulated sugar

1 cup/130 g all-purpose flour

½ tsp ground allspice

½ tsp ground cinnamon

½ tsp ground nutmeg

½ tsp salt

8 tbsp/120 g butter, melted

1 egg, lightly beaten

2 cups/500 mL milk

1 cup/250 mL water

1 tsp almond extract

1 tsp vanilla extract

½ cup/80 g raisins

Thaw the banana leaves and wipe each piece with a wet paper towel. Cut along the grain into rectangular strips the full width of the leaf by about 6 inches/15 cm high; you'll need at least 64 pieces in total. Cut 32 lengths of kitchen string 12 inches/30 cm long and set aside.

In a large bowl, combine the pumpkin, sweet potatoes, and coconut.

In a separate large bowl, combine the cornmeal, sugar, flour, allspice, cinnamon, nutmeg, and salt. Add the pumpkin mixture to the dry ingredients and stir to combine. Add the melted butter, egg, milk, water, and extracts and stir to combine. Gently fold in the raisins.

Arrange 2 pieces of banana leaf in the shape of a cross and place two large spoonfuls (about 5 tablespoons/75 g) of the pumpkin mixture where the leaves overlap. Fold in the edges of the topmost leaf, then fold over the edges of the bottom leaf to make a squarish pillow. Tie with kitchen string, wrapping once or twice both horizontally and vertically (see Tips).

Put 4 cups/1 L water into a large pot fitted with a deep steamer basket (or in a canning pot with a wire trivet).

Carefully place the conkies in the steamer basket (or stack in layers on the trivet). Bring to a boil and steam for 1 hour 45 minutes. Remove the conkies from the pot and place in a colander to drain and cool.

TIPS:
If you have a troublesome/leaking conkie (or cannot find banana leaves), wrap it in plastic wrap and then in foil.

Place a coin in the bottom of the pot when steaming; it will rattle while the water boils. Keep an ear out: if the coin stops rattling, you know you have to add more water to the pot.

KUTIA

Barley and Poppy Seed Pudding

Prep: 24-plus hr

Cook: 30 to 45 min

Makes: 4 servings

1 cup/140 g poppy seeds

½ cup/100 g pearl barley

1½ cups/350 mL whole milk, plus more as needed

½ cup/80 g raisins

½ cup/50 g walnuts, plus more for garnish

4 tbsp candied orange peel, plus more for garnish

4 tbsp honey, plus more for garnish

Maria first came to The Dep early on, ambitiously tackling a Berlin-style currywurst night with her friend Agata. Something must have clicked, because after a string of well-received events she went on to launch her own food business teaching and cooking Polish food. Her popular pierogi classes would always include a round of traditional Polish folk songs, weaving layers of culture, history, and folklore into the delicious food. She did a number of unforgettable Polish holiday meals, where she introduced me to this unique dessert of barley and poppy seeds sweetened with honey and topped with nuts and raisins.

Line a sieve with cheesecloth (see Tips), add the poppy seeds, and rinse with cold water. Transfer to a small bowl.

Remove the cheesecloth and add the barley to the sieve. Rinse with cold water. Rinse again with boiling water. Place in a separate small bowl.

Cover the poppy seeds with 1 cup/250 mL of milk. Cover the barley with ½ cup/125 mL of milk, making sure both are completely covered. Cover and refrigerate both bowls for 24 hours.

Transfer the barley mixture to a small pot and add additional milk as necessary to cover by ½ inch/1.3 cm. Cover and cook over medium heat until bubbling. Reduce the heat to medium-low, tilt the lid, and continue to simmer until the milk has been absorbed and the grains are tender, 30 to 45 minutes. Rinse the barley with cold water and set aside in a medium bowl.

Meanwhile, transfer the poppy seed mixture to a medium pot and add additional milk as necessary to cover by ½ inch/1.3 cm. Cover, and cook over medium heat until bubbling. Reduce the heat to medium-low, tilt the lid, and continue to simmer, stirring occasionally, until the milk has been absorbed, 30 to 45 minutes. Let cool.

Using a meat grinder (see Tips), grind the poppy seeds three times. Add to the barley and mix well.

In a small bowl, cover the raisins with very hot water and let sit for 1 minute. Drain and cover again with very hot water. Let rest for 5 minutes to plump up. Drain well.

Meanwhile, in a dry medium skillet, toast the walnuts over medium-low heat for 5 minutes, stirring frequently to prevent burning. Let cool and chop into small pieces.

Add the chopped walnuts, candied orange peel, drained raisins, and honey to the barley mixture and mix well.

Serve garnished with more walnuts, candied orange peel, and honey.

TIPS:

If you have a fine enough sieve, there is no need to use cheesecloth when rinsing the poppy seeds.

Use a mild-tasting honey or it can overpower the dish.

Chopped fresh figs can be used instead of raisins.

Orange zest can be used instead of candied peel.

A meat grinder with a fine plate works best for grinding the poppy seeds, but a mortar and pestle, coffee/spice grinder, powerful blender, or food processor can also work, with varying results. You may also be able to find preground poppy seeds at specialty shops.

The longer this dish sits the better, so make it ahead of time for maximum flavour.

 Art Liem

Maria Rozynska grew up in a Polish household alongside her mother, grandmother, and great-grandmother in the kitchen. Maria now teaches others how to make traditional Polish foods at her cooking school, Just Be Cooking. **@justbecooking**

Gardening just makes you respect your food a lot more. You cherish it. This morning we opened our second-to-last jar of black currant jam for our toast. As I was spreading it I was like, "I picked those!" I turned them into jam and we're eating it today, when the snow is falling. Immediately I'm transported back to being in the backyard with my music in my ears and the sun beating down.

Christine Manning is the founder of Manning Canning, a company preparing preserves from locally sourced produce. Christine also runs Manning Canning Kitchens, which offers rentable kitchens for local food entrepreneurs. @manningcanning

CHRISTINE MANNING

SEVILLE ORANGE MARMALADE

I adore marmalade, and getting Christine to share her award-winning recipe was something of a coup. Christine taught The Dep's canning and preserving classes for many years prior to opening up her own shop, Manning Canning Kitchens, which is both home to her own line of products, but also an incubator kitchen for many local food businesses—a bit of Dep DNA that she carried into her own space.

Using a citrus juicer, juice the oranges and lemon, ensuring you save the seeds. Set the orange rinds aside and discard the lemon rind. Set the juice aside.

Line a small bowl with a 12-inch/30 cm square of cheesecloth. Using a spoon, scrape the pith from inside the orange rinds and add to the bowl, along with the seeds. Gather up the cheesecloth and tie tightly with kitchen string. Set aside.

Slice the orange rind halves into quarters and then cut into short ribbons. You can cut these thinly or thickly, as you prefer.

In a medium pot, combine the ribbons of peel with enough water to cover. Bring to a boil over medium heat, then reduce the heat and simmer gently until the peel is tender, 20 to 30 minutes.

Drain and rinse, then return the softened peel to the pot. Add the reserved juice, the cheesecloth bag with pith/seeds, and the 5 cups/1.2 litres of water. Bring to a boil over medium heat, then reduce to a simmer. Cook, uncovered, stirring occasionally, for 1½ to 2 hours.

In a canning pot or stockpot, prepare a boiling water bath (see Tips).

To sterilize the canning jars, place six ½-pint/250 mL jars (without lids) in the canning pot. Bring to a boil

over medium-high heat. Boil the jars for 10 minutes. In a small saucepan, cover the lids with water and bring just to a simmer, until the rubber seal softens.

Using a slotted spoon, remove the cheesecloth bag from the peel mixture. Gently push down to squeeze out all the juice. Set aside. Add the sugar to the peel mixture and stir until fully dissolved. Turn the heat back up to medium and cook, stirring occasionally, until the mixture reaches 220°F/104°C or until the product has a thick shimmer on the surface, about 20 minutes. Remove from the heat.

Remove the jars from the canning pot (pouring the water back into the pot as you remove the jars) and set them on a clean towel or cutting board on your counter. Remove the lids and lay them beside the jars.

Funnel the marmalade into the prepared jars, leaving ¼ inch/6 mm of headspace. Wipe the rims, apply the lids and rings, and tighten finger-tip tight. Process in the boiling water bath for 10 minutes (see Tips).

Carefully remove the jars from the hot water and place on a wire rack, wooden board, or dish towel. Do not invert the hot jars. Allow to cool for 12 to 24 hours before checking the seals (see Tips).

Prep: 1 hr

Cook: 2½ to 3 hr

Makes: six ½-pint/ 250 mL jars

Vegan

---

2 lb/900 g Seville oranges (5 to 6), halved

1 lemon, halved

5 cups/1.2 L water

3 lb/1.4 kg sugar

TIPS:

Seville oranges are only available for a short window (late December to February), so be sure to check the market regularly.

Wash the oranges and lemon gently, being careful not to scrub the skin too hard.

To prepare a boiling water bath, place a metal rack in the bottom of a canning pot and fill until the water reaches 4 inches/

10 cm from the top. Cover and turn the heat to high or medium-high.

To water-bath can: Using a jar lifter, lower each filled jar into the pot and rest on the metal rack. Be sure to leave at least 1 inch/2.5 cm of space between the jars so hot water can circulate. Ensure the jars are covered by 1 to 2 inches/2.5 to 5 cm

of water. Cover the pot and bring to a boil. Once the water comes to a boil, start the timer and process for 10 minutes.

As the jars seal, you will hear a popping sound and the nipple on the lid will depress. If a jar does not seal properly, simply put that one in the fridge and eat it first!

ADOPT-A-RECIPE   Kate Marshall

The Story of Newcomer Kitchen

The Song of
the Kitchen

On a chilly Wednesday morning in mid-April 2016, a group of about a dozen women gathered in a dingy hotel lobby on the outskirts of Toronto. Refugees of the vicious Syrian civil war, they were bundled up against the still-wintery weather, several with one or two small children in tow. For many this would be their first excursion beyond the hotel, some on their first-ever trip on a subway. This small flock of brave souls were making a tentative foray into a strange new city, led by the faint call of the song of the kitchen.

For the previous few years, global awareness of the Syrian conflict and its escalating refugee crisis had been slowly building. The tragic death and viral image of the drowned body of three-year-old Alan Kurdi in September 2015 pushed the issue into that year's federal election, and the Canadian government committed to take in 25,000 Syrian refugees. Inundated, the Canadian immigration system struggled to process the massive influx of cases. By February 2016, many of the families found themselves stuck in remote hotels for several months, without kitchens or any way to make their own food.

As the local story grew louder, I, Cara Benjamin-Pace (whom I had just recently hired to help with business development), and a small group of concerned neighbours started to try and figure out if we might be able to help in some way.

I already had a peculiar kind of restaurant that invited strangers to come and cook. It didn't seem like much of a stretch to extend this invitation to those stuck in the hotels. If nothing else, it might provide a bit of a break from the tedium, and a chance to make and share a familiar meal. It was a gesture of hospitality, a small gift that would, in time, give back more than I could have ever imagined.

In early April, a stroke of luck brought The Dep's offer to the ears of a young Syrian couple, Rahaf Al Akbani and Esmaeel Aboufakher. Barely in their twenties, they had fled Sweida City in Southern Syria and ended up in a refugee camp in Turkey along with hundreds of thousands of others escaping the chaos and violence. They were now two of the lucky few who had found safe harbour in Canada. Their English proficiency and social work experience thrust them into the role of informal advocates for the other Syrian families in their hotel.

Esmaeel and Rahaf, herself a passionate and talented cook, took the idea back to their hotel. The prospect proved enticing, and in a matter of days an outing was organized, nicknamed "Trip and Cook." All of a sudden they found themselves on a voyage of trust, shepherding a group of women and children across an unfamiliar city to the doorstep of The Depanneur.

When they arrived, there was a hush of uncertainty as they took stock of the room. What was this peculiar place? Who were these strangers and what did they want? **Amid the awkward language gap we managed to get across a simple idea: Here's the kitchen, here are some ingredients, go ahead and make whatever you want. Cook first and we can talk later.** As this became clear, everything shifted; a rush of energy filled the room, and it was "Out of my way!" as the ladies stormed the kitchen. Suddenly the room was

Start where you are,
use what you have,
do what you can.
— *Arthur Ashe*

alive with the clamour of pots clanging, knives chopping, and animated chatter. There was a tangible outpouring of joy everyone could feel.

How long had it been since they had been able to cook their own food, breathe in the comforting smells, move in the ordinary dance of what had once been a mundane household task? I could only imagine after all the months of chaos and displacement, of camps, travel, and hotels, that to just be hanging out in the kitchen, making some familiar food, might have felt so . . . normal. In that moment, the simple, everyday happiness in the room felt like the most precious treasure imaginable.

In what seemed like no time at all, a glorious banquet spread out in front of us. A colourful bowl of chopped tomatoes, cucumbers, and onions tossed in lemon and garlic, crispy chips of pita and chickpeas under a rich blanket of tahini and yogurt, pooled with olive oil and decorated with little flowers cut from tomatoes. Roast chicken, fragrant with garlic and thyme sat alongside creamy slabs of feta and crunchy rubies of radishes.

In this moment, they became the hosts, generously offering the beautiful food they had made to us, their guests. Without a word, we had turned the whole social configuration upside down, making them the givers and us the receivers, allowing us to proffer thanks, and them to receive our gratitude. We sat, and we ate, and were nourished as much by simply eating together as by the food before us.

An Accidental Philanthropist

I posted a few pictures on social media, and they lit up unlike anything I had ever done before. It was clear that we were onto something important, something that embodied and amplified everything that The Dep was about. It felt like the culmination of all the things I had worked towards over the last five years—building community through food, fostering diversity and inclusion, lowering barriers to participation, celebrating cultures and human connections, creating social and economic opportunities. We quickly agreed to do it again the following week.

The days that followed were a blur of activity. My branding brain homed in on the word *newcomer*, which I felt spoke more to the present, to new beginnings and possibilities, and was not tied to any culture or gender. I much preferred it over *refugee*, which felt tied to the past, trauma and external forces, sympathy and charity. When I discovered that the *newcomerkitchen* domains were available, it felt like a digital omen, a kind of blessing on the project. I registered them immediately, and the project was officially christened. I set up a dedicated email address, a landing page on The Dep

Top
(L) *Our first visit to a super-market; for some this was their first outing into the city beyond the hotels.*
(R) *Rahaf and Esmaeel, both talented musicians, would regularly break into traditional Syrian songs, to which everyone would sing along as they cooked.*

Bottom
(L) *An early group of ladies seeing themselves in the newspaper for the first time.*
(R) *One of the first dinners we sold, with handmade thank-you cards prepared by the many kids we attempted to wrangle while the ladies cooked.*

website, and a public Facebook Group. By the weekend @NewcomerKitchen was on Twitter and Instagram, and a dedicated mailing list was starting to gather email addresses.

We did it again, and included a shopping trip to a local supermarket (a first for many of the ladies), and then made a plan to host the following week at a friend's restaurant, The Butler's Pantry. This was an important detail, as it implied that this idea of connecting newcomers and kitchens might be portable and scalable. It helped us begin to imagine a model that might have the potential to work with any newcomer community, in any kitchen willing to open its doors, in any city in the world.

Over the course of those first few weeks as we scrambled to bootstrap the project, the last of the families living in the hotels were finally relocated into homes. Now scattered across the city, this presented new logistical challenges. Moreover, now with kitchens of their own, the focus shifted. No longer just a field trip or social gathering, the question quickly became whether it might offer a way to generate any income for the participants.

I had the ability to sell tickets on my website, so we decided to try making additional meals and offering them for sale to The Dep community. The hope was that this could help offset the mounting food costs and provide an honorarium for the Syrian coordinators.

Any surplus profit would be divvied up among the ladies. Until now everything had been paid for out of a small fund compiled by the original group of neighbours, plus small donations from some local supermarkets, with me donating the space and picking up any shortfall.

In May we sold our first dozen meals, and in a matter of weeks had expanded to making and selling fifty meals a week. This earned enough to cover the food and packaging costs, and a respectable, above-minimum wage for about eight ladies each week. For a food project that was barely a month old, with cooks who didn't speak English, had no professional experience, and had been in Canada for a few months at most, it was a remarkable accomplishment, and a very encouraging suggestion of what might be possible.

The project had an immediate moral and emotional logic; it didn't take any explaining to see why it was a good thing. Syrian women were making friends, having fun, making delicious food, and getting paid. People who really wanted a way to help the newcomers had a quick, easy way to support them tangibly and directly, and get a wonderful meal in return. It offered an equitable exchange rather than a gesture of sympathy or charity. It highlighted the women's skills and talents, not the tragedy of their past or the challenges of their present. It dodged the hurdles of language and bureaucracy and found a path to directly engaging and supporting the people who needed it most. **By simply creating a space where they could do what they were already good at, the kitchen gave them a place to shine.**

For those who had been invisible for a long time, it was a way to be seen. It empowered them to tell a part of their story, to contribute to a more positive narrative about themselves and their culture than the one on the news. It was a feel-good story about a feel-bad situation and the press quickly caught the scent. The story quickly jumped from the local papers to the national and international media.

The next few weeks were a whirlwind of frantic coordination and high-profile events: a public pop-up serving nearly a thousand people at Luminato (one of Canada's largest art festivals), catering a Canada Day *iftar* (the evening meal that breaks the Ramadan fast) for the mayor, and more. An incredible constellation of people and organisations began to come into orbit around the project: LUSH cosmetics donated an entire pallet of products, Foodora

A group of ladies, under the mentorship of veteran Syrian chef Hiyam Samara, prepare 1000+ meals for the Luminato Festival in the FoodStarter industrial kitchen. Health regulations required they put hair nets over their hijabs!

Rahaf (front row left), Cara (front row right), and part of the crew at Luminato. It was outdoors in 35°C heat, in the middle of Ramadan. Most of the ladies were fasting and could not even drink water. They knew this was our high-profile public opportunity to launch our fundraising campaign. True grit on display.

offered to do free weekly meal deliveries. The whole thing vibrated with promise and potential.

Cara and I pulled together an ad hoc board of directors and began the arduous, bureaucratic process of incorporating a non-profit organisation. The pressure was growing: **despite all the attention, exposure, and public goodwill; the sold-out dinners and the uncountable hours of donated time and volunteer effort, the program was not breaking even.** The accumulated shortfall quickly snowballed into the five figures, and I found myself in the awkward position of being an accidental philanthropist, in way over my head.

Barely three months had passed since leaving the hotels. Still reeling from Luminato, with a fledgling fundraiser to promote, we took on an ambitious catering job for a Canada Day iftar *dinner; an A-list crowd with guest of honour Toronto Mayor John Tory. Everyone was exceptionally kind, gracious, and appreciative, but the fundraiser did not budge.*

Sofra Dayma

To keep the project alive, we needed to quickly find some way to raise enough funds to dig me out of the hole I had dug, and to buy enough time until we could find some kind of stable funding. I naively imagined that simply becoming a non-profit would enable us to tap into the funds earmarked to help refugees and new immigrants. In reality, this journey would ultimately turn out to be more challenging than launching Newcomer Kitchen in the first place.

Slightly desperate, I decided to attempt a crowdfunding campaign with little sense of what a staggering amount of work that entailed. It was a nail-biter of a ride, hitting its goal of $25,000 with just a few hours left on the clock. It was a reprieve, but we still needed to find a sustainable way to pay for the seemingly endless strategic, administrative, legal, financial, and regulatory work involved in keeping the project running.

One of our early gatherings, and the first of many times we made kibbeh.

Our first party and the others that would follow were the collective effort of a lot of incredible volunteers.

Photo: Sandy Nicholson

Still, a celebration was in order; we decided to host a "small" party. By the time we invited all fifty-plus women now involved in the program along with their families, and the many volunteers and donors, it had ballooned into a sprawling 350-plus person affair that taxed our logistical skills to the limit. Somehow, we managed to pull it off, bringing dozens of the families together to eat, socialize, and celebrate our remarkable accomplishments. As an unexpected bonus, renowned Canadian photographer Sandy Nicholson offered to take beautiful family portraits of all the families who attended.

By October we had our non-profit incorporation papers in hand. Unfortunately, it was becoming painfully clear that it would take many more months to wade through the gauntlet of unfamiliar grant applications and approvals. The short runway provided by what we had been able to fundraise was going to run out long before we got off the ground. Another financial stopgap was needed, and fast.

One of the board members suggested that we host a gala fundraiser. I had no idea where to begin—I had never even been to a gala fundraiser. Yet somehow, in a matter of weeks, with an unfathomable amount of work by an incredible team of volunteers and sponsors, we managed to pull it off. We called it *Sofra Dayma,* a Syrian phrase spoken in thanks when being fed by a host. Translating roughly to "May your table always be plentiful," it embodied the deeper, reciprocal lessons of hospitality we were all learning. Graciously sponsored by the Gladstone Hotel, it was an elegant, unforgettable night of music, food, and remarkable generosity. The money raised bought us a bit more time, and drove home the transformative potential of what had emerged.

In less than a year we had invented a novel model for creating social and economic opportunities for marginalized newcomers. We had sold thousands of meals, and put tens of thousands of dollars directly into the pockets of amazing Syrian women. The story would go on to garner international attention from *Time* magazine to the *Guardian*, the *New York Times* to Al Jazeera, and even bring Prime Minister Justin Trudeau to our doorstep. For the next two years we would continue to forge ahead, continue to innovate and expand, all the while struggling to stay afloat and remain on track to becoming a sustainable non-profit.

Sofra Dayma, our gala fundraiser at the Gladstone Hotel, showcased the incredible culinary skills of the women of Newcomer Kitchen, who worked alongside hotel staff, artists, and volunteers to put on a world-class event.

Cooking is my hobby; it's like self-esteem for me. I was always excited to share food with my friends and say, "Oh, I made that myself." That's a privilege for me. When the crisis hit in Syria, it affected many things in our lives, including food. The gas was cut off, so we used to cook on wood, and the lack of food supplies from the markets affected us greatly. We started cooking simple things like lentils and bulgur, many simple things until we reached the point that we did not even have wood to cook on. Then we decided to leave.
—Khadija

Breaking Bread

Behind the whirlwind of the weekly meals, the catering and workshops, the journalists and film crews, the subtler, more profound beauty of Newcomer Kitchen was slowly revealing itself. It was something not always visible from the outside, rarely explicitly articulated, but it was the luminous core that powered everything, and gave us all the strength to attempt the impossible, over and over again.

One of the first things to become apparent was this was far from a homogenous group of women. Syria was revealed to me as a deeply rooted, kaleidoscopic culture, highly regional by language, religion, history, geography, class, and education in ways hard to grasp in a fledgling country like Canada. These were not trivial differences, they were the fundamental material of identity, inexorably entangled in politics and history, in religion and ritual, tribalism and kinship. Every person in that room had seen their world disintegrated by conflict rooted in these differences.

Our cohort was diverse and multicultural in unexpected ways; there were Christians and Druze and Zoroastrians and Kurds. There were Shias and Sunnis and sects of Islam I had never heard of, each with its own cultural and culinary history. Here was a random selection of people pried from that mosaic, people who would likely have never met—never mind hung out together—back in Syria. Illiterate peasant farmers next to university-educated, urbanite professionals. Suddenly they are all around a table sharing something they all had in common: food. It was a new space, undefined and unfamiliar, cast in the shadow of history but illuminated by the possible.

Here, in the safety of the kitchen, the ladies met and cooked and ate and spoke. And slowly, through a cookie or a spoon of rice, they came to know each other. In small conversations I was not part of, in a language I did not speak, the real magic of Newcomer Kitchen quietly unfolded.

My son likes this dish a lot.
How old is your son?
He is 5.
My daughter is 6, maybe she will like it.

My mother used to make this.
Is she here?
No, she is still in the camp in Turkey.
I know someone there.

Have you tried this before?
Yes, my cousin's wife used to make it, she was from Aleppo.
My brother lived in Aleppo, but he was killed.
So was my cousin.

Here, around the table, unlikely new friendships took tenuous root in a soil of common ground. To eat together—to break bread—is to connect to a shared, fundamental humanity. That experience, of the other as not so different from us, quietly left The Dep and found its way home with each family. With it went the seeds of hope, of new beginnings, of things possible, of a gentle healing—led by women, growing from the bottom up, spreading out fragile tendrils into the world. For me, to bear witness to this was to be transformed by it.

I recall one lady explaining a particular dish she wanted to make: It was a beloved dish in her city, one they would always make for weddings or parties. Another lady, who had lived only a

My kids love Canadian food, fast food. And I can't forbid them from eating it so we let them have this once a week. But the rest of the week I cook for them and I will make sure to keep our culture through food. My kids have such good memories with their grandmother cooking for them so I'm trying my best to keep these dishes alive for them. I'm reminding them, "We had this, and we celebrated with this. Do you remember? We had it with your cousins and uncles, aunts?" All those foods remind us of home, I want to make sure to keep this culture, especially for my kids.
—Nesreen

few hours away, confessed that she had never even heard of this dish before. She said to me, "I like coming here, I get to learn new recipes. I am learning more about being Syrian." I told her that I also liked coming to the kitchen, that I was learning more about being Canadian.

The more I discovered about the food, its history, its stories and traditions, the more I realized how much we all had to learn. Syria, the heart of the Levant, was home to a true cuisine, a millennia-long experiment in what was sustainably extractable from a given ecosystem. **You don't get to have a 5,000-year-old culinary tradition if that tradition is not sustainable, generation after generation, century after century.** It encoded the aggregate wisdom of millennia of experience, a technology of sustainability, the culture in agriculture.

By comparison, settlers have been in Canada for a few hundred years at best. None of the food that I grew up eating reflected a meaningful relationship with the land upon which I lived, upon which we all depended. To look at the urban sprawl, the "development" of some of the most fertile and irreplaceable farmland in the county, and the larger global ecological disasters of industrialized farming and global warming was to realize how utterly we have broken the connection between our agriculture, our food, and ourselves.

Just maybe, we could begin to see this as being less about all the things we thought we needed to teach them—about English proficiency or resumé writing or computer literacy or whatever— but about what they might have to teach us. Maybe, if we could find a way to listen closely, we might get the most important lesson of our lives, at a moment when we need it more desperately than ever.

To mark the first anniversary of the Syrian refugees' arrival, the CBC hosted a televised round table with Prime Minister Justin Trudeau. Just as he was leaving, this group was returning to The Dep from another catering job.

Photo: Kelli Kieley

Shway Shway

In the years to come Newcomer Kitchen would face many more challenges and accomplish an equal number of remarkable things; it is simply not possible to list them all. The weekly meal program that started at The Depanneur ran for three years, expanding to multiple pickup locations around the city, serving tens of thousands of meals and putting over $150,000 into the pockets of more than eighty Syrian families before winding down in early 2019.

Along the way, it continued to do the amazing and impossible. We worked with emergency relief organisation Global Medic to develop culturally appropriate emergency meal kits for thousands of Syrian refugees still in camps around the world. Newcomer Kitchen was part of *The Canadian Dream,* Chevrolet's national advertising campaign. Filmmaker Kelli Kieley shot a feature-length documentary, *Shway Shway* ("slowly, slowly" or "step by step" in Arabic), tracing the whole story of the project that patiently awaits funding to be completed. Newcomer Kitchen taught cooking classes in schools and offered countless public and private workshops, animated corporate conferences, and academic symposia. In 2019 they were invited to collaborate with billionaire entrepreneur, philanthropist—and former refugee—Hamdi Ulukaya, to pilot an international Newcomer Kitchen program at his flagship Chobani factory in Twin Falls, Idaho.

It did all these things almost entirely without any official institutional or government support. There were more frantic, last-minute, fundraising drives, literal bake sales, and many other revenue-generating experiments, but it always teetered terrifyingly close to the edge. Eventually it received some stopgap support from the Propeller Project, a community-building initiative led by Toronto's Pearson International Airport. It was enough to help stabilize operations while Cara, now the official executive director, pursued the long and tortuous path towards government funding. A string of rejected grant applications taxed morale, stretched the skeleton staff to the breaking point, and strained relationships on the board. Cara, and her equally determined director of operations, Tamara Chaikin, worked unpaid for months on end.

But we persevered. Each week would be another powerful reminder of just how incredible the project really was, beyond metrics or revenue, funding or impact. One story illuminates this: We were approached by an educational conference to tie into their "experiential learning" stream with a hands-on cooking class led by some of the ladies. We invited Zoubaida, a grandmother in her seventies, to lead the class, assisted by a translator. During the class, **Zoubaida confessed that her greatest regret in life had been being too poor to go to school, and never having learned to read. We stopped the class for a moment to gently point out that, today, she was the one being paid to teach the teachers.** Through all the struggle, moments like this sustained us.

Finally, in September 2019, after more than three-and-a-half

Mohamed's first Canada Day

intense, nerve-wracking years, Newcomer Kitchen received a multi-year grant from Immigration, Refugees and Citizenship Canada to develop a food entrepreneurship training program for Newcomer women. It was built around Newcomer Kitchen's core idea: to create social and economic opportunity for newcomer women through food-based projects. It retained Newcomer Kitchen's central innovation: whatever proceeds were generated from entrepreneurial activities went to the ladies who did them, something to the best of my knowledge remains unique in any government-funded settlement or training program.

But its tone and timbre shifted; it was no longer a grassroots project that sought to tap the latent capacity of small businesses to support newcomers. The emphasis became more on training and entrepreneurial skills-building. It evolved, by necessity, into something different, something the government was willing to fund. The Depanneur had taken it as far as it could, then passed the baton to those more tenacious than me to carry it the rest of the way. I admire the strength, grit, and dedication of Cara and Tamara as they continue to push the project forward, navigating the winding road of uncertainty and bureaucracy.

Newcomer Kitchen remains the most personally important work I have ever done; I am incredibly proud of what it achieved and immeasurably grateful for the chance to have been a part of it. It was, in many ways, the ultimate expression of the vision and values of the Depanneur: to cultivate community through food, to foster more inclusion and diversity in my city, to support entrepreneurial opportunity, to create more meaningful experiences for cooks and diners, to use small business as an activist medium. It showed, by example, what is possible. It sang the song of the kitchen and the world sang it back.

NEWCOMER KITCHEN

Muhammara
Red Pepper and Walnut Dip

Mujadara
Bulgur, Lentil, and Caramelized Onion Pilaf

Fatayer Jibneh/ Sabanekh
Savoury Cheese or Spinach Pastries

Kousa Mahshi
Zucchinis Stuffed with Meat and Rice

Kibbeh Lahmeh
Fried Kibbeh with Beef and Pine Nuts

Kibbeh bil Sanieh
Baked Bulgur Pie with Pumpkin, Chickpea, and Pomegranate Filling

Maqluba
"Upside-Down" Casserole

S'fouf
Turmeric Cake

Ma'amoul
Date-Filled Shortbread Cookies

Qatayef
Yeasted Pancakes with Ricotta Filling and Syrup

Muhammara

Red Pepper and Walnut Dip

By now virtually everyone is familiar with hummus, the Levantine dip that has become a global phenomenon. But this is only one of many delicious dips that make up the Syrian repertoire of mezze, the collection of small dishes that start off most meals. *Muhammara* (meaning "red") is bright and tangy with a hint of smoky sweetness, and offers a beautiful contrast to hummus's pale, smooth creaminess. Serve the dip with pita bread, crackers, or crudités.

Chop the roasted red peppers into large chunks.

In a food processor, pulse the onion and garlic until minced. Add the roasted peppers, tomato paste, pepper paste (if using), Aleppo pepper, cumin, and salt and blend until smooth.

Add the walnuts and pulse to incorporate. You want to retain a bit of texture. Scrape into a bowl and stir in the nigella seeds, sesame seeds, lemon juice, and pomegranate molasses. Stir to combine; taste and adjust the seasoning.

Turn out onto a plate and spread out decoratively with a spoon. Garnish with a drizzle of olive oil and a sprinkling of the walnuts, nigella seeds, sesame seeds, and pomegranate seeds (if using). Decorate with some parsley sprigs if desired.

Tips:

Jarred or canned (but not pickled!) roasted peppers make this dish very fast and easy to put together, but you can roast your own fresh red peppers if you wish (you'll need about 3 large ones). Brush red bell peppers with olive oil. If you have a gas burner or BBQ, roast the peppers directly over the flame until blackened on all sides. (Alternatively, place on a foil-lined baking sheet and roast in a 450°F/230°C oven, turning occasionally, until the skin is blackened, about 20 minutes.) Put the blackened peppers in a paper or plastic bag, or in a bowl covered with a plate until cool enough to handle. Peel, remove the seeds, and place in a colander to drain.

Turkish red pepper paste, biber salçası, is available at most Middle Eastern markets. It comes in hot and sweet varieties; stick with the mild, but you can adjust to your spice level with the Aleppo pepper. Alternatively, you can substitute a mix of equal parts smoked paprika and tomato paste.

Aleppo pepper is a kind of ground red chili used in Syrian cooking to add heat; you can substitute cayenne pepper, chili flakes, or hot paprika.

Nigella seeds (also known as kalonji) and pomegranate molasses can be purchased at most Middle Eastern supermarkets.

In a pinch, you could substitute reduced balsamic vinegar and a bit of sugar for the pomegranate molasses, but it's worth having some on hand.

Prep: 30 min
Cook: 5 min
Makes: 1½ cups/ 375 mL

---

1 (380-ml) jar roasted red peppers, well drained (see Tips)

1 small onion, chopped

1 clove garlic, peeled

2 tbsp tomato paste

2 tbsp Turkish red pepper paste (optional; see Tips)

1 tsp Aleppo pepper (see Tips)

1 tsp ground cumin

½ tsp salt

3 tbsp chopped walnuts

1 tbsp plus 2 tsp nigella seeds (see Tips)

1 tbsp plus 2 tsp sesame seeds

1 tbsp fresh lemon juice

1 tbsp pomegranate molasses (see Tips)

Garnish:

Olive oil, for drizzling

1 tbsp chopped walnuts

1 tsp nigella seeds

1 tsp sesame seeds

1 tbsp pomegranate seeds (optional)

Parsley leaves, for garnish (optional)

Mujadara

Bulgur, Lentil, and Caramelized Onion Pilaf

This is a very ancient dish that has been enjoyed in the Middle East for millennia. Eaten by rich and poor alike, it is highly nutritious and fortifying, earning it the nickname "nail in the knees" for its ability to keep labourers standing all day. Completely vegan, it could also be served during periods of religious fasting.

Prep: 1 hr

Cook: 50 min

Makes: 4 main-dish servings or 6 side-dish servings

---

4 tbsp olive oil, plus more for serving (see Tips)

4 large yellow or red onions, finely sliced

2½ teaspoons salt

½ cup/100 g small brown lentils

6 cups/1.4 L water

1 cup/135 g coarse bulgur (#3)

Freshly ground black pepper, for serving

In a heavy-bottomed medium soup pot, heat the olive oil over medium heat. Add the onions and patiently brown them, stirring regularly. As they begin to darken, add ½ teaspoon of salt and continue to cook until they start to caramelize and some turn crispy golden brown, 15 to 20 minutes. Remove a generous ½ cup/125 mL of the onions and set aside for garnish.

Add the lentils to the onion mix and stir together for about 2 minutes. Add 3 cups/750 mL of water and 1 teaspoon of salt and bring to a boil. Reduce the heat to medium-low, cover, and simmer for 20 minutes.

Stir in the bulgur, the remaining 3 cups/750 mL water, and remaining 1 teaspoon salt. Bring back to a boil, then reduce the heat to medium-low, cover, and simmer until almost all the liquid is absorbed, about 15 minutes.

Uncover, remove from the heat, and let sit for another 10 minutes to let the last of the liquid absorb. The lentils and bulgur should be cooked but not mushy.

Fluff with a fork, and transfer to a serving bowl. Reheat the reserved onions in a small pan. Top each serving of the mujadara with a little pile of the caramelized onions, a light drizzle of olive oil, and a twist of black pepper.

Tips:

You can use a fair bit more oil to make the onions, pouring off and reserving the excess along with the reserved onions, then using that oil to reheat the onions and to drizzle over the finished dish.

This dish requires coarse bulgur and small brown lentils to get the right combination of textures and cooking time.

ADOPT-A-RECIPE Cara Benjamin-Pace

Fatayer Jibneh/Sabanekh

Savoury Cheese or Spinach Pastries

Fatayer are the perfect party food: easy to prepare, they can be made a day ahead, refrigerated, and then warmed to serve. These tidy, attractive little pastries can be filled with meat, cheese, spinach, or just za'atar, with different shapes based on the type of filling they contain. The convention is to shape meat *fatayer* into squares, cheese *fatayer* into boats, and spinach *fatayer* into triangles. Each filling recipe makes enough to fill one recipe of the dough.

Prep: 1½ hr

Cook: 30 to 40 min

Makes: 12 to 16 medium fatayer (6 servings)

Dough:

1 cup/250 mL warm water or 2% milk

1 (¼ oz/7 g) envelope active dry yeast

1 tsp sugar

3 cups/400 g all-purpose flour

½ tsp salt

¼ cup/60 mL vegetable oil

Jibneh (Cheese Filling):

3½ oz/100 g feta cheese, crumbled (about ¾ cup)

3½ oz/100 g akawi or Halloumi cheese, shredded (about 1 cup)

1 tbsp nigella seeds

3 to 4 sprigs parsley, chopped (optional)

1 chopped green onion (optional)

Sabanekh (Spinach Filling):

1 lb/450 g spinach (fresh or frozen)

Salt

2 tbsp vegetable oil

1 small white onion, finely diced

1 tbsp sumac

½ tsp baharat (aka "seven spice" mix; see Tips)

¼ tsp freshly ground black pepper

2 tbsp fresh lemon juice

½ cup/125 mL pomegranate seeds

¼ cup/60 mL chopped walnuts or pine nuts (optional)

Assembly:

1 egg, for brushing (optional)

1 tbsp nigella and/or sesame seeds, to decorate

Make the dough: In a small bowl, mix the water with the yeast and sugar. Let sit until foamy on top, about 10 minutes.

In a large bowl, mix the flour and salt and make a well in the centre. Gradually add the yeast mixture and the oil to the well and knead until you have a pliant but firm dough, about 8 minutes. Cover and let rise until doubled in volume, about 30 minutes.

Make the jibneh filling: In a bowl, stir together the cheeses and nigella seeds. If using parsley and green onion, stir them in as well.

Make the sabanekh filling: If using fresh spinach, chop coarsely, toss with some salt, and let sit for 10 minutes, then squeeze away the moisture. If using frozen, thaw thoroughly and squeeze out any water.

In a skillet, warm the oil over medium heat. Add the onion and sauté until translucent, about 5 minutes. Add the spinach, sumac, baharat, ½ teaspoon salt, and the pepper and cook until the spinach is wilted and all the remaining liquid has evaporated.

Remove from the heat and stir in the lemon juice, pomegranate seeds, and walnuts (if using).

Preheat the oven to 350°F/180°C.

To assemble: Punch down the dough and pinch off pieces the size of golf balls. You should get between 12 and 16. Let them rest, covered, for 15 minutes.

Roll out each ball into a thin round 4½ to 5 inches/ 11 to 13 cm in diameter. Spread about 2 table-spoons of the filling in the centre of the dough. Pinch both ends and lift up the sides to form a boat-shaped pastry, or pull three edges of the dough together over the filling and pinch to form a sort of low pyramid.

Place on a baking sheet. Brush with beaten egg if desired and sprinkle with nigella/sesame seeds. Bake until golden, about 30 minutes.

Tips:

You can find Arabic "seven spice" seasoning known as baharat *in spice shops or Middle Eastern markets.*

You can use a variety of cheeses to make the jibneh fatayer, *including ricotta, mozzarella, or any other of your favourites.*

The egg wash helps the pastries brown, but if you prefer to keep them vegan it need not be used.

These savoury pastries also freeze very well.

Kousa Mahshi

Zucchinis Stuffed with Meat and Rice

Stuffed vegetables of all kinds are popular throughout the Levant, so much so that there is even a dedicated tool called a *manakra* used to hollow them out. Small pale-green zucchini, sometimes called marrow, are especially well suited for this recipe.

Prep: 1 hr 45 min
Cook: 1 hr
Makes: 6 servings

---

1 cup/200 g basmati rice

12 small zucchinis

1 lb/450 g ground beef

1 small yellow onion, finely chopped

1 tbsp salt

1 tsp baharat (Arabic "seven spice" mix; see Tips)

1 tsp ground cumin

1 tsp freshly ground black pepper

½ tsp ground allspice

4 tbsp olive oil, plus more as needed

4 tbsp chopped fresh parsley

4 tbsp chopped fresh mint

1 (5.5 fl oz/156 mL) can tomato paste

½ cup/125 mL fresh lemon juice

Lemon wedges and olive oil, for serving

Set the rice aside in a bowl of water to soak while you prepare the zucchinis.

Trim off the stem ends of the zucchinis. Use a manakra or zucchini corer (an apple corer, or even a small spoon, like a grapefruit spoon, can also work) to twist into the zucchini the long way, slowly hollowing out the flesh of the zucchini and leaving a wall about ¼ inch/6 mm thick. Take care not to push all the way through the other end. You should have a nice, even, empty but firm shell to fill with the meat mixture. Save the flesh to use in another recipe.

Drain the rice and place in a large bowl. Add the ground beef, onion, salt, baharat, cumin, pepper, and allspice and mix well. Add the oil and combine until the mixture is moist. (Add more oil if necessary.) Add the chopped parsley and mint.

Using this mixture, stuff the zucchini, leaving about ½-inch/1.3 cm gap at the end. Don't pack it in too hard as it needs a bit of room to expand.

Carefully arrange the stuffed zucchini in a large shallow pot. In a small bowl, stir together the tomato paste and lemon juice. Pour over the zucchini, then add enough water to cover.

Cover the pot and bring to a boil. Reduce the heat and simmer, covered, for 30 minutes.

Uncover and simmer until the liquid is reduced by half, another 20 minutes, to finish cooking and thicken the sauce, adding a bit more water if needed to prevent the liquid from going below about half the original volume.

Serve hot or at room temperature, with a drizzle of olive oil and squeeze of lemon.

Tips:

Baharat, *aka "seven spice mix," is available online and at Middle Eastern markets.*

Some cooks like to score the length of the outside of the zucchini with the serrated edge of the manakra *or a fork to add a nice look; it also helps if the skin is a bit tough.*

This filling is used to stuff many other kinds of vegetable, too: small eggplants, tomatoes, peppers, onions, or parboiled potatoes.

Prep: 1½ hr

Cook: 30 min

Makes: 12 to 15 medium croquettes

Dough:

1½ cups/250 g fine bulgur (#1)

1 cup/250 mL hot water plus more as needed

1 small onion, quartered

¾ lb/340 g extra-lean ground beef (see Tips)

1 tsp salt

½ tsp freshly ground black pepper

¼ tsp ground cumin

¼ tsp baharat (optional; see Tips)

Filling:

1 tbsp vegetable oil

1 small onion, chopped

½ lb/225 g lean ground beef

⅓ cup/80 mL chopped walnuts or pine nuts, lightly toasted

1 tsp salt

Pinch of freshly ground black pepper

2 tsp pomegranate molasses

2 tbsp pomegranate seeds

Assembly:

Neutral oil, for deep-frying

Kibbeh Lahmeh

Fried Kibbeh with Beef and Pine Nuts

Making and stuffing kibbeh is a group activity just about every Syrian woman would have participated in—virtually no major occasion occurs without the appearance of a platter (or mountain) of kibbeh at the table. Bulgur, finely ground meat, and spices are combined into a dough to be carefully stuffed and formed into small football-shaped dumplings that are then fried to a crisp, dark auburn.

Make the dough: Place the bulgur in a large bowl and gradually add 1 cup of hot water. Cover and wait 15 minutes. If it feels very dry you may need to add another ¼ cup/60 mL water and wait until it has been fully absorbed.

In a food processor, combine the onion, beef, salt, pepper, cumin, and baharat (if using) and process to a very smooth paste. (Alternatively, run through a meat grinder; see Tips.)

Add the meat mixture to the soaked bulgur and use damp hands to knead to make a smooth, evenly combined dough. Cover and refrigerate while you prepare the filling.

Make the filling: In a skillet, heat the oil over medium to medium-high heat. Add the onion and sauté until golden, 5 to 10 minutes. Add the ground beef and cook until browned, breaking up the meat. Add the toasted nuts, salt, pepper, and pomegranate molasses and stir to combine. Remove from the heat and let cool. Stir in the pomegranate seeds.

To assemble: Keep a small bowl of water next to you so you can keep your hands damp (see Tips).

Take the dough from the refrigerator and have a baking sheet or platter ready to put the kibbeh on once formed.

With dampened hands, pinch off about 2 tablespoons of the dough and form into a squat cone. Using your finger, make a well in the base of the cone while rotating the dough around your finger to deepen and expand the hole until you create a thin (¼-inch/6 mm) shell. It will look something like the bowl of a wineglass with a slightly pointed bottom.

Add about 1 tablespoon of the filling into this dough "cup," seal the dough around the filling, and form to create a football or torpedo shape, making sure there are no cracks in the shell. Repeat this process until all the ingredients are used up.

Refrigerate the kibbeh balls for at least 1 hour.

Pour 3 to 4 inches/7 to 10 cm oil into a deep heavy-bottomed pan and heat to about 325°F/163°C. Fry the kibbeh, a few at a time, for 5 to 6 minutes until dark brown. Remove to a wire rack or a plate lined with paper towels.

Tips:

At a Middle Eastern butcher you can request meat ground extra fine specifically for making kibbeh.

Baharat, aka "seven spice mix," is available online and at Middle Eastern markets.

You can get extra-fine plates for meat grinders specifically for making kibbeh.

Make sure you keep your hands moist and try to keep the dough cool as you work with it as it will be much easier to make it stick together and prevent cracking.

ADOPT-A-RECIPE   Stephanie Thomas

Kibbeh bil Sanieh

Baked Bulgur Pie with Pumpkin, Chickpea, and Pomegranate Filling

A staple of every Syrian party, kibbeh comes in a vast array of shapes and flavours—Aleppo alone is purported to have nearly twenty different kinds. This recipe, a vegetarian kibbeh traditionally baked in a large round tray, is much faster and easier than hand-forming and deep-frying scores of individual kibbehs.

Prep: 45 min

Cook: 45 min

Makes: 4 to 6 main-dish servings; 8 to 12 appetizer servings

Dough:

½ large potato, peeled and quartered

1½ cups/250 g fine bulgur (#1)

1 tsp salt, plus more to taste

1½ cups/375 mL warm water

¼ red onion, finely chopped (about ⅓ cup/80 mL)

½ cup plus 2 tbsp/155 mL pumpkin purée (add more if the mixture feels dry)

½ tsp dried basil

½ tsp cayenne pepper or chili powder

½ tsp ground cumin

Freshly ground black pepper

Filling:

1 tbsp olive oil

1 medium onion, finely diced

2 cups/500 mL diced squash, such as butternut, acorn, kabocha, etc. (fresh or frozen)

1 (18 fl oz/540 mL) can chickpeas, drained and rinsed

¼ cup/60 mL pomegranate seeds (fresh or frozen)

½ tsp ground cumin

Salt and freshly ground black pepper

Assembly:

¼ cup/60 mL melted butter or ghee, for brushing

Make the dough: In a medium pot of boiling water, cook the potato until tender, about 20 minutes. Drain and mash roughly with a fork.

In a large bowl, combine the bulgur and 1 teaspoon of salt. Add 1 cup/250 mL of warm water and let soak for 5 minutes. Gradually add the remaining ½ cup/125 mL water until the liquid is absorbed and the texture is soft but not wet. (You may not need all the water.) This should take about 15 minutes.

Add the cooked potato, onion, pumpkin purée, basil, cayenne, and cumin to the bulgur. Season with more salt and pepper to taste. Stir to combine (using your hands lets you really mix everything together well).

Transfer the mixture to a meat grinder or food processor and process by pulsing until a smooth dough is formed. The dough should hold its shape if you squeeze a ball of it in your hands. Set aside.

Make the filling: In a medium saucepan, heat the oil over medium heat. Add the onion and sauté until translucent, about 5 minutes. Add the squash and cook until softened, 2 to 3 minutes. Add the chickpeas, pomegranate seeds, and cumin. Season with salt and pepper.

Preheat the oven to 350°F/180°C. Line a 9-inch/23 cm springform pan with parchment paper and spray the pan with cooking spray.

To assemble: Gently press half of the dough into the pan and pat down into an even layer about ½ inch/1.3 cm thick. Spoon the filling evenly on top. Press the rest of the dough on top so that the filling is sandwiched in between the two layers of bulgur dough.

Score the top of the "pie" with whatever design you like (keeping in mind that the finished kibbeh will be cut along those lines). Brush with the melted butter.

Bake until golden, about 45 minutes.

Let it sit to cool for at least 10 minutes before releasing the springform pan. Cut into wedges to serve.

Tips:

The ladies would often make this with a mushroom, spinach, and walnut filling as well; a meat filling can also be used.

Bulgur, or burghul, is sold in fine, medium, and coarse grinds, which are sometimes numbered: #1, #2, and #3 respectively. For kibbeh, it is important to use the finest grind available.

Decorative cuts, often diamond shapes, are scored onto the dough before baking. This not only makes the dish very attractive, but also makes it much easier to cut/portion after it's baked.

Chicken and Broth:

1 whole small or ½ large chicken, cut into rough pieces

1 small onion, halved

1 celery stalk, halved

1 carrot, halved

1 dried lemon (optional)

1 bay leaf

1 tsp kosher salt

Freshly ground black pepper

8 cups/2 L water

Eggplant and Filling:

2 large eggplants, cut lengthwise into ½-inch/1.3 cm slices

Salt

½ cup/125 mL olive oil

½ head cauliflower, cut into bite-size pieces

2 large carrots, peeled and cut on the diagonal into ½-inch/1.3 cm slices

2 cups/400 g short-grain rice, such as Calrose, or sushi rice

Garnish:

½ pound/225 g lean ground beef

1 tsp baharat

½ tsp ground cumin

Salt and black pepper

¼ cup slivered almonds

2 tbsp pine nuts

Maqluba

"Upside-Down" Casserole

This is a festive dish served at parties and family celebrations. The word *maqluba* means "upside down," a reference to the dramatic moment when the pot is inverted onto a plate and then lifted to reveal the dish —usually to great applause—before being decorated with ground meat and nuts. It can be made with a variety of ingredients layered with rice, but the eggplant case gives it's essential structure.

Make the chicken and broth: In a soup pot, combine the chicken pieces, onion, celery, carrot, dried lemon, bay leaf, salt, pepper to taste, and the water. Bring to a boil. Skim off the foam as it rises to the top. Reduce the heat to medium and simmer for 1½ hours.

Remove the chicken and set aside to cool. Strain the broth through a sieve, pressing down on the vegetables to extract all the flavours. If using immediately, keep the pot handy.

When the chicken is cool enough to handle, pull the meat off the bones. Tear the meat into bite-size pieces. Both white and dark meat should be in the mix. The dish will require 2 cups/500 mL.

Measure the chicken broth and add enough water (if needed) to come to 4½ cups/1 L. The broth and chicken can be prepared in advance and reserved separately in the fridge.

Prepare the eggplant and filling: Place the eggplant slices on a clean tea towel. Sprinkle each side with some salt and leave for 15 minutes.

In a large heavy skillet, heat the olive oil over medium heat. Add the eggplant slices and cook until soft and golden, 3 to 5 minutes. Drain on a paper towels to absorb any excess oil. Reserve the pan and any leftover oil for making the garnish.

In the original broth cooking pot or in a large saucepan, bring 4 cups/950 mL of the chicken broth to a boil. Add the cauliflower and carrots and cook for 10 minutes. Remove the vegetables with a slotted spoon and set aside to cool.

Rinse the rice, drain, and then add it to the broth. Add 1 teaspoon salt to the broth. Set the broth over medium-low heat, cover with a tight-fitting lid, and simmer until the liquid has evaporated, about 20 minutes. Turn off the heat and let sit covered for another 10 minutes.

Preheat the oven to 300°F/150°C.

You'll want a round deep ovenproof dish or pan about 10 inches/25 cm wide, 4 to 6 inches/10 to 15 cm deep, with a bit of a lip and/or handles–a medium-size Pyrex bowl, deep casserole dish, or a small pot with 2 side handles would work. Carefully line the pan with the eggplant slices, overlapping them to form a complete casing. Start at the bottom of the pan and work up the sides with the slices placed outward from the centre like flower petals. When the slices reach the top of the pan, trim to create an even edge.

Spread one-third of the rice over the bottom of the casserole. Make a layer of 1 cup/250 mL of the shredded chicken and then 1 cup/250 mL of the cauliflower and carrots. Press down firmly on each layer as you add it to create cohesion to the "cake." Repeat with another layer of rice and chicken, and finish with the last one-third of the rice. Drizzle an additional ½ cup/125 mL of the chicken broth over the top and let it run down into the filling.

Cover tightly with a lid (or a sheet of heavy-duty foil). Bake in the oven for 25 minutes. Take out of the oven and let sit for 15 minutes. Remove the lid or foil.

Meanwhile, prepare the garnish: In the skillet and oil (left over from the eggplant) over medium to medium-high heat, add the ground beef, season with the baharat, cumin, and salt and pepper to taste and cook until browned and a little crispy, 8 to 10 minutes. Set aside, keeping warm.

In a small dry skillet, slowly toast the slivered almonds and pine nuts over medium-low heat until golden, about 7 minutes. Shake the pan often to prevent burning. Set aside.

When ready to serve, transfer the fried ground beef and toasted nuts to decorative bowls. Get a platter that is larger in diameter than the dish or pot containing the layered rice. Bring to the table and place the platter face down over the dish. Holding the lip of the casserole and the platter together, give it a few gentle shakes side to side to loosen. Then in a single, fluid, courageous gesture, flip the maqluba over onto the platter. Give it one more little jiggle, then with a little fanfare, carefully lift off the pan to reveal the dish! It is traditional–and kind of irresistible–that guests clap at the unveiling.

Generously sprinkle some of the ground beef and nuts over top of the "cake." With a sharp knife, cut the maqluba into generous slices and scoop onto serving plates. Any extra meat or nuts can be passed around for guests to garnish their plates.

ADOPT-A-RECIPE **Tamara Chaikin**

S'fouf

Turmeric Cake

This delicate, not-too-sweet cake gets its beautiful golden colour and complex, earthy, slightly spicy flavour from ground turmeric. Coconut, nigella, and sesame seeds add texture and intriguing flavour notes. It became one of Newcomer Kitchen's signature dishes.

Prep: 15 min
Cook: 25 to 35 min
Makes: 8 to 12 generous servings

2 cups/300 g medium-grind semolina flour (see Tips)

1½ cups/195 g all-purpose flour

1½ cups/300 g granulated sugar

1 tbsp baking powder

1 cup/80 g unsweetened shredded coconut

4 tbsp sesame seeds

2 tbsp nigella seeds (see Tips)

1½ tbsp ground turmeric

2 cups/475 mL 2% milk

8 tbsp/120 g butter

1 tsp vanilla extract

Softened butter, for the pan

2 tbsp honey

2 tbsp chopped pistachios

In a large bowl, whisk together the semolina, all-purpose flour, sugar, baking powder, coconut, sesame seeds, nigella seeds, and turmeric.

In a medium saucepan, heat the milk over medium heat until almost boiling. Remove from the heat and add the butter, stirring until melted. Cool to lukewarm and then stir in the vanilla.

Add the milk mixture to the flour mixture and mix well.

Line the bottom of a 9-inch/23 cm square cake pan with parchment paper. Grease well with softened butter. Scrape the batter into the prepared pan and allow to sit for at least 20 minutes so that the semolina can absorb the liquid.

Meanwhile, preheat the oven to 350°F/180°C.

Bake until a toothpick inserted in the centre comes out clean, 25 to 35 minutes.

Warm the honey slightly in the microwave for 10 seconds or submerge the jar in a small saucepan filled with water over low heat. Brush over the still-warm cake. Sprinkle with the pistachios.

Tips:

Wheat semolina comes in several grinds. The medium grind provides the best texture for this cake.

Nigella seeds, also known as kalonji or black cumin, can be purchased at any Middle Eastern or Asian market.

Ma'amoul

Date-Filled Shortbread Cookies

These buttery stuffed cookies are popular in the Middle East during religious holidays, for both Muslims and Christians. *Ma'amoul* are traditionally formed in special decorative carved wooden moulds—sometimes family heirlooms passed down through generations of women—but the cookies can also be formed and decorated entirely by hand.

Prep: 50 min, including 30 min | resting time for dough | **Cook:** 15 min | **Makes:** 24 cookies

Dough:

2 cups/260 g all-purpose flour

½ cup/85 g fine semolina

¼ cup/50 g sugar

½ tsp vanilla powder

Pinch of mahleb (optional; see Tips)

½ cup/125 mL ghee, melted

1 tbsp rose water or orange blossom water (optional)

¼ cup/60 mL water

Filling:

1 cup/305 g date paste (see Tips)

To finish:

2 to 3 tbsp powdered sugar (optional)

Make the dough: In a deep bowl, combine the flour, semolina, sugar, vanilla powder, and mahleb (if using). Add the ghee, rose water (if using), and water and mix with your hands until the dough is soft, crumbly, and can be rolled into a ball. Cover with a tea towel or plastic wrap and let sit for at least 30 minutes.

Make the filling: In a microwave-safe bowl, microwave the date paste until pliable, about 20 seconds. Divide the paste into 24 equal portions (about 2 teaspoons each) and roll into balls. Set aside.

Preheat the oven to 350°F/180°C.

Roll the dough in your hands until it is soft and pliable. Divide into 24 equal portions (about 20 to 25 g each) and roll into balls; they should be slightly larger than the date balls.

Flatten each dough ball into a disc and place a ball of date paste in the centre. Wrap the dough around the date ball, forming one larger ball. Using decorative tongs or a fork, gently imprint a decorative pattern on top of each ball. (Alternatively, gently press each ball into a traditional ma'amoul mould to create a pattern, then invert and tap to release.)

Arrange on a baking sheet and bake until lightly golden, 10 to 15 minutes.

Let cool, then dust with the powdered sugar. Store in an airtight container.

Tips:

Date paste is simply pitted dates that have been skinned and mashed into a paste. You can make your own by blanching or steaming, pitting, and pureeing whole dates, but this is quite time-consuming. It is much easier to purchase premade date paste at any Middle Eastern grocery store. If it is too stiff, you can add a bit of vegetable oil to soften the paste.

Mahleb (aka mahlab or mahalepi) is made from grinding the seeds of a species of cherry, and adds an almondy fragrance, and is also available online or at specialty shops.

Wooden or plastic ma'amoul moulds can be found online or at specialty Middle Eastern shops.

ADOPT-A-RECIPE Yvonne Hilder

Qatayef

Yeasted Pancakes with Ricotta Filling and Syrup

These elegant little pancakes, filled with ricotta cheese and decorated with nuts, are a beloved part of the holiday table during Ramadan and Eid.

Prep: 45 min

Cook: 10 min

Makes: 12 to 14 pancakes (4 servings)

½ cup/65 g all-purpose flour

½ cup/85 g fine semolina

½ tbsp granulated sugar

½ tsp baking powder

¼ tsp instant yeast

⅛ tsp salt

1¼ cups/295 g warm water

¾ cup/175 mL ricotta cheese (see Tips)

1 tbsp rose water or orange blossom water (optional; see Tips)

4 tbsp simple syrup (see Tips) or honey, plus more for drizzling

4 tbsp ground pistachios

In a large bowl, combine the flour, semolina, sugar, baking powder, yeast, and salt. Add the warm water and mix until well incorporated. Cover with plastic wrap or a damp cloth and let rest in a warm place for 20 to 30 minutes, to allow the yeast to activate and the semolina to absorb the liquid.

Meanwhile, in a small bowl, mix the ricotta, rose water (if using), and simple syrup to taste. The filling can be unsweetened or lightly sweet as it will get a further drenching of syrup before serving.

Heat a nonstick medium skillet over medium heat. Add 2 tablespoons of batter per pancake and cook on one side only until bubbles appear and there are no visible wet spots. Do not flip!

As you work, transfer the pancakes to a large plate and cover with a slightly damp cloth to keep them from drying out.

When cool enough to handle, fold and pinch the edges of each pancake together about two-thirds of the way down to form a small cone.

Fill the cone opening with 1 to 2 teaspoons of the ricotta mixture and then dip the open side into the ground pistachios.

Arrange on a serving platter and generously drizzle with the simple syrup just before serving.

Tips:

For a special treat, substitute kaymak, a kind of Arabic clotted cream available in Middle Eastern shops, for some or all of the ricotta.

Rose water and orange blossom water can be found at most stores that stock Middle Eastern or Asian ingredients.

Simple syrup can be made by boiling 2 parts sugar to 1 part water until the sugar is dissolved. A squeeze of lemon juice makes it even nicer!

Pomegranate seeds, crumbled dried rose petals, or little dollops of rose petal jam make exquisite special garnishes.

These pancakes freeze well, so make extra. Pack them in pairs, uncooked sides touching, separated with wax paper, and place in sealed plastic bags. Then simply thaw and stuff with fresh filling when you want a special treat.

ADOPT-A-RECIPE   Kirsten Hanson

DIGESTIF

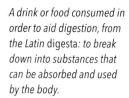

A drink or food consumed in order to aid digestion, from the Latin digesta: *to break down into substances that can be absorbed and used by the body.*

WHEREIN I REFLECT ON LESSONS LEARNED

ENOUGH

Enough is as good as a feast.

Not the wisdom of Wing's Fortune Cookie Company, but rather attributed to Greek philosopher Euripides, c. 500 BCE.

Around 2009, I happened upon a fortune cookie that read "Enough is as good as a feast." It resonated with me enough that I taped it to my laptop screen as I set out on the strange, winding adventure that became The Depanneur. The journey began at a time of personal upheaval and uncertainty. My professional life had come unravelled, and I had grown disenchanted with the received wisdom concerning entrepreneurial ambition and success. I wanted a new direction, but did not know where to begin.

I started by taking stock of what I had to work with: my skills, my relative privilege, and a lifelong love of food, travel, and conviviality. I decided that rather than pursue whatever avenue might make the most possible money, I'd try to get to *enough* in the funnest, most interesting way I could. It helped that *enough*, for me, wasn't much. I was lucky enough to have modest needs, no dependents, and a place to live. I was an educated, straight, white male, able-bodied and neuro-typical, riding the coattails of a middle-class upbringing. What emerged was an attempt at a kind of privilege ju-jitsu: an experiment to see if I might be able to use the inertia of my own advantage to try and help make things better for others, or at least resist making them worse.

It's a self-help cliché that cultivating gratitude is a key to being happier; to actually *feel* grateful is indeed a very powerful antidepressant. Fortunately, gratitude—like love,

293

Ginger Dean (R) ran The Dep's brunch in the early days. Occasionally she'd team up with her twin sister, Yvonne, for a Drop-In Dinner. It was always a bit of a trip to watch them work, with movements and mannerisms that were eerily synchronized. Ginger was also a talented gardener, and helped me plant my first vegetable garden in my tiny front yard.

kindness, generosity, and happiness—is not a zero-sum game. The more you give away, the more you get in return; this abundance is what makes it inherently radical and subversive in an extractive, capitalist world. **The Dep became a tool to pay forward and amplify what I had, a process for turning privilege into gratitude.**

When The Dep started, and I put out the call for people to donate stuff to our kitchen drive, I tried a private experiment I called Give & Take. Back at my design firm I had been hunting around for an alternative to perfunctory client gifts and discovered Kiva, an organisation that facilitates small loans to people around the world who do not have easy access to credit. Now, if someone donated something especially useful or valuable to The Dep, I would make small loans to women food entrepreneurs in the developing world in return.

Over time Give & Take would become a quiet but important part of The Dep's DNA. Later, when things were going badly, when sales were AWOL or some new crisis was unfolding, I would dig up a few more dollars to lend. However hard I thought I had it, I knew that every one of them had it much harder than me. It was an exercise in

gratitude, a recalibration of entitlement, a reminder of my own good fortune and privilege in the moments when I felt it the least.

Over the years, these little loans slowly accumulated; there are now hundreds of them, thousands of dollars quietly at work in more than forty countries. If there is one distant fantasy buried deep in my heart, it would be to one day go visit some of these women, sit down at their little village kiosks or market stalls, taste their food, and hear their stories.

Photo: Sandy Nicholson

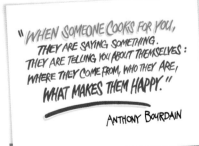

"WHEN SOMEONE COOKS FOR YOU, THEY ARE SAYING SOMETHING. THEY ARE TELLING YOU ABOUT THEMSELVES: WHERE THEY COME FROM, WHO THEY ARE, WHAT MAKES THEM HAPPY."

ANTHONY BOURDAIN

DEPANNEUR

WE'RE ALL IN THIS TOGE-THER!

A PLACE WHERE INTERESTING FOOD THINGS HAPPEN

Photo: Jyll Simmons

Photos: Hanna Slotterback

SMALLNESS

Starting from a place of *enough* lends itself to smallness. The Dep was only about 450 square feet, renovated and outfitted for less than what some places might spend on an espresso machine. The one room contained the open kitchen, storage, sinks, fridges, and the dining area, reflecting both the project's modest ambitions and very real financial constraints.

Smallness also made sense if I intended to showcase amateur and home cooks. The Dep could fit twenty-four people, around the limit of what I imagined was realistically achievable by an enthusiastic non-professional cook. If you could make a big holiday dinner for your family, you could probably do this. It was also small enough that if things went wrong, they could only go so bad. Going bigger risked excluding the very people and food I wanted to feature in the first place.

Smallness was also about operating at a human scale, one that afforded intimacy and connection. As a Depanneur guest, you ate in the same room as the person who cooked your food; you saw them, and they saw you. You could see if they were struggling to get something done or were beaming with pride as they brought a platter to the table.

Even the silly conceit of the Supper Club, that one paid for a membership but the meal was free, quietly nudged the experience away from the transactional. Communal, family-style dining meant you weren't being *served*; something was being shared with you, and you in turn were sharing it with others. The open kitchen centred the cooks as people, more real and present than nameless, faceless workers toiling away behind unseen closed doors. It offered a bi-directional connection between the cooks and the diners, something that had been largely, perhaps intentionally, obscured in most restaurant settings. This made guests more patient, compassionate, and understanding when things were a bit slow or imperfect.

Part of The Dep was me shaking my tiny fist at the values of fine-dining, a rebuttal of notions of luxury, decadence, or obsequious service. **Instead of using food to highlight and widen the inequality gap, I was trying to close it with human connection, storytelling, and food.** To embrace smallness was to reject the idea that a great experience had to be defined by how much it cost—and by extension, the idea that value itself, personal or professional, had to be measured in dollars. The Dep asked: Could it be *enough* to just be small and cheap?

Smallness also lowered the barriers to participation and helped make it more inclusive. The result was a flourishing of diverse culinary voices. It helped create a welcoming space for those often pushed to the margins, for women and immigrants and visible minorities. It showed that it was possible to support greater equity and opportunity simply by moving obstacles out of the way. Nature abhors a vacuum; where there are affordable spaces, creativity and talent will rush in to fill them.

It wasn't always fun or easy, but its modest ambitions and low overhead gave

The Dep a remarkable resilience. To simply survive more than ten years as a food business in a rapidly gentrifying city like Toronto is itself not a trivial matter. How to stay small without becoming expensive, how to eke out *enough* amidst ever-rising rents, is a big question for the future of The Dep. Embracing smallness is an act of resistance to the voracious ambition of capitalism and its delusion of limitless growth in a finite world.

Danielle Mitrovic was a treat to work with. Funny, smart, cute as a button, and communist AF, she'd make short work of a busy weekend brunch service. She also hosted her own occasional pop-up, with fantastic cupcakes, baklava, and cabbage rolls.

" START WHERE YOU ARE. USE WHAT YOU HAVE. DO WHAT YOU CAN. "

ARTHUR ASHE

THE MACGUFFIN

Sharing a meal is probably among the most universal of all human experiences—there has never been a person who does not eat. Food, like art and music, is one of those rare things that can leap across age, race, gender, culture, history, and geography; this is its superpower. To me, most restaurant meals feel like a missed opportunity to do something much more interesting. The Dep was about looking for that something and trying to make it the centre of the experience.

The Supper Clubs, the family-style dinner party where guests sat and shared food with people they didn't know, was the heart of The Dep. Food came to the table and people served each other; this was fundamental to what made it different from a regular restaurant. You got to share a meal and an experience, meet new people, maybe discover a new culture or try an unfamiliar dish, possibly even make some new friends along the way. Sometimes it was a bit too loud, or too warm, or too crowded; sometimes the kitchen was too smoky or the timing was off. It wasn't for everyone, but it was always interesting and memorable.

It was a place where chefs had the freedom to explore and tell their stories through their food. The meals offered a way to reach beyond simply what was on the plate, to find a point of contact between the person in the kitchen and the person at the table. Sharing these experiences acted as a kind of resonating chamber, amplifying the signal. The cooks were in the room, interacting with the diners, watching people enjoy themselves,

giving and receiving hospitality, manifesting a kind of reciprocal care and generosity. **In many restaurant kitchens, the only feedback a chef might get is a complaint; at The Dep it was not uncommon for a cook to get a round of applause.**

Depanneur meals were intentionally affordable, but they were exclusive in ways that cannot come from simply a high price tag. Each dinner was a small, unique event for just a handful of people; miss it and it was gone forever. In this way I could create something precious; create value without having to make it expensive. Moreover, they were authentic experiences; not in the red-herring way of how one might imagine an "authentic" recipe, a mirage of provenance that dissolves as you approach it. They were authentic because they were not a commodity, but rather a genuine manifestation of someone's passion and personality, a gift to be shared.

There were a thousand of these little dinner parties, an eclectic mix of one-offs and perennial favourites that wove the fabric of The Depanneur. Little delighted me more than being able to present a dinner from a cuisine I had never tried before. It offered a chance to try the kind of home-cooked family meals that intimately embody a place in a way that restaurants rarely do. I couldn't get a seat at a dinner table in Albania or Azerbaijan, Kazakhstan or Kenya, Ghana or Guangxi, but I could bring them to my

Jonna Pederson, the Dep's resident brunchatrix from 2013 to 2015, spent many years teaching English in Korea, where she also became interested in the tradition of vegetarian Korean Temple Food. She taught several popular kimchi workshops, and would occasionally blow the mind of an unsuspecting ajumma (middle-aged Korean housewife) at the local Korean supermarket by responding to their skeptical commentary in fluent Korean.

"PEOPLE WHO GIVE YOU THEIR FOOD GIVE YOU THEIR HEART."

CESAR CHAVEZ

Natalia "Cookie" Martinez
*brought a lot of infectious
laughter and a fair bit of
mischief into The Dep
kitchen, with her cookies,
and later, ice cream
sandwiches, which would
become a popular Dep treat.
She would eventually open
a stall at the Scadding Court
Market 707–an innovative
urban project of food stalls
made from converted
shipping containers–before
opening her own restaurant,
Cookie Martinez Colombian
Street Food.*

kitchen. I found a way to travel the world without leaving my neighbourhood.

The Dep allowed for a deeper dive into culinary traditions, offering up a context and a sense of how dishes connected to individuals, cultures, or geographies. Sometimes this was implicit, conveyed through family recipes and personal food memories. Other times it was more explicit, like Chantal Véchambre's multi-year culinary voyage through all eighteen regions of France, each dinner showcasing the specialities of a distinct terroir in a particular season (see her Basque Country Chicken on page 161).

The Dep encouraged cooks to explore the complex intersections that reflected themselves and their lives in a cosmopolitan city. So many people came from mixed-culture backgrounds, and their food offered a way to engage and celebrate their unique combinations. The results were as diverse as the people who cooked them: Mexican-Thai, or Portuguese-Russian, or Franco-Korean, or Scottish-Haitian, or Jamaican-Italian, or Yemeni-Kenyan. There was always something new to discover, for me, for the diners, and often for the cooks themselves. Encountering the depth, complexity, and idiosyncrasies of real people adds dimension to a world flattened by stereotypes and clichés. It closes the distance between others and ourselves, forges a connection that is a small cobblestone in the road to compassion.

Back in my university days in Montreal, I took a film studies class at Concordia. I learned that Alfred Hitchcock used something called a MacGuffin to move the story along—an object, device, or event that is necessary to the plot and the motivation of the characters, but insignificant in itself. Think of the Maltese Falcon—the fact that it happened to be Maltese, or a falcon, is completely irrelevant. Many restaurateurs or chefs may say, "It is all about the food," but food was my MacGuffin. I have come to believe that I was never really in the restaurant business at all. I was in the business of trying to create meaning and human connection, and I chose food because it seemed the easiest and most accessible way to approach it.

"FOOD IS OUR COMMON GROUND."
JAMES BEARD

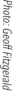

Photo: Geoff Fitzgerald

LOOPHOLE HUNTING

Smallness offers a way to lower risk, and this helps afford more creative freedom. It enables people to take more chances, to do more fun, interesting things. A Scottish-Haitian fusion menu? An ancient Roman banquet? A dinner of only black and white ingredients with a black and white dress code? These would probably not fly as full-time restaurant concepts, but we could get away with them for one night.

Low overhead freed The Dep from having to pander to the latest trend or the lowest common denominator. It let me make mistakes, learn from them, pick myself back up, and try again. This ability to fail gently, non-catastrophically, is essential to taking the kind of creative risks that underlie innovation. Soaring rents and overhead costs demand ever greater, faster success to just survive. This leaves even less room to experiment, to take genuine creative chances. To innovate means to risk failing, yet failing in such a context becomes disastrous. The end result is a lot of derivative, copycat concepts that are ultimately dull and uninspired, chasing whatever is trendy at the moment.

To play a different game, one in opposition to traditional definitions of success, can be a risky endeavour. Anything genuinely innovative, disruptive, radical, or subversive will likely run afoul of rules somewhere along the way. A lot of what The Depanneur did was against those rules, some theoretical (you can't have a restaurant with a different chef every night), some real (you can't host BYOB events without a liquor licence). The rules became the parameters of the problem within which the solution had to be found, and sometimes creativity flourishes within constraints that focus its energy.

In the wildly over-regulated food space of Toronto, my experience of the first few years of The Dep was largely defined by hunting for—or outright inventing—loopholes. Finding them was necessary to allow me to do many of the things I wanted to do. This required getting a good handle on what the rules were and then hunting for the cracks through which the light famously gets in. For example: I once came up with the notion to save a bit of money by churning my own organic butter, using the leftover "free" buttermilk to make the bread pudding for brunch. I'd use some of the butter to cook and thought I'd just sell any surplus. **When I found out it was technically forbidden to sell homemade butter, I put an $8 "butter sandwich" on the menu: a slice of toast that came with ¼ pound of butter on the side, to go.**

Part of the challenge of doing something innovative is that it may take you into uncharted territory. Very few "out of the box" things happen in Toronto, because the box is rigidly built to only accommodate things expressly designed to fit in it. This begs the questions: Who decides on the shape of the box, and who benefits from it being that shape? Keeping things small, modest, and under the radar all helped expand the freedom I had to explore new ideas. It takes advantage of the fact that large systems often become preoccupied with maintaining or expanding their domains of control. This means they may not even bother to care about little things on the margins, or are so glacially slow to react that often by the time they even figure out what is going on, it is already done.

Lisa Kates was an important mentor and supporter of The Dep from the very beginning. With a background in food and social issues in Ottawa, she "got" what The Dep was all about from the get-go. She ran a soup catering business out of the Dep's kitchen for several years, along with numerous pop-ups, like this one with her two daughters, Olivia and Katie, both of them food entrepreneurs as well. Lisa later went on to join forces with another food activist in Toronto, Darcy Higgins, to found Building Roots, a non-profit that fights food insecurity in some of Toronto's most underserved communities through affordable produce markets and innovative urban agriculture projects.

"IT'S EASIER TO ASK FORGIVENESS THAN IT IS TO GET PERMISSION."

— GRACE MURRAY HOPPER

VENTURE COMMUNISM

*In 2013, **Quinn Cruise** was the only deaf woman to have graduated from George Brown Culinary College. But even after an internship in Shanghai, and months of searching, no one would hire her, and she was getting discouraged. Fortunately her weekly pop-up at The Dep got written up in the paper, which led to a full-time gig as a chef. Then, in 2014, she was invited to represent Canada in the Deaf Culinary Olympics in Copenhagen. Here she's in the kitchen with her mom, journalist Alison Griffiths.*

All this rule-bending was a calculated gamble based on research into the rules themselves, an estimation of the possible consequences, and an inherent appetite for risk without which no entrepreneurial venture is possible. Of course, I cannot officially condone people doing things that they know are explicitly illegal, but I have a lot of room for the idea of making "good trouble," rattling the cages that confine us, especially when they feel like they are arbitrary, unjust, or manifestations of deeper systemic issues.

Bending the rules can be a kind of protest, a form of civil disobedience. Intention is important; a lot depends on who benefits and who might suffer harm. I realize this is a combination of optimism, privilege, and survivor bias talking. It is easier to ask forgiveness from a position of privilege, but this is just one more reason that the privileged should be the ones doing that asking and taking those risks; this is part of the jujitsu.

In running The Dep, I was willing to take a lot of personal risk. I was likely wildly underinsured for the things that went on there. There is a bit of impetuous foolhardiness in this kind of entrepreneurship, but to my mind the official systems' obsession with liability and ass-covering is anathema to creativity, experimentation, and innovation. Often rules are turned into barriers to participation, another way of insulating the status quo from disruption. **How can we discover new ways of doing things if we are only allowed to do it the way it is already being done?** Sometimes breaking the rules is breaking our chains.

The Dep, and definitely Newcomer Kitchen, was born of a certain personal and entrepreneurial impatience. In both cases, I did not have patience to wait for the glacial process of political, systemic, or market transformation to enable what I wanted to do. I found myself in a situation where I felt something needed to be done, *now*. This kind of entrepreneurship became a type of direct action, manifestation of agency, what my friend and fellow radical restaurateur Shamez Almani calls venture communism. In this way I believe that small business can be an activist medium. By then helping facilitate this for others, I could amplify the signal even further.

"IF YOU ARE FREE, YOU NEED TO FREE SOMEBODY ELSE. IF YOU HAVE SOME POWER, THEN YOUR JOB IS TO EMPOWER SOMEBODY ELSE."

— TONI MORRISON

LITTLE THINGS

I guess I was always drawn to the kitchen.

Even as I set out to try and engage with issues I cared about, it was obvious to me that there is no way I, or anyone, could begin to fix everything that was broken. Instead, I decided to just try and focus on creating something that felt a little less broken, and tend to it as best I could. Years after I started The Dep, I encountered the idea of *tikkun olam*, a Jewish concept of "repairing the world." Rabbi Tarfon describes it this way: **"It is not your responsibility to finish the work of perfecting the world, but you are not free to desist from it either."** Any hope of even beginning to address big problems starts by finding a way, however small, to push in the opposite direction. The Dep offered me a small way to direct my energy towards something I believed in, a small act of rebellion.

The Dep touched many people's lives, directly and indirectly. It enriched the community where I lived, connected people, birthed friendships, and created opportunities. It offered me a path to my goal: to get to *enough* in a fun and interesting way. By letting me use my privilege constructively, it afforded me the greatest privilege of all: to get up each day and work on something I genuinely cared about, with and for people I liked, in a way that felt worthwhile.

The Dep and Newcomer Kitchen were, at their core, gestures of hospitality. The word itself is layered with meaning, coming from the Latin *hospes*, meaning both "host" and "guest." This itself is derived from *ghostis*, meaning "stranger" or "enemy," as in hostile. Yet it is also the root of words like host, hospital, or hospice. This etymology tells a compelling story of the power of hospitality: how a small act of trust can transform strangers into guests, enemies into friends. The word itself embodies the bridge that a little kindness, food, and drink can build.

Food has forever been close to the

spiritual. To say a small prayer of thanks before a meal is to take a moment to consciously invoke gratitude. In English this is literally called *grace*, just in case we're a bit dense. It infuses the mundane task of feeding ourselves with something more profound. It doesn't take much to elevate a bite of food into a morsel of meaning; this is what gives comfort food its comfort, soul food its soul.

Anonymous, expendable, commodity cooks are going to create anonymous, expendable, commodity food. One could extend this to so many things in our world that have become cheap and disposable. Inversely, making quality into a luxury or status symbol further divides the world along the lines of wealth. The Dep was an attempt to push in the opposite direction, towards something more inclusive. It strove to show that food did not have to be expensive to be delightful, memorable, and meaningful. In this small way, it tried to reframe the ideas that reduce a cook's worth to just their wage, or the value of their food to simply its price tag. By extension, maybe we could see everything, including ourselves, a little differently, measured in terms of something other than money or status.

Around the table, over a glass of wine and the clink of cutlery, The Dep hinted at the possibility of another world. Maybe, together, we could turn our privilege into gratitude, our gratitude into hospitality, and our hospitality into a world that is a little bit kinder. It doesn't need to be a lot; it just needs to be *enough*.

"MANY LITTLE PEOPLE, IN LITTLE PLACES, DOING LITTLE THINGS, CAN CHANGE THE WORLD."

EDUARDO GALEANO

LEFTOVERS

Running The Dep for more than a decade meant, among other things, that I rarely went out for dinner and I inevitably had a random assortment of leftovers kicking around. Being a cheap and lazy cook who hates wasting food, pretty much everything I ate during those years was some variation of leftovers ("Encore presentations," as one wag put it), each ingredient a prompt for a creative improvisation. The resulting recipes are by their nature necessarily very flexible and accommodating, allowing me to incorporate whatever I had on hand.

BREAD PUDDING FRENCH TOAST

FRITTATA

FRIDGE CLEANER MINESTRONE

KIMCHI FRIED RICE

CHILAQUILES

BREAD PUDDING FRENCH TOAST

This popular fixture of The Dep's early brunches was a direct response to the reality of selling bread: whatever you didn't sell can easily eat up all of the profit (or more) of whatever you did. I'd cut up unsold loaves, along with ends and heels and toss them in the freezer, where they'd wait until I had a chance to whip up a batch of this bread pudding.

This recipe, in addition to being very tasty, is very flexible, allowing you to mix and match any kind of neutral or sweet bread. Once made, the bread pudding can be sliced and refrozen, then fried up straight from the freezer any time you want a decadent breakfast treat or luxe dessert served with ice cream.

Prep: 20 min (less if your bread is already cut up), plus 10 min rest

Cook: 45 min, plus cooling and final fry-up

Makes: 6 servings

6½ cups/1.5 L bread cubes (1 inch/ 2.5 cm), about a whole loaf's worth (see Tips)

3¼ cups/750 mL milk

2 tbsp/30 g unsalted butter, plus more for greasing pan

½ cup/100 g granulated sugar

1 tsp vanilla extract

¼ tsp ground nutmeg

Generous pinch of salt

3 large eggs

1 to 2 tbsp demerara sugar (optional)

Preheat the oven to 350°F/180°C. Pour 1 inch/2.5 cm water into a roasting pan or baking dish (about 2 quarts/2 litres) and set the water bath into the oven to preheat.

Place the bread in a large bowl.

In a medium saucepan, combine the milk, butter, sugar, vanilla, nutmeg, and salt. Heat over medium heat until the butter is melted and the mix is hot but not boiling. Remove from the heat and let cool a bit.

In a medium bowl, beat the eggs. Add a ladle or so of the warm milk to temper the eggs, then add the warmed eggs back to the rest of the milk and stir to combine. Pour the custard over the bread, toss to incorporate, and let sit for about 10 minutes to absorb.

If you want, you can customize at this point (see Tips).

Generously butter a 9 × 5-inch/23 × 13 cm loaf pan.

Transfer the bread mix to the pan, jiggle and pat down a bit so it's more or less even. Sprinkle the top with demerara sugar (if using).

Set the loaf pan in the water bath and bake until firm, but with a bit of wobble left, about 45 minutes. If you like it crustier, turn on the broiler for 2 to 3 minutes, but keep an eye on it, and be careful it does not burn!

Take out to cool.

To serve warm:

You can eat it like this, still warm, by the scoop, with ice cream, warm custard sauce, boozy hard sauce, and/or fruit compote.

To serve later:

Let cool; ideally refrigerate overnight. Slide a knife around all sides to release and turn out onto a cutting board. Slice about ¾ inch/2 cm thick for 12 slices in total. At this point it can be frozen (see Tips) or quickly pan-fried to finish.

In a nonstick skillet, heat 1 teaspoon butter over medium heat. If cooking from refrigerated, fry a few slices over medium heat until golden, 3 to 4 minutes. If cooking from frozen, reduce the heat to medium-low and cook for 2 to 3 minutes longer. Serve like French toast with whipped cream and maple syrup, and/or jam, candied nuts, or fresh fruit. Dust with cinnamon or icing sugar if that's your thing.

TIPS:

I especially like fruit/nut breads, like walnut-raisin, or cranberry-pumpkin seed for this. Alternatively, challah or brioche makes for a more delicate version, perfect for adding stuff to.

Customize as you wish by tossing in things like dried cranberries or cherries, walnuts or pecans, frozen blueberries, rum-soaked raisins, chocolate chips, etc.

Unused slices can be put on a tray on wax paper and frozen; once solid, transfer to a zip-seal plastic bag.

ADOPT-A-RECIPE   John Hanson

FRITTATA

Frittata is the perfect vehicle for just about any savoury bits and bobs you have kicking around in the fridge at the end of the week: bits of veg, cold cuts, cheese, herbs, you name it. . . . The result is a great brunch main hot out of the oven, and the leftover leftovers make great breakfast sandwiches.

Pro tips: Recipe can be doubled in a deep tray, and triangular wedges fit perfectly on diagonally cut toast.

Prep: 20 min
Cook: 20 min
Makes: 8 wedges

The basic idea: Eggs + stuff: something rich and salty: cheese, meat; something bulky, light, colourful: veggies; something aromatic: herbs, spices, garlic, etc.

Sauté "stuff" in an ovenproof skillet, mix it into the eggs, pour it back into the still-warm pan, and bake. Serve it with mayonnaise spiked with any kind of condiment that complements what's in your frittata.

Herbed Zucchini, Leek, Spinach, and Feta

1 tsp butter, plus more as needed

1 tsp olive oil, plus more as needed

1 medium leek, chopped

Salt and black pepper

1 zucchini, chopped

2 cloves garlic, finely chopped

½ cup/125 mL frozen spinach, thawed, liquid squeezed, chopped

1 tsp thyme, dried or fresh

10 large eggs

¼ cup/60 mL 10% cream

1/3 cup/50 g crumbled feta cheese

Preheat the oven to 350°F/180°C.

In a 10-inch/25 cm cast-iron or ovenproof skillet, heat 1 teaspoon of butter and 1 teaspoon of oil over medium heat. Add the leek, season with salt and pepper, and sauté until soft, 8 to 10 minutes.

Add the zucchini, garlic, spinach, and thyme and season with salt and pepper. Continue cooking until the vegetables are soft, another 5 to 8 minutes.

In a large bowl, beat the eggs and cream. Add the feta and season with salt and pepper. Mix in the cooked vegetables and toss to combine.

Scrape the skillet clean with a silicone spatula. Add 1 teaspoon butter or oil. Pour the egg/veg mix back into the same, still-warm pan, scraping the bowl with the spatula. Even it out, sprinkling with a little extra feta if you like.

Transfer to the oven and bake until set, 15 to 20 minutes.

Roasted Pepper, Red Onion, Potato, and Sausage

2 tbsp plus 1 tsp olive oil

1 cup red onion, about 1 cup, thinly sliced

½ cup/125 mL smoked chorizo sausage, chopped/sliced

2 cloves garlic, finely chopped

1/3 cup/80 g jarred roasted red peppers

2 cups/300 g cooked potatoes, diced

12 large eggs

2 tbsp fresh chives, chopped

2 tbsp grated parmesan cheese

Salt and freshly ground black pepper

Preheat the oven to 350°F/180°C.

In a 10-inch/25 cm cast-iron or other ovenproof skillet, heat 1 tablespoon of oil over medium heat. Add the onion, chorizo, and garlic to the skillet and continue cooking for 8 to 10 minutes.

Add the roasted red peppers, potatoes, and 1 tablespoon of olive oil, stir to coat with the oil and warm through. Remove from the heat and set aside.

In a bowl, beat the eggs with the chives, 1 tablespoon of parmesan, and a pinch each of salt and pepper.

Scrape the potato mix into the eggs with a rubber spatula and stir to combine.

Add the remaining 1 teaspoon olive oil to the pan and pour the egg mix into the pan. Even out and sprinkle any remaining parmesan.

Transfer to the oven and bake until set, 15 to 20 minutes.

TIPS:
You can substitute 10% cream with sour cream, crème fraîche, full-fat (3.5%) yogurt, plant milk, or melted diluted cream cheese.

It can also be made in muffin tins for individual mini-frittatas, with a shorter cooking time.

Lean towards slightly underdone as it will continue cooking a bit more after you remove it from the oven.

Some flavour combinations:

Zucchini or asparagus, peas, mint, chèvre

Mushroom, bacon, chives, jalapeño, Havarti

Sun-dried/oven-dried tomatoes, caramelized onions, basil, Gouda

Broccoli, green onion, thyme, cheddar

Spinach, chard, onions, oregano, feta

Olives, artichokes, rosemary, ricotta

Poblanos or chipotles, tomato, chorizo, scallions

Leeks, shallots, potato, tarragon, Brie

Garlic scapes/chives, cherry tomatoes, basil, mozzarella

Arugula, pancetta, parmesan, truffle oil

Edamame, shiitake, green onion, shrimp, nori (try substituting dashi for cream)

Options for your spiked mayo:

Aioli (mashed garlic)

Chipotle peppers in adobo

Tapenade (sun-dried tomato or olive)

Pesto

Kimchi + gochujang

Oyster sauce + hoisin

Cilantro + jalapeño + lime

Indian pickles or chutney

Preserved lemon (minced)

Wasabi + mirin

Za'atar + extra-virgin olive oil

Roasted garlic + parmesan

Truffle paste

Miso

FRIDGE CLEANER MINESTRONE

Prep: about 20 min

Cook: about 50 min (using an electric or regular pressure cooker will cut the time in half)

Makes: 16 cups/ 4 L (12 to 16 servings)

This soup is almost infinitely forgiving. It is the saviour of whatever straggly odds and ends you have slowly dying in your vegetable crisper. Like most soups, it gets better the next day. It can go lighter and brothier in the springtime—leaning towards more fast-cooking veg, greens, and fresh herbs—or heartier in the fall with more root veg, beans, and pasta. It's the perfect great place to use up a parmesan rind if you have one kicking around (it's worth saving just for this!). Basically, everything past the base and tomatoes is optional; any combination works, all measurements are approximate—use up what you have, that's the whole point. And with basically nothing but veg, it is super healthy and light, even though it is a very hearty bowl.

Make the base: In a large heavy-bottomed pot or Dutch oven, heat the olive oil over medium heat. Add the onion, carrot, celery, garlic, salt, and pepper and sauté, stirring occasionally, until softened, about 10 minutes.

Add the slow-cooking veg and crumble the bouillon cube over the mix and sauté until it dissolves and adds a bit of colour to the pan, 1 to 2 minutes. Deglaze with the white wine.

Add the tomatoes, breaking them up by hand as you add them. Pour in the juice and then fill the empty can with water or vegetable stock (hold on to the can; you'll use it again) and add that along with the bay leaf, dried or fresh herbs, chili flakes (if using), and parmesan rind (if you have one).

Bring to a boil, then reduce the heat to medium and simmer for 15 to 20 minutes, stirring occasionally. (Or cook for 7 minutes on high pressure in an electric pressure cooker, then quick release.)

Add the fast-cooking veg, spinach, cooked beans, and dry pasta. Top up with one more tomato can's worth of veggie stock (or water plus 1 teaspoon salt), bring back to a boil, then reduce to medium-low and simmer, stirring occasionally, for another 15 to 20 minutes. (Or another 7 minutes in the pressure cooker, then quick release.)

Add a little more stock or water if it is too thick. Fish out the parmesan rind and bay leaf, add a few generous twists of black pepper, adjust the salt, and add a splash of vinegar to taste.

Garnish with fresh herbs and/or a splash of olive oil and/or grated parmesan or crumbled feta. It's also really nice with garlicky croutons or a spoon of pesto. Serve it with some crusty bread and you're good to go.

The Base:

1 tbsp olive oil

1 onion, diced

1 carrot, diced

1 celery stalk, diced

2 cloves garlic, minced

½ tsp salt

¼ tsp freshly ground black pepper

Slow-Cooking Vegetables:

~ 3 cups/ 750 mL medium-diced slow-cooking veg, ~ ½ cup/125 mL each, any combination of: bell peppers, green cabbage, potato, parsnip or turnip, daikon or radishes, kale or collards, mushrooms, fennel, etc.

1 veg or mushroom bouillon cube

½ cup/125 mL white wine

1 (28 fl oz/796 mL) can whole peeled tomatoes, undrained

1 large or 2 small bay leaves

1 tsp Italian seasoning or herbes de Provence, and/or any fresh herb ends that need using up

¼ tsp crushed chili flakes (optional)

Parmesan rind, if you have one (optional)

Fast-Cooking Vegetables:

~ 2 cups/ 500 mL medium-diced fast-cooking veg, ~ ½ cup/ 125 mL each, any combination of: zucchini, sweet potato, chard (add chopped stems to the slow-cooking veg), squash, fresh or frozen peas, corn, green beans, etc.

½ package frozen spinach or 1 to 2 handfuls/60 g fresh

½ cup/125 mL canned/cooked chickpeas, red or white beans, and/ or cooked green or brown lentils

½ cup/125 mL small, sturdy pasta, like macaroni or tubetti

Vegetable stock or water

Salt and freshly ground black pepper

Balsamic or sherry vinegar

Optional Garnishes:

Any fresh herbs

Olive oil

Grated parmesan or crumbled feta chese

Garlicky croutons

Pesto

TIPS:

Lentils and pasta will keep absorbing broth after cooking, so any leftover soup will get very thick; you'll need to add more water or stock and taste for salt when reheating.

If you have any cooked pasta leftovers (even if it has sauce), you can add it, roughly chopped, at the very end instead of adding dried pasta.

KIMCHI FRIED RICE

Fried rice is amazing, and I eat it a lot. You can bend it in almost any direction depending on what you throw in. I like ending up with lots of colour, texture, and flavour variations to keep each bite interesting, and I love topping it with a sunny-side up egg. This particular dish goes to Koreatown with the addition of kimchi and gochujang, but you could just as easily substitute Thai curry paste, some hoisin or oyster sauce, Indian curry paste, a bit of diluted miso, and on and on. . . . The point is if you always make extra rice, you're never more than a few minutes away from a great lunch.

Short-grain sushi rice or brown jasmine work well; regular long-grain is also fine; basmati is a bit delicate for this recipe but will work in a pinch. This recipe really needs cold, next-day rice; it does not work so well with hot/fresh rice.

Prep: 15 min   **Cook:** 15 min   **Makes:** 4 servings

1 tbsp gochujang (Korean red pepper paste)

2 tablespoons juice from a jar of kimchi

1 tbsp mirin or ½ tsp sugar

2 to 3 slices bacon, cut crosswise into ¼-inch/6 mm strips (optional)

2 tbsp oil or butter or a combo (omit if using bacon)

1 small onion, diced

2 cloves garlic, minced

2 tsp grated fresh ginger

Optional protein (if you didn't use bacon): ½ cup/ 125 mL coarsely chopped leftover Korean beef or pork; ham or Spam (popular in Korea!), cut into small cubes; ¼ cup/60 mL small dried shrimp

4 shiitake mushrooms, sliced (fresh or rehydrated dried)

1 carrot, cut into 1-inch/2.5 cm matchsticks

½ bunch kale, chard, or choi, tough stems removed and leaves chopped

2 to 3 radishes, finely diced

1 cup/250 mL kimchi, squeezed, coarsely chopped

4 cups/640 g cold leftover rice

3 tbsp soy sauce

1 tbsp sesame oil

Fried Eggs:

4 eggs

1 tsp butter (or ½ tsp neutral oil plus ½ tsp sesame oil)

Garnishes:

4 tbsp nori strips

2 green onions, thinly sliced

1 tbsp white and/or black sesame seeds

1 tbsp gochujang, stirred with 1 tsp water (optional)

In a small bowl, whisk together the gochujang, kimchi juice, and mirin or sugar. Set aside.

In a large wok, cast-iron, or other nonstick skillet, cook the bacon (if using) over medium heat until almost crisp and the fat has rendered, about 5 minutes. If not using bacon, in the wok or skillet, heat the oil or oil/butter mix.

To the bacon fat or oil/butter mix in the skillet, add the onion, garlic, ginger, and any other protein (if using) and cook, stirring frequently, until the onion has become a bit translucent, 2 to 3 minutes.

Stir in the vegetables, kimchi, and kimchi juice/ gochujang mixture and cook, stirring constantly, until the vegetables have softened and the sauce has evaporated a bit, about 5 minutes.

Add the cold rice and break up clumps with a wooden spoon or spatula, tossing to coat. Add the soy sauce and sesame oil and toss to coat. Keep cooking, stirring, and tossing until thoroughly mixed and piping hot, 2 to 3 minutes.

Reduce the heat to low and let sit to brown a bit while you fry the eggs sunny-side up in butter or a neutral/sesame oil mix.

When the eggs are ready, scrape up the rice, hopefully with a few little browned bits, and fill a medium soup bowl with one-quarter of the rice. Place a plate on top of the bowl and then invert to produce a dome of rice. Garnish with a fried egg, a nori strip, and some green onions and sesame seeds. If you like it spicier, drizzle with a bit of the diluted gochujang.

Repeat for the remaining portions of rice.

CHILAQUILES

aka Brunch "Nachos"

The leftovers of a lot of Mexican meals can become the foundation for chilaquiles, one of my favourite brunch dishes. It is basically totopos (fried tortilla chips), tossed in a warm salsa, topped with fried eggs and a mix of colourful garnishes. It's a very flexible dish, but you want a nice mix of toppings; crunchy, tangy, creamy, spicy, savoury. Try and serve it fast, when the chips are at the magical place between soft and crunchy.

Prep: 20 min

Cook: 20 to 40 min (see Tips)

Makes: 4 generous servings

Totopos:

1 cup/250 mL vegetable oil, for frying

12 corn tortillas, cut into 4 or 6 wedges (see Tips)

Salt

Assembly:

2 cups/ 475 mL salsa roja, homemade or store-bought (see Tips)

4 eggs (8 if you are in a 2-eggs-per-person kind of mood)

Salt and black pepper

Hot sauce

Quartered limes

Toppings of your choice (see page 319)

Salsa Roja

1 dried guajillo, ancho, or pasilla pepper (optional)

3 tomatoes, halved

1 small onion, unpeeled, ends trimmed, cut into quarters

1 to 2 medium jalapeños, halved

4 cloves garlic, unpeeled

½ tsp salt, plus more if needed

2 tbsp neutral oil

1 cup/250 mL stock, or water

Make the totopos: Line a tray with paper towels. In a large skillet, heat the oil over medium-high heat. Test with a little piece of tortilla; it should sizzle and bubble when it goes in. Fry half the tortilla wedges, tossing occasionally until crispy and bubbles recede but before they turn dark, 3 to 4 minutes. Remove to the paper towels to drain, sprinkle with salt while still warm, and repeat with the remaining tortillas. Try not to eat them all. Put the pan aside with the leftover oil (you'll need it for the eggs and if you are making your own salsa roja).

If making your own salsa roja, make it now. If using a store-bought sauce, proceed to making the eggs.

Fry the eggs: Line a plate with paper towels. Reheat the pan with the oil from the tortillas over medium-high heat. When shimmery, crack in the eggs one at a time, trying to keep them separate. They should bubble up, and after 15 seconds or so use a fork or spatula to loosen them from the bottom of the pan so they can move around. When the whites are almost, but not completely set, around 1 minute, remove to the paper towels to drain (they'll firm up a bit more on their own). Repeat if you're doing 8 eggs. Tent lightly with foil while you prepare the chilaquiles. I guess you could also use poached eggs, but you are basically having nachos for breakfast so who are you kidding?

To assemble one plate at a time: Heat a skillet (or use the pan from making the salsa roja) over medium heat, and add ½ cup/125 mL of the sauce. Drop in one-quarter of the totopos and toss to coat and warm through, about 1 minute. You want to get them just starting to soften, but still a bit crispy.

Scrape it all onto a plate, garnish with an egg(s), a bit of all your toppings, a sprinkle of salt and pepper, a nice splash of hot sauce, and a wedge of lime on the side. Eat ASAP.

To assemble family-style: Pour all the sauce into a skillet and when warmed through, add all the totopos, tossing to coat, 1 to 2 minutes. Pile on all the toppings and eggs, a bit of salt and pepper, and a few lashings of hot sauce. Bring to the table with lime wedges for sharing and applause.

Salsa Roja

Heat a dry heavy-bottomed skillet (cast-iron works best) over medium-high heat. (You can also do this on a BBQ, or a traditional Mexican comal/griddle.) If you're using the dried pepper, toast it on both sides in the dry pan, then set aside to cool. Break open, remove and discard the stems and seeds, then crumble or roughly chop.

Add the tomatoes, onion, jalapeños, and garlic to the hot pan and let sit for 2 to 3 minutes. You want to get a bit of black char going; flip with tongs and let sit for another 2 to 3 minutes to get some char on the other sides. Take off the heat, but don't wash the pan.

Drop the tomatoes and jalapeños into a food processor or blender. Put the onion and garlic on a cutting board and when cool enough to handle, remove the skins and add to the tomatoes and jalapeños. Add the salt and crumbled toasted chili pepper (if using). Process until relatively uniform, but not completely smooth.

Add the oil to the pan you just used to char the vegetables. Warm the oil over medium heat, pour in the tomato purée, scrape up any charred bits from the skillet, and cook, stirring, about 5 minutes, until it incorporates the oil and darkens a bit.

Thin the sauce with the stock or water until the consistency of heavy cream. Taste for salt and add a bit if needed.

TIPS:

Home-fried totopos are really the best for this. Most lightweight supermarket tortilla chips will just turn to mush. Stale tortillas from dinner a few nights ago, or some old ones languishing in the back of your freezer will work just fine.

You can use any canned/bottled enchilada sauce, red or green, instead of making your own, but the salsa roja is quick to whip up and really works well. Don't use jarred salsa; it is usually too chunky and sweet. That said, if you happen to have some leftover salsa, you might as well throw it in; that's kind of the point.

You can turn the salsa roja into salsa verde by replacing the tomatoes with tomatillos and the dried chilies with poblanos or jalapeños, plus a big handful of cilantro.

If you make extra salsa roja, add a few more cups of stock and you have yourself the base of a great Sopa Azteca (tortilla soup).

Toppings

Use any combination of the following, in pretty much any quantity. The point is to use up what you have lying around:

Avocado, sliced or cubed, or guacamole

Crema, sour cream, crème fraîche, or thick yogurt (I fake a passable Mexican-style crema by watering down sour cream with a bit of lime juice and a pinch of salt.)

Cubed queso fresco, crumbled Cotija, or feta cheese

Shredded chicken, pork, or beef

Chopped or sliced radishes, jalapeños, and/or bell peppers

Roughly chopped fresh cilantro

Chopped or sliced red onion or sliced green onions

Pickled jalapeños or pickled red onions

ACKNOWLEDGEMENTS

The hardest part of writing this book has been the impossibility of acknowledging everyone who played a role in making The Depanneur. The Dep was the collective product of a huge community of cooks and customers, employees and volunteers, friends and mentors, collaborators and sponsors, without whom it would not have existed. This book is an expression of gratitude to all of you for the gift of being able to spend the last decade learning what food had to teach me.

Photo: Merlin Boissonneault

The Depanneur Cookbook
Thank you to everyone who helped make this book possible:

Ksenija Hotic: For your elegant styling, beautiful photography, unwavering support, and invaluable collaboration

Miriam Davidson: For your generosity of spirit, kindness, and patience as I struggled to untangle my voice

Raluca Cojocariu: For your enthusiasm, support, and indispensable help in getting this enormous project done

Buffy Childerhose: For interviewing all the cooks and panning through the endless transcripts for the nuggets of gold

Carole Nelson Brown: For patiently and diligently testing recipes, plus being a true Depaneer through and through

Carline Haurie: For your gorgeous plates and bowls, worthy containers, and beautiful frames for the cooks' art

Amy Wilson: For props and styling assistance, encouragement over the years, and artistic inspiration

Hilary McMahon: For doing your best to manage my expectations, and keeping a watchful eye on my best interests

Kirsten Hanson: For stewarding the book through the gauntlet, from proposal to product

Katherine Gibson: For encouraging and supporting me as the endless story kept pouring out

Plus all the cooks and Kickstarter contributors: Without you there would have been no book.

The Depanneur

Thank you to all the people who helped inspire, build, and support The Dep over the years.

Andy Dowey
Charlene Rowland
Cory Oulette
Dana Kelly
Danielle Mitrovic
Dougie Kerr and Honest Ed's
Emily Zimmerman
Ginger Dean
Jiva Mackay
John Kipphoff
John Szucs
Jonna Pederson
Katie Krelove
Lisa Kates
Malka Elkin
Marisa Blankier
Marius Lombrea
Monique Ganon
Ran Goel
Ryan Andrade
Sara Power
Skeeter Jones
Sue and Axel Young
Tanya Surman and CSI
The Bentway

Plus everyone who ever cooked or ate or taught or spoke or got married at The Dep: Without you there would have been no Dep.

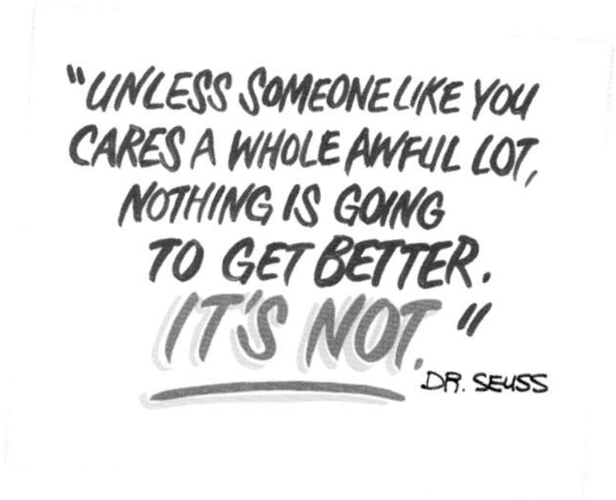

Newcomer Kitchen

Thank you to those who poured their hearts and souls into this project.

Rahaf Alakbani and **Esmaeel Aboufakher**
Cara Benjamin-Pace and **Tamara Chaikin**
Anissa Helou
Anne Gentleman
Atique Azad and Maha Gafar
Aysha Teja
Caroline Keenan
Céline Lamarre
Christina Zeidler and The Gladstone Hotel
Dan Rose
David Sax
Donna MacDonald
Faizan Ashraf
Foodora
Hamdi Ulukaya
Hiyam Samara
IRCC
Jack Huang
Jeannie Baxter and Toronto Image Works
John Hanna
John Rosenthal
Joshna Maharaj
Kashif Kahn
Kelli Keiley
Kirstine Stewart and Zaib Shaikh
Leslie Feist
LUSH Cosmetics
Marcella Tomas
Michelle Krasny
Mohamad Fakih
Mohammad Al Zaibak
Monica Abdelkader
Sandy Nicholson
The Propeller Project
Tolga Ay and Murat Ozsuvari
Westbank

Plus all the talented ladies who cooked with us and taught me so much about why food matters: Without you there would have been no Newcomer Kitchen.

"UNLESS SOMEONE LIKE YOU CARES A WHOLE AWFUL LOT, NOTHING IS GOING TO GET BETTER. IT'S NOT." DR. SEUSS

The Depanneur Cookbook Kickstarter

Thank you to all those who supported the project and helped bring this book to life.

Special Dedication
John Hanson

VIP Patrons
Art Liem
Brent Mclaughlin
Capri Cafaro
Cara Benjamin-Pace
Donna Macdonald
Gianni Chiappetta
Ingo Holzinger
James Adams
Kirsten Hanson
Matthew Clark
Momoyo Yoshida
No One
Peter Hanson
Sean Moore

Sponsors
Alicia Peres
Andrea M
Ann Ball
Carl Bloom
Carolyn Humphreys
Christine Manning
Colette Snyder
Constance Dykun
Derek Ruth
Elisa Shenkier
Elizabeth Howson
Emcb
Francine
Gale Rubenstein
Gordon Goldschleger
Graeme
Greg Clow
Gregory Bent
Jacqueline Tam
Jane French
Janet Polivy
Herman
Jillian Brant
Joe Adelaars
John Hanna
John Leeson
Julie Mcphail
Kari Romaniuk
Kate Marshall
Kevin
Lesley Ciarula Taylor
Lisa Kates
Lisa Singer
Loretta Chang
Marcella Tomas
Marcia Ross
Marna Yates
Marnie Sohn
Mary Hulbert
Mary Machamer
Mess Hall
Michael Hierlihy
Michael Zimmerman
Monika Rau
Niky Senater
Pete
Peter Voore
Richard Joy
Robert Elliott
Ruth
Salimah Y. Ebrahim
Sandy Nicholson
Stephanie Thomas
Stephen Bulger
Tamara Chaikin
Tobaron Waxman
Tom Yim
Vivien Cy Wong
Yvonne Hilder

"MAKE IT SIMPLE. INCREASE CONTACT. REMOVE BARRIERS."

MARINA ABRAMOVIĆ

Supporters

A
A Lee
Aaron
Aaron Dewitt
Abel Cartaya
Abokichi
Adrian
Adrianna Knight
Aidan Nulman
Ailsa Robinson
Ainsley
Alan Zweig
Aldona Satterthwaite
Aleb
Alex Fitzgerald
Alex Mlynek
Alex Neumann
Alfredo Suarez
Alice Luong
Alison
Alison Broverman
Alison Crouse
Alison Stevenson
Aliya Somani
Aliza
Allison Magpayo
Alyshah
Aman Vellani
Amanda Darrach
Amanda White
Amira Eskenazi
Amit Ajwani
Amreen Omar
Amy V
Ana Bailao
Anais Mathers
Anastasia Ali
Andi Cuddington
Andi Curtis and Nick Saul
Andrea Jean Brown
Andrea Parnell
Andreas Duess
Andrew Hwang
Andrew Usher
Angela
Angela Harvey
Angela Leung
Anna Khimasia
Anne
Anne Brown
Anne Cairns
Annemarie Baynton
April
Arlene Stein
Asif Rashid
Asim Fayaz
Barbara Howson
Barbato Martiniello

Bari Zittell
Becca
Bénédicte Ronfard
Benita
Bennett Mccardle
Beth
Bethany
Beverly Wooding
Bill Vanderclock
Bonnie Stern
Brendan Powell
Brian Desrosiers-Tam
Brigitte Rabazo
Brooke M
Bruce M Williams
Bryan Swift
Cameron Grant
Canadork
Carey Taschuk
Carlos M. Gárate
Carly Dunster
Carol Gordon
Carol Mark
Carole Nelson Brown
Caroline Haurie
Caroline Keenan
Caroline Park
Carolyn Ramos
Carolyn Scotchmer
Catherine Gui
Catherine Solyom
Cathy Knights
Cathy Vine
Cecily
Celine Lamarre
Chantal Véchambre
Charlyn W
Chef Dave Mottershall
Cheryl Fretz
Chris Dunne
Chris Thomas
Christen
Christina Rousseau
Christina Verdurmen
Christina Zeidler
Christine May
Christine Robertson
Christopher
Christopher
Mudiappahpillai
Christopher Paul Lawson
Christopher Tran
Claire
Clara T
Claude
Claude Vezina
Claudia Fuchs
Clement Kent
Cody Mares

Colin Geddes
Colin Kelly
Cookbook
Corbin Venida
Corinne Chamney
Cory Kirchhofer
Craig Ruttan
Craig Small
Cristina Petrucci
Cynthia Pruss
Dan Wood
Dana
Daniel Demsky
Daniel Rose
Danielle
Darcelle
Darcy Higgins
David Arie
David Armstrong
David Carrier
David Ess You
David Fernandez
David Kua
David Senater
Davinder Singh
Dean Goodman
Debbie Bunze
Deborah Abbott
Dee Brooks
Denise Pinto
Derek Leebosh
Didi Psomopoulos
Dimcd
Djuna Day
Donna Lypchuk
Donnalu Macdonald
Doris Fin
Dorothy De Val
Doug Pritchard
Drew Skinner
Duncan Reith
Dylan Carlson
Ed Lui
Eden Spodek
Eldrida Ruiz
Elena Ferranti
Elissa Gelleny
Elita Rocka
Elizabeth
Elizabeth Caione
Elizabeth Kenny
Elizabeth Laboone
Elizabeth Ryerson
Elle Crevits
Elyse
Elyssa Kaplan
Emily Boucher
Emily Dela Cruz
Emily Heung

Emily Hurson
Emma Grenon
Emmab
Erika
Erin
Erin Haggett
Eva Bruketa
Eva Tentere De Metz
Eva-Lynn Jagoe
Eve-Lynn Stein
Farida Bogosoff
Fergus Heywood
Folkard Fritz
Françoise Briet
Frank Vinodolac
Frederick Peters
Gabriella Gwendolen
Gabrielle Leith
Gail Gordon Oliver
Gary Chapple
Gary Tsim
Gaye Zimmerman-Huycke
Geraldine Bowman
Glen Cuthbert
Gracie Carroll
Grayling Brown
Hao Ngo
Hassel Aviles
Heather
Heather Kelly
Heather Macdonald
Helen
Hiromi
Holger Boeckner
Holly
Hormuz Dadabhoy
Ian Busher
Ian Swartz
Ianmerringer
India A
Ines Popovic
Ingrid Hein
Irene Efston
Isbrand
J. Kim
Jaclyn Law
Jaime Sugiyama
Jake Risk
James
James Harpley
James Scott
Jan Keck
Janet Forbes
Janet Fung
Janet Haddock
Janice Roberts
Jannie Tsang
Jared Chadwick
Jared Kligerman

Jasia Kiersnowski
Jasmine Grewal
Jasmine Kochar
Jason
Jason Charters
Jason Dong
Jason Tannis
Jean Brown
Jeanne-Marie Robillard
Jen
Jen Rogers
Jena Roy
Jenna N
Jennifer And Steve Horton
Jennifer Ramsay
Jenny Hartin
Jeremy Kojima
Jessica Tsang
Jiliyan Milne
Jill Mckay
Jill Parsons
Jillian Lum
Jj Fueser
Joan Malcolmsen
Joan Weed
Joanne Blanchette
Joanne Lawrence
Jodi Carman
Jodi Pudge
Joebanh
Joel Harrower
Joel Slonetsky
Johanna Braden
John C Forde
John Haynes
John Noyes
John T O'connell
John Thiessen
Jonas Crawley
Jonathan Bouchard
Jonathan Kim
Jonathan Moneta
Jones
Jos Rehli
Josh Apostolopoulos
Joshna Maharaj
Joy Levine
Judy Brunsek
Judy Perry
Julia K
Julian Sleath
Julianna Wronski
Julie M Foley
Juliette Nicolet
Juniper Locilento
Justin Bull
Justin Stephenson
Justine Turner
Karen Chisvin

Karen Dubinsky
Karen Leiva
Karen Tam
Kashif Khan
Kathi Ziolkowski
Kathryn Tanaka
Katie
Katie Hagan
Katie Mccool
Katya Osadchin
Kay Compagnoni
KB
Keith Bryan
Kelli Kieley
Kelly Bray
Kelly Cook
Ken Aucoin
Ken Bereskin
Kerri C
Kevin Taylor
Kieran Wyatt
Kim
Kim Hamilton
Koel Loyer
Krisstell Bonilla
Kristi
Kristin Nelson
Kyle
L Humphreys
L Nathan
Lana Tibbetts
Lara Brooks
Laura
Laura
Laura
Laura Alper
Laura Brehaut
Laura Cappe
Laura McDonald
Laura Repo
Laura Rumkle
Laurel Carter
Laurie Barker
Lea Carlson
Leila
Leo Baduria
Leo Moncel
Leona Breslaw
Leslie Ambedian
Leslie Lorette
Lilie Zendel
Lily Champniss
Linda Bronfman
Linda Julia Paolucci
Lindsey Lenters
Lindy
Lisa
Lisa
Lisa Elchuk

Lisa Ellenwood
Lisa Shamata
Lise Buisson
Liz
Lori Brown
Lori Myers
Lorna Novosel
Lucy
Lucy
Luke Sargent
Lynda Balogh
Malka
Manicmarauder
Mankee Mah
Marc Hébert
Marc-André Laurence
Mardi Michels
Maria Rozynska
Marianne Senater
Marie-Louise Fitrion
Marilyn Steinkopf
Marion Kane
Mark
Mark Lapowich
Mark Valdmanis
Marlene
Marni
Martha Friendly
Mary Holding
Mary-Margaret Jones
Matias R
Matt
Matt Dodge
Matthew Mcmillan
Maureen Carter-Whitney
Mazzuca
Meg Bowie
Meggen Janes
Megumi Overton
Melanie Houselog
Melvin Se
Michael
Michael Cosby
Michael Di Caro
Michael Franklin
Michael Katz
Michael Temple
Michaela
Michèle Bussières
Michelle
Michelle C.
Michelle Chan
Michelle Munk
Michelle Shariff
Mike Brcic
Mike Cheatley
Mike Wanless
Mikka Gia
Milly Casey

Mina Hanna
Mirelle Blassnig
Miriam Davidson
Moira Grant
Molly Helferty
Molly Whalen
Monica
Monty
Murray Bryant
Nadia
Nadia Bragagnolo
Nancy Matsumoto
Natalie
Natalie
Natalie Currie
Natascha Swyrydenko
Natasha
Natasha Bijelich
Neil Sitka
Nelson Tam
Nichjolas Parker
Nicholas Sidhu
Nicole Bennett
Nicole Leaper
Nidia
Nik Beeson
Nikhil Nair
Noelle Elia
Nored Englebers
Oswin Chang
Pamela Lagamba
Patricia Baranek
Patricia Meindl
Patrick Charron
Patrick Dinnen
Patrick Robinson
Paul Butler
Paul Carew
Paul Decampo
Paul Habert
Paula Costa
Peter Cuff
Peter Mcclusky
Peter Sanagan
Phil Liberbaum
Philipp Angermeyer
Pippimd
Pma
RP
Rachael Costa
Rachel
Ralu
Ramona Ramlochand
Rebecca
Rebecca Nelson
Rebecca Smollett
Rebecca Tischart
Renee Anne Mckenzie
Rhea

Rhoma Akosua Spencer
Richard Rossi
Richard Yampolsky
Rick Innis
Rick Madge
Rie Ueda
Rime Luu
Rissi
Robert Kwak
Ron Nash
Ron Sissel
Roohi Qureshi
Rose Zgodzinski
Ruth Gangbar
Ruth Hannah
Ruth Wilford
Ryan
Ryan
Ryan Matheson
Ryan West
Saffron Beckwith
Saira Qureshi
Sam Mooney
Samantha Doedens
Samantha Gawron
Samantha Thompson
Samara Gottesman
Sarah Clarke
Sarah Compton
Sarah Demb
Sarah Margolius
Sarah Power
Sari Papular
Sawyer
Scott Myhal
Scott Thorner
Sean Browne
Sean Copeman
Serena Yi
Sergio Elmir
Seth Goren
Shangeetha Jeyamanohar
Sharon Lea Whitton
Shauna
Shawn Kirkup
Shelley S
Shinji Yamaguchi A.K.A
Mr. Gushi
Shoshana Teitelman
Sillygwailo
Siobhan Mccann
Smash Arts
Snjezana Pruginic
Sonia
Stef
Stephanie Morrison
Stephanie Senater
Stephanie Wessely Rose
Stephen C.

Stephen Chanasyk
Stephen Johns
Stephen Walker
Stephenie Sam
Steve Mcnally
Steve Pontet
Sujala Balaji
Susan Philpott
Susan Usher
Susanne Wickstrom
Suzanne Manvell
Sybil Eastman
Tad Michalak
Teresa Toten
Teri Mcmahon
Terri
Tess Chen
The Tucker Family
Therese
Tim Collingwood
Tim Kearns
Tomasz
Tonya Surman
Tygacil
Tyler Burton
Valerie Tung
Vandana Taxali
Vanessa Allen
Vicki Clough
Vicky Forster
Victor Meng
Victoria Stegle
Vijay Khurana
Vladimir
Waleed Nassar
Wendy
Wendy Iles
Wendy Mullinder
Wenzie Ng
William Robertson
William Stefancic
Wilson Truong
Xave
Xavier Chaillot
Yuliya Tsoy
Zach Anderson
Zachery Oman
Zahra Ebrahim
Zdenka Goralikova

"YOU DON'T NEED A SILVER FORK TO EAT GOOD FOOD."

PAUL PRUDHOMME

EPILOGUE

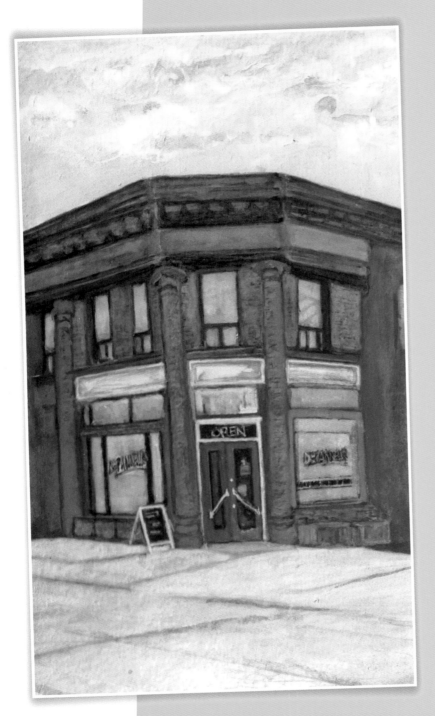

Watercolour by Jeanne-Marie Robillard

The creation of this book was an adventure all its own. More than three years in the making, it was, in its own way, as difficult and as rewarding as The Dep ever was. My original story was easily five times longer, and having to choose what to omit, what stories not to tell, which people not to acknowledge was impossibly hard. The long and winding process taught me a lot of things, helped me see and appreciate The Dep in new ways, revealing themes and patterns that have woven through my whole life.

There were many times when it felt like it was going off the rails, when the plot was getting lost, the point missed, the spirit flattened. Ironically it was in those moments of conflict when I felt most deeply my responsibility to the stories and voices that been entrusted to me, and found the courage to fight for what The Dep really meant. Here is a little of what I learned.

The Dep did not try to be popular, or classy, or elegant. It was, at its heart, a critique of those notions, and of the power structures that hold them in place. It aimed to show that people's authentic food, embodying their stories and personality and culture, did not have to be "elevated" to be valid, that it was wonderful as it was, and could proudly shine without having to compromise or conform. The Dep was my tiny *cri de coeur* against the commodification and a gentrification of everything. Against apathy and homogeneity and the status quo, against slickness and pretention and elitism, against the ubiquity of bland, white, Canadian mediocrity.

It did not aspire to be fancier or trendier than it was. It was recycled and resourceful and quirky; old, mismatched cutlery, junk turned into art. It packed a lot into a tiny space, and imbued it with hospitality and generosity and abundance. It was loud and enthusiastic, friendly and welcoming. If it erred, it erred on the side of excess. Its big, messy heart offered a safe place for vulnerability and connection. There were those who found it crowded or uncomfortable, amateurish or vulgar. But those that loved it, loved it because of the authentic human experiences it fostered and celebrated.

The Dep was a lot of things, but it was never boring or generic. It was something different, something unlikely and odd and imperfect. It was about celebrating people and encouraging them to take chances, about biting off more than you can chew and chewing really hard. It was not safe or easy; I often took ill-advised risks and regularly fell into uncharted, sometimes precarious territory.

There is an old cliché that the personal is political; I believe it is also economic. As a business, The Dep sought to sustain itself by enriching those who participated in it. It was bottom-up, not top-down; the cooks were the true source of value, and my job was to use what privilege I had to help facilitate its expression in the world. **The Dep was not only a critique but an experiment in creating an alternative, a new kind of arrangement between restaurants and cooks and diners that might put more into the world than it extracted from it.**

This idea was validated by the all those who supported The Dep, as guests and through the campaign to create this book. It was the Dep community that breathed life into this project, and for whom it was created in gratitude.

For all that I have tasted, for all that I have learned, for all that I have grown— thank you.

—LEN

My nieces, Lucy and Grace, with Loki, 2021

INDEX

Recipe Index
Alphabetical by Cook

"SHAKE THE HAND THAT FEEDS YOU."
MICHAEL POLLAN

Recipe Index
Alphabetical by Recipe

Index